THE CAPTURE
OF ATLANTA
AND
THE MARCH
TO THE SEA

THE CAPTURE OF ATLANTA

OF ATLANTA

AND

THE MARCH TO THE SEA

From Sherman's Memoirs

General William T. Sherman

Dover Publications, Inc.
Mineola, New York

Bibliographical Note

This Dover edition, first published in 2007, is an unabridged republication of Chapters 15 through 20 of Volume II of the *Memoirs of General William T. Sherman,* originally published by D. Appleton and Company, New York, 1876.

Library of Congress Cataloging-in-Publication Data

Sherman, William T. (William Tecumseh), 1820–1891.
    [Memoirs of General William T. Sherman. volume 2 Chapter 15-20]
    The capture of Atlanta and the March to the Sea : from Sherman's memoirs / General William T. Sherman.
        p. cm.
    "This Dover edition, first published in 2007, is an unabridged republication of chapters 15 through 20 of volume II of the Memoirs of General William T. Sherman, originally published by D. Appleton and Company, New York, 1876"—T.p. verso.
    ISBN 0-486-45477-0 (pbk.)
    1. Atlanta Campaign, 1864—Personal narratives. 2. Sherman's March to the Sea—Personal narratives. 3. Sherman, William T. (William Tecumseh), 1820–1891. 4. United States—History—Civil War, 1861–1865—Personal narratives. 5. Generals—United States—Biography. I. Title.

E476.7.S45 2007
973.7'731092—dc22

                              2006053151

Manufactured in the United States of America
Dover Publications, Inc., 31 East 2nd Street, Mineola, N.Y. 11501

GENERAL W. T. SHERMAN

TO

HIS COMRADES IN ARMS,

VOLUNTEERS AND REGULARS.

NEARLY ten years have passed since the close of the civil war in America, and yet no satisfactory history thereof is accessible to the public; nor should any be attempted until the Government has published, and placed within the reach of students, the abundant materials that are buried in the War Department at Washington. These are in process of compilation; but, at the rate of progress for the past ten years, it is probable that a new century will come before they are published and circulated, with full indexes to enable the historian to make a judicious selection of materials.

What is now offered is not designed as a history of the war, or even as a complete account of all the incidents in which the writer bore a part, but merely his recollection of events, corrected by a reference to his own memoranda, which may assist the future historian when he comes to describe the whole, and account for the motives and reasons which influenced some of the actors in the grand drama of war.

I trust a perusal of these pages will prove interesting to the survivors, who have manifested so often their intense love of the "cause" which moved a nation to vindicate its own authority; and, equally so, to the rising generation, who therefrom may learn that a country and government such as ours are worth fighting for, and dying for, if need be.

If successful in this, I shall feel amply repaid for departing from the usage of military men, who seldom attempt to publish their own deeds, but rest content with simply contributing by their acts to the honor and glory of their country.

WILLIAM T. SHERMAN,

General.

St. Louis, Missouri, *January* 21, 1875.

CONTENTS.

MEMOIRS

OF

GENERAL WILLIAM T. SHERMAN.

CHAPTER XV.

ATLANTA CAMPAIGN—NASHVILLE AND CHATTANOOGA TO KENESAW.

MARCH, APRIL, AND MAY, 1864.

On the 18th day of March, 1864, at Nashville, Tennessee, I relieved Lieutenant-General Grant in command of the Military Division of the Mississippi, embracing the Departments of the Ohio, Cumberland, Tennessee, and Arkansas, commanded respectively by Major-Generals Schofield, Thomas, McPherson, and Steele. General Grant was in the act of starting East to assume command of all the armies of the United States, but more particularly to give direction in person to the Armies of the Potomac and James, operating against Richmond; and I accompanied him as far as Cincinnati on his way, to avail myself of the opportunity to discuss privately many little details incident to the contemplated changes, and of preparation for the great events then impending. Among these was the intended assignment to duty of many officers of note and influence, who had, by the force of events, drifted into inactivity and discontent. Among these stood prominent Generals McClellan, Burnside, and Fremont, in the East; and Generals Buell, McCook, Negley, and Crittenden, at the West. My understanding was that General Grant thought it wise and prudent to give all these officers appropriate commands, that would enable them to regain the influence they had lost; and, as a general reorganization of all the armies was then necessary, he directed me to keep in mind especially the claims of Generals Buell, McCook, and Crittenden, and endeavor to give them commands that would be as near their rank and dates of commission as possible; but I was to do nothing until I heard further from him on the subject, as he explained that he would have to consult the Secretary of War before making final orders. General Buell and his officers had been subjected to a long ordeal by a court of inquiry, touching their conduct of the campaign in Tennessee and Kentucky, that resulted in the battle of Perryville, or Chaplin's Hills, October 8, 1862, and they had been substantially acquitted; and, as it was manifest that we were to have some hard fighting, we were anxious to bring into harmony every man and every officer of skill in the profession of arms. Of these, Generals Buell and McClellan were prominent in rank, and also by reason of their fame acquired in Mexico, as well as in the earlier part of the civil war.

After my return to Nashville I addressed myself to the task of organization and preparation, which involved the general security of the vast region of the South which had been already conquered, more especially the several routes of supply and communication with the active armies at the front, and to organize a large army to move into Georgia, coincident with the advance of the Eastern armies against Richmond. I soon received from Colonel J. B. Fry—now of the Adjutant-General's Department, but then at Washington in charge of the Provost-Marshal-General's office—a letter asking me to do something for General Buell. I answered him frankly, telling him of my understanding with General Grant, and that I was still awaiting the expected order of the War Department, assigning General Buell to my command. Colonel Fry, as General Buell's special friend, replied that he was very anxious that I should make specific application for the services of General Buell by name, and inquired what I proposed to offer him. To this I answered that, after the agreement with General Grant that he would notify me from Washington, I could not with propriety press the matter, but if

General Buell should be assigned to me specifically I was prepared to assign him to command all the troops on the Mississippi River from Cairo to Natchez, comprising about three divisions, or the equivalent of a *corps d'armée*. General Grant
never afterward communicated to me on the subject at all; and
I inferred that Mr. Stanton, who was notoriously vindictive in
his prejudices, would not consent to the employment of these
high officers. General Buell, toward the close of the war, published a bitter political letter, aimed at General Grant, reflecting
on his general management of the war, and stated that both
Generals Canby and Sherman had offered him a subordinate
command, which he had declined because he had once out-
ranked us. This was not true as to me, or Canby either, I
think, for both General Canby and I ranked him at West Point
and in the old army, and he (General Buell) was only superior
to us in the date of his commission as major-general, for a short
period in 1862. This newspaper communication, though aimed
at General Grant, reacted on himself, for it closed his military
career. General Crittenden afterward obtained authority for
service, and I offered him a division, but he declined it for the
reason, as I understood it, that he had at one time commanded
a corps. He is now in the United States service, commanding
the Seventeenth Infantry. General McCook obtained a command under General Canby, in the Department of the Gulf,
where he rendered good service, and he is also in the regular
service, lieutenant-colonel Tenth Infantry.

I returned to Nashville from Cincinnati about the 25th of
March, and started at once, in a special car attached to the regular train, to inspect my command at the front, going to Pulaski,
Tennessee, where I found General G. M. Dodge; thence to
Huntsville, Alabama, where I had left a part of my personal
staff and the records of the de artment during the time we had
been absent at Meridian; and there I found General McPherson, who had arrived from Vicksburg, and had assumed command of the Army of the Tennessee. General McPherson accompanied me, and we proceeded by the cars to Stevenson,
Bridgeport, etc., to Chattanooga, where we spent a day or two

with General George H. Thomas, and then continued on to Knoxville, where was General Schofield. He returned with us to Chattanooga, stopping by the way a few hours at Loudon, where were the headquarters of the Fourth Corps (Major-General Gordon Granger). General Granger, as usual, was full of complaints at the treatment of his corps since I had left him with General Burnside, at Knoxville, the preceding November; and he stated to me personally that he had a leave of absence in his pocket, of which he intended to take advantage very soon. About the end of March, therefore, the three army commanders and myself were together at Chattanooga. We had nothing like a council of war, but conversed freely and frankly on all matters of interest then in progress or impending. We all knew that, as soon as the spring was fairly open, we should have to move directly against our antagonist, General Jos. E. Johnston, then securely intrenched at Dalton, thirty miles distant; and the purpose of our conference at the time was to ascertain our own resources, and to distribute to each part of the army its appropriate share of work. We discussed every possible contingency likely to arise, and I simply instructed each army commander to make immediate preparations for a hard campaign, regulating the distribution of supplies that were coming up by rail from Nashville as equitably as possible. We also agreed on some subordinate changes in the organization of the three separate armies which were destined to take the field; among which was the consolidation of the Eleventh and Twelfth Corps (Howard and Slocum) into a single corps, to be commanded by General Jos. Hooker. General Howard was to be transferred to the Fourth Corps, vice Gordon Granger to avail himself of his leave of absence; and General Slocum was to be ordered down the Mississippi River, to command the District of Vicksburg. These changes required the consent of the President, and were all in due time approved.

The great question of the campaign was one of supplies. Nashville, our chief depot, was itself partially in a hostile country, and even the routes of supply from Louisville to Nashville by rail, and by way of the Cumberland River, had to be guarded.

Chattanooga (our starting-point) was one hundred and thirty-six miles in front of Nashville, and every foot of the way, especially the many bridges, trestles, and culverts, had to be strongly guarded against the acts of a local hostile population and of the enemy's cavalry. Then, of course, as we advanced into Georgia, it was manifest that we should have to repair the railroad, use it, and guard it likewise. General Thomas's army was much the largest of the three, was best provided, and contained the best corps of engineers, railroad managers, and repair parties, as well as the best body of spies and provost-marshals. On him we were therefore compelled in a great measure to rely for these most useful branches of service. He had so long exercised absolute command and control over the railroads in his department, that the other armies were jealous, and these thought the Army of the Cumberland got the lion's share of the supplies and other advantages of the railroads. I found a good deal of feeling in the Army of the Tennessee on this score, and therefore took supreme control of the roads myself, placed all the army commanders on an equal footing, and gave to each the same control, so far as orders of transportation for men and stores were concerned. Thomas's spies brought him frequent and accurate reports of Jos. Johnston's army at Dalton, giving its strength anywhere between forty and fifty thousand men, and these were being reënforced by troops from Mississippi, and by the Georgia militia, under General G. W. Smith. General Johnston seemed to be acting purely on the defensive, so that we had time and leisure to take all our measures deliberately and fully. I fixed the date of May 1st, when all things should be in readiness for the grand forward movement, and then returned to Nashville; General Schofield going back to Knoxville, and McPherson to Huntsville, Thomas remaining at Chattanooga.

On the 2d of April, at Nashville, I wrote to General Grant, then at Washington, reporting to him the results of my visit to the several armies, and asked his consent to the several changes proposed, which was promptly given by telegraph. I then addressed myself specially to the troublesome question of transportation and supplies. I found the capacity of the railroads from Nashville forward to Decatur, and to Chattanooga, so small, especially in the number of locomotives and cars, that it was clear that they were barely able to supply the daily wants of the armies then dependent on them, with no power of accumulating a surplus in advance. The cars were daily loaded down with men returning from furlough, with cattle, horses, etc.; and, by reason of the previous desolation of the country between Chattanooga and Knoxville, General Thomas had authorized the issue of provisions to the suffering inhabitants.

We could not attempt an advance into Georgia without food, ammunition, etc.; and ordinary prudence dictated that we should have an accumulation at the front, in case of interruption to the railway by the act of the enemy, or by common accident. Accordingly, on the 6th of April, I issued a general order, limiting the use of the railroad-cars to transporting only the essential articles of food, ammunition, and supplies for the army proper, forbidding any further issues to citizens, and cutting off all civil traffic; requiring the commanders of posts within thirty miles of Nashville to haul out their own stores in wagons; requiring all troops destined for the front to march, and all beef-cattle to be driven on their own legs. This was a great help, but of course it naturally raised a howl. Some of the poor Union people of East Tennessee appealed to President Lincoln, whose kind heart responded promptly to their request. He telegraphed me to know if I could not modify or repeal my orders; but I answered him that a great campaign was impending, on which the fate of the nation hung; that our railroads had but a limited capacity, and could not provide for the necessities of the army and of the people too; that one or the other must quit, and we could not until the army of Jos. Johnston was conquered, etc., etc. Mr. Lincoln seemed to acquiesce, and I advised the people to obtain and drive out cattle from Kentucky, and to haul out their supplies by the wagon-road from the same quarter, by way of Cumberland Gap. By these changes I nearly or quite doubled our daily accumulation of stores at the front, and yet even this was not found enough.

I accordingly called together in Nashville the master of transportation, Colonel Anderson, the chief quartermaster, General J. L. Donaldson, and the chief commissary, General Amos Beckwith, for conference. I assumed the strength of the army to move from Chattanooga into Georgia at one hundred thousand men, and the number of animals to be fed, both for cavalry and draught, at thirty-five thousand; then, allowing for occasional wrecks of trains, which were very common, and for the interruption of the road itself by guerrillas and regular raids, we estimated it would require one hundred and thirty cars, of ten tons each, to reach Chattanooga daily, to be reasonably certain of an adequate supply. Even with this calculation, we could not afford to bring forward hay for the horses and mules, nor more than five pounds of oats or corn per day for each animal. I was willing to risk the question of forage in part, because I expected to find wheat and corn fields, and a good deal of grass, as we advanced into Georgia at that season of the year. The problem then was to deliver at Chattanooga and beyond one hundred and thirty car-loads daily, leaving the beef-cattle to be driven on the hoof, and all the troops in excess of the usual train-guards to march by the ordinary roads. Colonel Anderson promptly explained that he did not possess cars or locomotives enough to do this work. I then instructed and authorized him to hold on to all trains that arrived at Nashville from Louisville, and to allow none to go back until he had secured enough to fill the requirements of our problem. At the time he only had about sixty serviceable locomotives, and about six hundred cars of all kinds, and he represented that to provide for all contingencies he must have at least one hundred locomotives and one thousand cars. As soon as Mr. Guthrie, the President of the Louisville & Nashville Railroad, detected that we were holding on to all his locomotives and cars, he wrote me, earnestly remonstrating against it, saying that he would not be able with diminished stock to bring forward the necessary stores from Louisville to Nashville. I wrote to him, frankly telling him exactly how we were placed, appealed to his patriotism to stand by us, and advised him in like manner to hold on to all trains coming into

Jeffersonville, Indiana. He and General Robert Allen, then quartermaster-general at Louisville, arranged a ferry-boat so as to transfer the trains over the Ohio River from Jeffersonville, and in a short time we had cars and locomotives from almost every road at the North; months afterward I was amused to see, away down in Georgia, cars marked "Pittsburg & Fort Wayne," "Delaware & Lackawanna," "Baltimore & Ohio," and indeed with the names of almost every railroad north of the Ohio River. How these railroad companies ever recovered their property, or settled their transportation accounts, I have never heard, but to this fact, as much as to any other single fact, I attribute the perfect success which afterward attended our campaigns; and I have always felt grateful to Mr. Guthrie, of Louisville, who had sense enough and patriotism enough to subordinate the interests of his railroad company to the cause of his country.

About this time, viz., the early part of April, I was much disturbed by a bold raid made by the rebel General Forrest up between the Mississippi and Tennessee Rivers. He reached the Ohio River at Paducah, but was handsomely repulsed by Colonel Hicks. He then swung down toward Memphis, assaulted and carried Fort Pillow, massacring a part of its garrison, composed wholly of negro troops. At first I discredited the story of the massacre, because, in preparing for the Meridian campaign, I had ordered Fort Pillow to be evacuated, but it transpired afterward that General Hurlbut had retained a small garrison at Fort Pillow to encourage the enlistment of the blacks as soldiers, which was a favorite political policy at that day. The massacre at Fort Pillow occurred April 12, 1864, and has been the subject of congressional inquiry. No doubt Forrest's men acted like a set of barbarians, shooting down the helpless negro garrison after the fort was in their possession; but I am told that Forrest personally disclaims any active participation in the assault, and that he stopped the firing as soon as he could. I also take it for granted that Forrest did not lead the assault in person, and consequently that he was to the rear, out of sight if not of hearing at the time, and I was told by hundreds of our men, who were at various times prisoners in

Forrest's possession, that he was usually very kind to them. He had a desperate set of fellows under him, and at that very time there is no doubt the feeling of the Southern people was fearfully savage on this very point of our making soldiers out of their late slaves, and Forrest may have shared the feeling.

I also had another serious cause of disturbance about that time. I wanted badly the two divisions of troops which had been loaned to General Banks in the month of March previously, with the express understanding that their absence was to endure only one month, and that during April they were to come out of Red River, and be again within the sphere of my command. I accordingly instructed one of my inspector-generals, John M. Corse, to take a fleet steamboat at Nashville, proceed *via* Cairo, Memphis, and Vicksburg, to General Banks up the Red River, and to deliver the following letter of April 3d, as also others, of like tenor, to Generals A. J. Smith and Fred Steele, who were supposed to be with him :

HEADQUARTERS MILITARY DIVISION OF THE MISSISSIPPI, }
NASHVILLE, TENNESSEE, *April* 3, 1864. }

Major-General N. P. BANKS, *commanding Department of the Gulf, Red River.*

GENERAL : The thirty days for which I loaned you the command of General A. J. Smith will expire on the 10th instant. I send with this Brigadier-General J. M. Corse, to carry orders to General A. J. Smith, and to give directions for a new movement, which is preliminary to the general campaign. General Corse may see you and explain in full, but, lest he should not find you in person, I will simply state that Forrest, availing himself of the absence of our furloughed men and of the detachment with you, has pushed up between the Mississippi and Tennessee Rivers, even to the Ohio. He attacked Paducah, but got the worst of it, and he still lingers about the place. I hope that he will remain thereabouts till General A. J. Smith can reach his destined point, but this I can hardly expect; yet I want him to reach by the Yazoo a position near Grenada, thence to operate against Forrest, after which to march across to Decatur, Alabama. You will see that he has a big job, and therefore should start at once. From all that I can learn, my troops reached Alexandria, Louisiana, at the time agreed on, viz., March 17th, and I hear of them at Natchitoches, but cannot hear of your troops being above Opelousas.

Steele is also moving. I leave Steele's entire force to coöperate with you and the navy, but, as I before stated, I must have A. J. Smith's troops now as soon as possible.

I beg you will expedite their return to Vicksburg, if they have not already started, and I want them if possible to remain in the same boats they have used up Red River, as it will save the time otherwise consumed in transfer to other boats.

All is well in this quarter, and I hope by the time you turn against Mobile our forces will again act toward the same end, though from distant points. General Grant, now having lawful control, will doubtless see that all minor objects are disregarded, and that all the armies act on a common plan.

Hoping, when this reaches you, that you will be in possession of Shreveport, I am, with great respect, etc.,

W. T. SHERMAN, *Major-General commanding.*

Rumors were reaching us thick and fast of defeat and disaster in that quarter; and I feared then, what afterward actually happened, that neither General Banks nor Admiral Porter could or would spare those two divisions. On the 23d of April, General Corse returned, bringing full answers to my letters, and I saw that we must go on without them. This was a serious loss to the Army of the Tennessee, which was also short by two other divisions that were on their veteran furlough, and were under orders to rendezvous at Cairo, before embarking for Clifton, on the Tennessee River.

On the 10th of April, 1864, the headquarters of the three Armies of the Cumberland, Tennessee, and Ohio, were at Chattanooga, Huntsville, and Knoxville, and the tables on page 16, *et seq.*, give their exact condition and strength.

The Department of the Arkansas was then subject to my command, but General Fred Steele, its commander, was at Little Rock, remote from me, acting in coöperation with General Banks, and had full employment for every soldier of his command; so that I never depended on him for any men, or for any participation in the Georgia campaign. Soon after, viz., May 8th, that department was transferred to the Military Division of "the Gulf," or "Southwest," Major-General E. R. S. Canby commanding, and General Steele served with him in the subsequent movement against Mobile.

In Generals Thomas, McPherson, and Schofield, I had three generals of education and experience, admirably qualified for the work before us. Each has made a history of his own, and I need not here dwell on their respective merits as men, or as commanders of armies, except that each possessed special qualities of mind and of character which fitted them in the highest degree for the work then in contemplation.

By the returns of April 10, 1864, it will be seen that the Army of the Cumberland had on its muster-rolls—

	Men.
Present and absent	171,450
Present for duty	88,883

The Army of the Tennessee—

	Men.
Present and absent	134,763
Present for duty	64,957

The Army of the Ohio—

	Men.
Present and absent	46,052
Present for duty	26,242

The department and army commanders had to maintain strong garrisons in their respective departments, and also to guard their respective lines of supply. I therefore, in my mind, aimed to prepare out of these three armies, by the 1st of May, 1864, a compact army for active operations in Georgia, of about the following numbers:

	Men.
Army of the Cumberland	50,000
Army of the Tennessee	35,000
Army of the Ohio	15,000
Total	100,000

and, to make these troops as mobile as possible, I made the strictest possible orders in relation to wagons and all species of incumbrances and impedimenta whatever. Each officer and soldier was required to carry on his horse or person food and clothing enough for five days. To each regiment was allowed but one wagon and one ambulance, and to the officers of each company one pack-horse or mule.

Transcript from the Tri-Monthly Return of the Department of the Cumberland, commanded by Major-General THOMAS, for April 10, 1864.

COMMANDS.	No. of Regiments	No. of Companies	For Duty: General Officers	For Duty: General Staff-Officers	For Duty: Field, Staff, and Company Officers	For Duty: Total commissioned	For Duty: Enlisted Men	Aggregate	Special, Extra, or Daily Duty: Comm. Officers	Special, Extra, or Daily Duty: Enlisted Men	Sick: Comm. Officers	Sick: Enlisted Men	In Arrest or Confine't: Comm. Officers	In Arrest or Confine't: Enlisted Men	Aggregate	On Detached Service, Within the Dept.: Comm. Officers	On Detached Service, Within the Dept.: Enlisted Men	On Detached Service, Without the Dept.: Comm. Officers	On Detached Service, Without the Dept.: Enlisted Men	With Leave: Comm. Officers	With Leave: Enlisted Men
Department Staff	…	…	8	19	…	22	…	22	…	…	…	…	…	…	22	1	1	1	…	2	…
Fourth Army Corps	75	751	6	17	826	849	15,323	16,172	80	1,505	27	726	5	82	18,597	801	4,494	95	884	752	8,266
Fourteenth Army Corps	60	600	7	18	636	706	18,981	19,687	126	1,866	53	1,210	11	1,182	23,085	326	4,828	114	457	408	5,724
Eleventh and Twelfth Ar'y Corps*	55	561	9	46	864	919	20,028	20,947	82	1,874	87	1,878	11	1,161	24,491	207	2,628	120	627	189	2,614
District of Nashville	18	196	5	8	896	409	8,820	9,229	74	2,221	26	907	9	216	12,682	104	1,431	80	175	23	796
Cavalry Command	26	293	1	12	542	555	10,472	11,027	49	1,442	28	404	6	72	13,023	175	2,762	13	847	186	1,899
Reserve Artillery	…	12	…	…	81	81	1,023	1,104	…	17	1	85	…	8	1,162	5	10	…	…	6	159
Tenth Ohio Sharp-shooters	1	14	…	…	80	80	596	626	5	154	…	50	1	18	854	4	57	…	…	2	12
Post of Chattanooga	…	…	1	8	128	197	8,153	8,230	18	296	5	155	…	49	8,803	88	574	17	76	21	842
Engineer Brigade	…	…	…	…	30	30	1,020	1,050	18	845	…	58	…	…	1,469	17	102	10	86	40	520
Unassigned Infantry	4	40	…	…	102	102	2,975	3,077	16	282	…	824	4	24	3,723	25	152	…	11	86	559
" Cavalry	4	42	…	…	79	79	1,558	1,667	8	204	…	168	1	26	2,051	9	184	4	5	4	108
" Artillery	8	9	…	…	20	20	811	891	…	…	9	38	…	4	953	5	4	6	8	4	145
Signal Corps	…	…	…	24	…	24	130	154	…	16	2	1	…	…	155	8	86	…	…	…	4
Grand Total	252	2,626	82	142	3,720	8,903	84,950	88,883	467	10,222	158	5,449	49	797	106,050	1,215	17,807	478	2,627	1,653	21,148

* Consolidated, and named Twentieth Army Corps.

Transcript from the Tri-Monthly Return of the Department of the Cumberland—(Continued.)

COMMANDS	Absent Sick — Com'd Officers	Absent Sick — Enlisted Men	Without Authority — Com'd Officers	Without Authority — Enlisted Men	Present and Absent — Com'd Officers	Present and Absent — Enlisted Men	Present and Absent — Aggregate	Aggregate Last Return	Present for Duty Equipped — Infantry Com'd Officers	Present for Duty Equipped — Infantry Enlisted Men	Present for Duty Equipped — Cavalry Com'd Officers	Present for Duty Equipped — Cavalry Enlisted Men	Present for Duty Equipped — Artillery Com'd Officers	Present for Duty Equipped — Artillery Enlisted Men	Horses — Serviceable	Horses — Unserviceable	Guns — Number	
Department Staff	1				27		27	27										Brig.-Gen. W. D. Whipple.
Fourth Army Corps	82	5,685	27	408	2,248	36,863	89,111	89,112	785	14,115			12	851	295	25	24	Maj.-Gen. O. O. Howard.
Fourteenth Army Corps	50	4,004	26	369	1,820	37,516	89,336	88,941	686	18,406			23	782	664	52	42	Maj.-Gen. J. M. Palmer.
Eleventh and Twelfth Army Corps																		Maj.-Gen. J. Hooker.
District of Nashville	41	3,728	11	871	1,618	83,409	85,027	84,858	888	18,297	1	50	25	988	802	44	52	Maj.-Gen. L. H. Rousseau.
Cavalry Command	7	983	5	357	693	15,906	16,599	15,074	862	8,006	2	89	24	789	589	10	65	Brig.-Gen. K. Garrard.
Reserve Artillery	44	2,800	17	237	1,067	20,935	22,002	22,002	104	1,376	363	6,786	6	188	9,022	1,969	12	Brig.-Gen. J. M. Brannan.
Fourth Ohio Sharp-shooters	1	116	2	49	59	1,470	1,529	3,074					27	940	481	4	38	
Post of Chattanooga		48	2	8	46	933	979	980	80	596			20	1,050	218		89	Capt. G. M. Barber.
Engineer Brigade		518	31	35	255	5,198	5,453	3,981	56	1,189						7		Maj.-Gen. J. B. Steedman.
Unassigned Infantry		270	1	15	115	2,429	2,544	2,572	80	1,020								Gen. O. M. Poe.
		244		40	181	4,611	4,792	4,010	96	8,001								Maj.-Gen. Carl Schurz.
Cavalry		174		70	112	2,527	2,639	2,265			79	1,204			658	545		{ In the field with other divisions of cavalry.
Artillery	1	88		8	89	1,172	1,211	775					20	871	54	11	28	Col. J. Barnett, 1st Ohio L.A.
Signal Corps		1		1	28	173	201	192										Capt. P. Babcock, Jr.
Grand Total	236	18,649	124	1,963	8,808	163,142	171,450	170,863	2,987	66,006	445	8,129	165	5,989	12,733	2,661	350	

GEO. H. THOMAS, *Major-General commanding.*

Official: E. D. TOWNSEND, *Adjutant-General.*

Transcript from the Tri-Monthly Return of the Department and Army of the Tennessee, commanded by Major-General McPHERSON, for April 10, 1864.

COMMANDS.	Number of Regiments.	Number of Companies.	PRESENT. For Duty. General Officers.	General Staff-Officers.	Field, Staff, and Company Officers.	Total commissioned.	Enlisted Men.	Aggregate.	Special, Extra, or Daily Duty. Commissioned Officers.	Enlisted Men.	Sick. Commissioned Officers.	Enlisted Men.	In Arrest or Confine't. Commissioned Officers.	Enlisted Men.	Aggregate.	ABSENT. On Detached Service. Within the Department. Commissioned Officers.	Enlisted Men.	Without the Department. Commissioned Officers.	Enlisted Men.	With Leave. Commissioned Officers.	Enlisted Men.	Sick. Commissioned Officers.	Enlisted Men.
Department Staff			1	4		5		5							5								
Fifteenth Army Corps	56	571	9	18	723	750	14,919	15,669	94	1,925	52	1,802	7	152	19,201	215	3,055	102	854	394	5,069	56	3,816
Sixteenth Army Corps	71	811	10	35	1,355	1,400	31,345	32,745	169	4,402	81	3,042	28	198	40,655	299	8,191	195	1,560	494	8,298	84	4,058
Seventeenth Army Corps	58	627	6	30	598	634	15,890	16,524	76	2,184	58	2,348	15	96	21,251	461	7,660	128	594	660	10,148	28	1,585
Signal Detachment						1	18	14							14	1	7	1	2	1			
Total Force—Department and Army of the Tennessee	185	2,009	26	82	2,651	2,790	62,167	64,957	889	8,461	191	6,692	45	441	81,128	976	18,913	426	2,450	1,549	23,515	163	9,059

Transcript from the Tri-Monthly Return of the Department and Army of the Tennessee—(Continued.)

COMMANDS	ABSENT. Without Authority		PRESENT AND ABSENT.			Aggregate Last Return.	PRESENT FOR DUTY EQUIPPED. Infantry.		Cavalry.		Artillery.		HORSES.		GUNS.	
	Commissioned Officers.	Enlisted Men.	Commissioned Officers.	Enlisted Men.	Aggregate.		Commissioned Officers.	Enlisted Men.	Commissioned Officers.	Enlisted Men.	Commissioned Officers.	Enlisted Men.	Serviceable.	Unserviceable.	Number.	
Department Staff			5		5	5										Colonel W. T. Clark.
Fifteenth Army Corps	19	262	1,689	30,354	32,043	31,522	689	11,053	27	850	31	1,165	1,086	243	57	Major-General J. A. Logan.
Sixteenth Army Corps	23	966	2,768	57,055	59,823	58,245	554	11,107	152	3,651	80	2,840	5,779	1,064	173	Major-General G. M. Dodge.
Seventeenth Army Corps	14	395	2,060	40,790	42,850	42,859	400	8,545	91	2,187	50	2,005	2,911	1,016	58	Major-General Frank P. Blair.
Signal Detachment		7	4	29	33	26							81			Captain O. H. Howard.
Total Force—Department and Army of the Tennessee	56	1,680	6,535	128,228	134,763	182,057	1,643	30,705	270	6,168	170	6,010	9,807	2,823	288	

Official: E. D. TOWNSEND, *Adjutant-General.*   J. B. McPHERSON, *Major-General commanding.*

Transcript from the Tri-Monthly Return of the Department of the Ohio, commanded by Major-General SCHOFIELD, *for April 10, 1864.*

COMMANDS.	No. of Regiments	No. of Companies	PRESENT — For Duty: General Officers	General Staff-Officers	Field, Staff, and Company Officers	Total commissioned	Enlisted Men	Aggregate	Special, Extra, or Daily Duty: Com. Officers	Enlisted Men	Sick: Com. Officers	Enlisted Men	In Arrest or Confinem't: Com. Officers	Enlisted Men	Aggregate	ABSENT — On Detached Service, Within the Dept: Com. Officers	Enlisted Men	Without the Dept: Com. Officers	Enlisted Men	With Leave: Com. Officers	Enlisted Men	Sick: Com. Officers	Enlisted Men
Twenty-third Army Corps	24	826	4	7	675	686	14,733	15,419	88	1,068	50	1,490	8	818	19,336	221	3,865	15	188	86	512	24	2,408
Cavalry Corps	14	167	1	4	209	214	5,419	5,633	42	678	19	557	4	87	6,965	141	1,660	14	85	32	270	29	1,875
District of the Clinch	4	37	1	8	79	88	1,406	1,489	9	118	5	120	2	21	1,764	9	69	1	14	4	8	5	229
Defenses of Knoxville	2	42			123	123	3,507	3,630	19	354	4	552	4	16	4,579	31	814	8	78	7	54	4	441
Newport Barracks					2	2	69	71		5		1		10	87						1		1
Total Force—Department of the Ohio	44	572	6	14	1,088	1,108	25,134	26,242	158	3,118	78	2,720	18	897	32,731	402	5,408	33	260	79	840	62	4,454

Transcript from the Tri-Monthly Return of the Department of the Ohio—(Continued.)

COMMANDS.	ABSENT. Without Authority.		PRESENT AND ABSENT.			Aggregate Last Return.	PRESENT FOR DUTY EQUIPPED.						HORSES.		GUNS.	
							Infantry.		Cavalry.		Artillery.				Number.	
	Commissioned Officers.	Enlisted Men.	Commissioned Officers.	Enlisted Men.	Aggregate.		Commissioned Officers.	Enlisted Men.	Commissioned Officers.	Enlisted Men.	Commissioned Officers.	Enlisted Men.	Serviceable.	Unserviceable.		
Twenty-third Army Corps	18	970	1,141	25,892	27,088	26,999	545	11,500	76	1,180	49	1,614	427	67	...	Major-General J. D. Cox.
Cavalry Corps	9	814	504	10,340	10,844	10,844	57	1,184	125	2,017	...	...	1,888	424	...	Major-General G. Stoneman.
District of the Clinch	1	873	119	2,353	2,472	2,478	54	897	16	245	9	291	5	...	...	Brig.-General T. T. Garrard.
Defenses of Knoxville	8	99	198	5,415	5,613	5,613	21	455	...	...	57	1,584	12	...	602	Brigadier-General D. Tillson.
Newport Barracks	...	1	2	88	90	224	...	...	...	...	...	...	...	...	...	Colonel J. P. Sanderson.
Total Force—Department of the Ohio	26	1,757	1,964	44,088	46,052	46,158	677	14,086	217	4,342	115	3,789	2,082	491	602	

J. M. SCHOFIELD, *Major-General commanding.*

Official: E. D. TOWNSEND, *Adjutant-General.*

Each division and brigade was provided a fair proportion of wagons for a supply-train, and these were limited in their loads to carry food, ammunition, and clothing. Tents were forbidden to all save the sick and wounded, and one tent only was allowed to each headquarters for use as an office. These orders were not absolutely enforced, though in person I set the example, and did not have a tent, nor did any officer about me have one; but we had wall tent-flies, without poles, and no tent-furniture of any kind. We usually spread our flies over saplings, or on fence-rails or posts improvised on the spot. Most of the general officers, except Thomas, followed my example strictly; but he had a regular headquarters-camp. I frequently called his attention to the orders on this subject, rather jestingly than seriously. He would break out against his officers for having such luxuries, but, needing a tent himself, and being good-natured and slow to act, he never enforced my orders perfectly. In addition to his regular wagon-train, he had a big wagon which could be converted into an office, and this we used to call "Thomas's circus." Several times during the campaign I found quartermasters hid away in some comfortable nook to the rear, with tents and mess-fixtures which were the envy of the passing soldiers; and I frequently broke them up, and distributed the tents to the surgeons of brigades. Yet my orders actually reduced the transportation, so that I doubt if any army ever went forth to battle with fewer impedimenta, and where the regular and necessary supplies of food, ammunition, and clothing, were issued, as called for, so regularly and so well.

My personal staff was then composed of Captain J. C. McCoy, aide-de-camp; Captain L. M. Dayton, aide-de-camp; Captain J. C. Audenried, aide-de-camp; Brigadier-General J. D. Webster, chief of staff; Major R. M. Sawyer, assistant adjutant-general; Captain Montgomery Rochester, assistant adjutant-general. These last three were left at Nashville in charge of the office, and were empowered to give orders in my name, communication being generally kept up by telegraph.

Subsequently were added to my staff, and accompanied me in the field, Brigadier-General W. F. Barry, chief of artillery;

Colonel O. M. Poe, chief of engineers; Colonel L. C. Easton, chief quartermaster; Colonel Amos Beckwith, chief commissary; Captain Thos. G. Baylor, chief of ordnance; Surgeon E. D. Kittoe, medical director; Brigadier-General J. M. Corse, inspector-general ; Lieutenant-Colonel C. Ewing, inspector-general; and Lieutenant-Colonel Willard Warner, inspector-general.

These officers constituted my staff proper at the beginning of the campaign, which remained substantially the same till the close of the war, with very few exceptions; viz.: Surgeon John Moore, United States Army, relieved Surgeon Kittoe of the volunteers (about Atlanta) as medical director; Major Henry Hitchcock joined as judge-advocate, and Captain G. Ward Nichols reported as an extra aide-de-camp (after the fall of Atlanta) at Gaylesville, just before we started for Savannah.

During the whole month of April the preparations for active war were going on with extreme vigor, and my letter-book shows an active correspondence with Generals Grant, Halleck, Thomas, McPherson, and Schofield on thousands of matters of detail and arrangement, most of which are embraced in my testimony before the Committee on the Conduct of the War, vol. i., Appendix.

When the time for action approached, viz., May 1, 1864, the actual armies prepared to move into Georgia resulted as follows, present for battle :

Army of the Cumberland, Major-General THOMAS.

	Men.
Infantry	54,568
Artillery	2,377
Cavalry	3,828
Aggregate	60,773

Number of field-guns, 130.

Army of the Tennessee, Major-General McPHERSON.

	Men.
Infantry	22,437
Artillery	1,404
Cavalry	624
Aggregate	24,465

Guns, 96.

Army of the Ohio, Major-General SCHOFIELD.

	Men.
Infantry	11,183
Artillery	679
Cavalry	1,697
Aggregate	13,559

Guns, 28.

Grand aggregate, 98,797 men and 254 guns.

These figures do not embrace the cavalry divisions which were still incomplete, viz., of General Stoneman, at Lexington, Kentucky, and of General Garrard, at Columbia, Tennessee, who were then rapidly collecting horses, and joined us in the early stage of the campaign. General Stoneman, having a division of about four thousand men and horses, was attached to Schofield's Army of the Ohio. General Garrard's division, of about four thousand five hundred men and horses, was attached to General Thomas's command; and he had another irregular division of cavalry, commanded by Brigadier-General E. McCook. There was also a small brigade of cavalry, belonging to the Army of the Cumberland, attached temporarily to the Army of the Tennessee, which was commanded by Brigadier-General Judson Kilpatrick. These cavalry commands changed constantly in strength and numbers, and were generally used on the extreme flanks, or for some special detached service, as will be hereinafter related. The Army of the Tennessee was still short by the two divisions detached with General Banks, up Red River, and two other divisions on furlough in Illinois, Indiana, and Ohio, but which were rendezvousing at Cairo, under Generals Leggett and Crocker, to form a part of the Seventeenth Corps, which corps was to be commanded by Major-General Frank P. Blair, then a member of Congress, in Washington. On the 2d of April I notified him by letter that I wanted him to join and to command these two divisions, which ought to be ready by the 1st of May. General Blair, with these two divisions, constituting the Seventeenth Army Corps, did not actually overtake us until we reached Acworth and Big Shanty, in Georgia, about the 9th of June, 1864.

In my letter of April 4th to General John A. Rawlins, chief of staff to General Grant at Washington, I described at length all the preparations that were in progress for the active campaign thus contemplated, and therein estimated Schofield at twelve thousand, Thomas at forty-five thousand, and McPherson at thirty thousand. At first I intended to open the campaign about May 1st, by moving Schofield on Dalton from Cleveland, Thomas on the same objective from Chattanooga, and McPherson on Rome and Kingston from Gunter's Landing. My intention was merely to threaten Dalton in front, and to direct McPherson to act vigorously against the railroad below Resaca, far to the rear of the enemy. But by reason of his being short of his estimated strength by the four divisions before referred to, and thus being reduced to about twenty-four thousand men, I did not feel justified in placing him so far away from the support of the main body of the army, and therefore subsequently changed the plan of campaign, so far as to bring that army up to Chattanooga, and to direct it thence through Ship's Gap against the railroad to Johnston's rear, at or near Resaca, distant from Dalton only eighteen miles, and in full communication with the other armies by roads behind Rockyface Ridge, of about the same length.

On the 10th of April I received General Grant's letter of April 4th from Washington, which formed the basis of all the campaigns of the year 1864, and subsequently received another of April 19th, written from Culpepper, Virginia, both of which are now in my possession, in his own handwriting, and are here given entire. These letters embrace substantially all the orders he ever made on this particular subject, and these, it will be seen, devolved on me the details both as to the plan and execution of the campaign by the armies under my immediate command. These armies were to be directed against the rebel army commanded by General Joseph E. Johnston, then lying on the defensive, strongly intrenched at Dalton, Georgia; and I was required to follow it up closely and persistently, so that in no event could any part be detached to assist General Lee in Virginia; General Grant undertaking in like manner to keep

Lee so busy that he could not respond to any calls of help by
Johnston. Neither Atlanta, nor Augusta, nor Savannah, was
the objective, but the "army of Jos. Johnston," go where it
might.

[PRIVATE AND CONFIDENTIAL.]

HEADQUARTERS ARMIES OF THE UNITED STATES, }
WASHINGTON, D. C., April 4, 1864. }

Major-General W. T. SHERMAN, *commanding Military Division of the Mississippi.*

GENERAL: It is my design, if the enemy keep quiet and allow me to
take the initiative in the spring campaign, to work all parts of the army
together, and somewhat toward a common centre. For your information
I now write you my programme, as at present determined upon.

I have sent orders to Banks, by private messenger, to finish up his present expedition against Shreveport with all dispatch ; to turn over the defense of Red River to General Steele and the navy, and to return your
troops to you, and his own to New Orleans ; to abandon all of Texas, except the Rio Grande, and to hold that with not to exceed four thousand
men ; to reduce the number of troops on the Mississippi to the lowest number necessary to hold it, and to collect from his command not less than
twenty-five thousand men. To this I will add five thousand from Missouri.
With this force he is to commence operations against Mobile as soon as he
can. It will be impossible for him to commence too early.

Gillmore joins Butler with ten thousand men, and the two operate against
Richmond from the south side of James River. This will give Butler thirty-
three thousand men to operate with, W. F. Smith commanding the right
wing of his forces, and Gillmore the left wing. I will stay with the Army
of the Potomac, increased by Burnside's corps of not less than twenty-five
thousand effective men, and operate directly against Lee's army, wherever
it may be found.

Sigel collects all his available force in two columns, one, under Ord and
Averill, to start from Beverly, Virginia, and the other, under Crook, to start
from Charleston, on the Kanawha, to move against the Virginia & Tennessee Railroad.

Crook will have all cavalry, and will endeavor to get in about Saltville,
and move east from there to join Ord. His force will be all cavalry, while
Ord will have from ten to twelve thousand men of all arms.

You I propose to move against Johnston's army, to break it up, and to
get into the interior of the enemy's country as far as you can, inflicting all
the damage you can against their war resources.

I do not propose to lay down for you a plan of campaign, but simply to
lay down the work it is desirable to have done, and leave you free to exe-

cute it in your own way. Submit to me, however, as early as you can, your plan of operations.

As stated, Banks is ordered to commence operations as soon as he can. Gillmore is ordered to report at Fortress Monroe by the 18th inst., or as soon thereafter as practicable. Sigel is concentrating now. None will move from their places of rendezvous until I direct, except Banks. I want to be ready to move by the 25th inst., if possible; but all I can now direct is that you get ready as soon as possible. I know you will have difficulties to encounter in getting through the mountains to where supplies are abundant, but I believe you will accomplish it.

From the expedition from the Department of West Virginia I do not calculate on very great results; but it is the only way I can take troops from there. With the long line of railroad Sigel has to protect, he can spare no troops, except to move directly to his front. In this way he must get through to inflict great damage on the enemy, or the enemy must detach from one of his armies a large force to prevent it. In other words, if Sigel can't skin himself, he can hold a leg while some one else skins.

I am, general, very respectfully, your obedient servant,

U. S. GRANT, *Lieutenant-General.*

HEADQUARTERS MILITARY DIVISION OF THE MISSISSIPPI, NASHVILLE, TENNESSEE, *April* 10, 1864.

Lieutenant-General U. S. GRANT, *Commander-in-Chief, Washington, D. C.*

DEAR GENERAL: Your two letters of April 4th are now before me, and afford me infinite satisfaction. That we are now all to act on a common plan, converging on a common centre, looks like enlightened war.

Like yourself, you take the biggest load, and from me you shall have thorough and hearty coöperation. I will not let side issues draw me off from your main plans in which I am to knock Jos. Johnston, and to do as much damage to the resources of the enemy as possible. I have heretofore written to General Rawlins and to Colonel Comstock (of your staff) somewhat of the method in which I propose to act. I have seen all my army, corps, and division commanders, and have signified only to the former, viz., Schofield, Thomas, and McPherson, our general plans, which I inferred from the purport of our conversation here and at Cincinnati.

First, I am pushing stores to the front with all possible dispatch, and am completing the army organization according to the orders from Washington, which are ample and perfectly satisfactory.

It will take us all of April to get in our furloughed veterans, to bring up A. J. Smith's command, and to collect provisions and cattle on the line of the Tennessee. Each of the armies will guard, by detachments of its own, its rear communications.

At the signal to be given by you, Schofield, leaving a select garrison at

Knoxville and Loudon, with twelve thousand men will drop down to the Hiawassee, and march against Johnston's right by the old Federal road. Stoneman, now in Kentucky, organizing the cavalry forces of the Army of the Ohio, will operate with Schofield on his left front—it may be, pushing a select body of about two thousand cavalry by Ducktown or Elijah toward Athens, Georgia.

Thomas will aim to have forty-five thousand men of all arms, and move straight against Johnston, wherever he may be, fighting him cautiously, persistently, and to the best advantage. He will have two divisions of cavalry, to take advantage of any offering.

McPherson will have nine divisions of the Army of the Tennessee, if A. J. Smith gets here, in which case he will have full thirty thousand of the best men in America. He will cross the Tennessee at Decatur and Whitesburg, march toward Rome, and feel for Thomas. If Johnston falls behind the Coosa, then McPherson will push for Rome; and if Johnston falls behind the Chattahoochee, as I believe he will, then McPherson will cross over and join Thomas.

McPherson has no cavalry, but I have taken one of Thomas's divisions, viz., Garrard's, six thousand strong, which is now at Columbia, mounting, equipping, and preparing. I design this division to operate on McPherson's right, rear, or front, according as the enemy appears. But the moment I detect Johnston falling behind the Chattahoochee, I propose to cast off the effective part of this cavalry division, after crossing the Coosa, straight for Opelika, West Point, Columbus, or Wetumpka, to break up the road between Montgomery and Georgia. If Garrard can do this work well, he can return to the Union army; but should a superior force interpose, then he will seek safety at Pensacola and join Banks, or, after rest, will act against any force that he can find east of Mobile, till such time as he can reach me.

Should Johnston fall behind the Chattahoochee, I will feign to the right, but pass to the left and act against Atlanta or its eastern communications, according to developed facts.

This is about as far ahead as I feel disposed to look, but I will ever bear in mind that Johnston is at all times to be kept so busy that he cannot in any event send any part of his command against you or Banks.

If Banks can at the same time carry Mobile and open up the Alabama River, he will in a measure solve the most difficult part of my problem, viz., "provisions." But in that I must venture. Georgia has a million of inhabitants. If they can live, we should not starve. If the enemy interrupt our communications, I will be absolved from all obligations to subsist on our own resources, and will feel perfectly justified in taking whatever and wherever we can find.

I will inspire my command, if successful, with the feeling that beef and salt are all that is absolutely necessary to life, and that parched corn once fed General Jackson's army on that very ground.

As ever, your friend and servant,

W. T. Sherman, *Major-General.*

HEADQUARTERS ARMIES IN THE FIELD, }
CULPEPPER COURT-HOUSE, VIRGINIA, *April* 19, 1864. }

Major-General W. T. Sherman, *commanding Military Division of the Mississippi.*

GENERAL : Since my letter to you of April 4th I have seen no reason to change any portion of the general plan of campaign, if the enemy remain still and allow us to take the initiative. Rain has continued so uninterruptedly until the last day or two that it will be impossible to move, however, before the 27th, even if no more should fall in the mean time. I think Saturday, the 30th, will probably be the day for our general move.

Colonel Comstock, who will take this, can spend a day with you, and fill up many little gaps of information not given in any of my letters.

What I now want more particularly to say is, that if the two main attacks, yours and the one from here, should promise great success, the enemy may, in a fit of desperation, abandon one part of their line of defense, and throw their whole strength upon the other, believing a single defeat without any victory to sustain them better than a defeat all along their line, and hoping too, at the same time, that the army, meeting with no resistance, will rest perfectly satisfied with their laurels, having penetrated to a given point south, thereby enabling them to throw their force first upon one and then on the other.

With the majority of military commanders they might do this.

But you have had too much experience in traveling light, and subsisting upon the country, to be caught by any such *ruse.* I hope my experience has not been thrown away. My directions, then, would be, if the enemy in your front show signs of joining Lee, follow him up to the full extent of your ability. I will prevent the concentration of Lee upon your front, if it is in the power of this army to do it.

The Army of the Potomac looks well, and, so far as I can judge, officers and men feel well. Yours truly,

U. S. Grant, *Lieutenant-General.*

HEADQUARTERS MILITARY DIVISION OF THE MISSISSIPPI, }
NASHVILLE, TENNESSEE, *April* 24, 1864. }

Lieutenant-General Grant, *commanding Armies of the United States, Culpepper, Virginia.*

GENERAL : I now have, at the hands of Colonel Comstock, of your staff, the letter of April 19th, and am as far prepared to assume the offensive as possible. I only ask as much time as you think proper, to enable me to get up McPherson's two divisions from Cairo. Their furloughs will expire about this time, and some of them should now be in motion for Clifton, whence they will march to Decatur, to join General Dodge.

McPherson is ordered to assemble the Fifteenth Corps near Larkin's, and to get the Sixteenth and Seventeenth Corps (Dodge and Blair) at Decatur at the earliest possible moment. From these two points he will direct his forces on Lebanon, Summerville, and Lafayette, where he will act against Johnston, if he accept battle at Dalton; or move in the direction of Rome, if the enemy give up Dalton, and fall behind the Oostenaula or Etowah. I see that there is some risk in dividing our forces, but Thomas and Schofield will have strength enough to cover all the valleys as far as Dalton; and, should Johnston turn his whole force against McPherson, the latter will have his bridge at Larkin's, and the route to Chattanooga *via* Wills's Valley and the Chattanooga Creek, open for retreat; and if Johnston attempt to leave Dalton, Thomas will have force enough to push on through Dalton to Kingston, which will checkmate him. My own opinion is that Johnston will be compelled to hang to his railroad, the only possible avenue of supply to his army, estimated at from forty-five to sixty thousand men.

At Lafayette all our armies will be together, and if Johnston stands at Dalton we must attack him in position. Thomas feels certain that he has no material increase of force, and that he has not sent away Hardee, or any part of his army. Supplies are the great question. I have materially increased the number of cars daily. When I got here, the average was from sixty-five to eighty per day. Yesterday the report was one hundred and ninety-three; to-day, one hundred and thirty-four; and my estimate is that one hundred and forty-five cars per day will give us a day's supply and a day's accumulation.

McPherson is ordered to carry in wagons twenty day's rations, and to rely on the depot at Ringgold for the renewal of his bread. Beeves are now being driven on the hoof to the front; and the commissary, Colonel Beckwith, seems fully alive to the importance of the whole matter.

Our weakest point will be from the direction of Decatur, and I will be forced to risk something from that quarter, depending on the fact that the enemy has no force available with which to threaten our communications from that direction.

Colonel Comstock will explain to you personally much that I cannot commit to paper. I am, with great respect,

W. T. SHERMAN, *Major-General.*

On the 28th of April I removed my headquarters to Chattanooga, and prepared for taking the field in person. General

Grant had first indicated the 30th of April as the day for the simultaneous advance, but subsequently changed the day to May 5th. McPherson's troops were brought forward rapidly to Chattanooga, partly by rail and partly by marching. Thomas's troops were already in position (his advance being out as far as Ringgold—eighteen miles), and Schofield was marching down by Cleveland to Red Clay and Catoosa Springs. On the 4th of May, Thomas was in person at Ringgold, his left at Catoosa, and his right at Leet's Tan-yard. Schofield was at Red Clay, closing upon Thomas's left; and McPherson was moving rapidly into Chattanooga, and out toward Gordon's Mill.

On the 5th I rode out to Ringgold, and on the very day appointed by General Grant from his headquarters in Virginia the great campaign was begun. To give all the minute details will involve more than is contemplated, and I will endeavor only to trace the principal events, or rather to record such as weighed heaviest on my own mind at the time, and which now remain best fixed in my memory.

My general headquarters and official records remained back at Nashville, and I had near me only my personal staff and inspectors-general, with about half a dozen wagons, and a single company of Ohio sharp-shooters (commanded by Lieutenant McCrory) as headquarters or camp guard. I also had a small company of irregular Alabama cavalry (commanded by Lieutenant Snelling), used mostly as orderlies and couriers. No wall-tents were allowed, only the flies. Our mess establishment was less in bulk than that of any of the brigade commanders; nor was this from an indifference to the ordinary comforts of life, but because I wanted to set the example, and gradually to convert all parts of that army into a mobile machine, willing and able to start at a minute's notice, and to subsist on the scantiest food. To reap absolute success might involve the necessity even of dropping all wagons, and to subsist on the chance food which the country was known to contain. I had obtained not only the United States census-tables of 1860, but a compilation made by the Controller of the State of ͏ͻ͏ia for the purpose of taxation, containing in consideral the "population and statistics" of every county in Georgia. One of my aides (Captain Dayton) acted as assistant adjutant-general, with an order-book, letter-book, and writing-paper, that filled a small chest not much larger than an ordinary candle-box. The only reports and returns called for were the ordinary tri-monthly returns of "effective strength." As these accumulated they were sent back to Nashville, and afterward were embraced in the archives of the Military Division of the Mississippi, changed in 1865 to the Military Division of the Missouri, and I suppose they were burned in the Chicago fire of 1870. Still, duplicates remain of all essential papers in the archives of the War Department.

The 6th of May was given to Schofield and McPherson to get into position, and on the 7th General Thomas moved in force against Tunnel Hill, driving off a mere picket-guard of the enemy, and I was agreeably surprised to find that no damage had been done to the tunnel or the railroad. From Tunnel Hill I could look into the gorge by which the railroad passed through a straight and well-defined range of mountains, presenting sharp palisade faces, and known as "Rocky Face." The gorge itself was called the "Buzzard Roost." We could plainly see the enemy in this gorge and behind it, and Mill Creek which formed the gorge, flowing toward Dalton, had been dammed up, making a sort of irregular lake, filling the road, thereby obstructing it, and the enemy's batteries crowned the cliffs on either side. The position was very strong, and I knew that such a general as was my antagonist (Jos. Johnston), who had been there six months, had fortified it to the maximum. Therefore I had no intention to attack the position seriously in front, but depended on Mc-Pherson to capture and hold the railroad to its rear, which would force Johnston to detach largely against him, or rather, as I expected, to evacuate his position at Dalton altogether. My orders to Generals Thomas and Schofield were merely to press strongly at all points in front, ready to rush in on the first appearance of "let go," and, if possible, to catch our enemy in the confusion of retreat.

All the movements of the 7th and 8th were made exactly as

ordered, and the enemy seemed quiescent, acting purely on the defensive.

I had constant communication with all parts of the army, and on the 9th McPherson's head of column entered and passed through Snake Creek, perfectly undefended, and accomplished a complete surprise to the enemy. At its farther *débouché* he met a cavalry brigade, easily driven, which retreated hastily north toward Dalton, and doubtless carried to Johnston the first serious intimation that a heavy force of infantry and artillery was to his rear and within a few miles of his railroad. I got a short note from McPherson that day (written at 2 P. M., when he was within a mile and a half of the railroad, above and near Resaca), and we all felt jubilant. I renewed orders to Thomas and Schofield to be ready for the instant pursuit of what I expected to be a broken and disordered army, forced to retreat by roads to the east of Resaca, which were known to be very rough and impracticable.

That night I received further notice from McPherson that he had found Resaca too strong for a surprise; that in consequence he had fallen back three miles to the mouth of Snake-Creek Gap, and was there fortified. I wrote him the next day the following letters, copies of which are in my letter-book; but his to me were mere notes in pencil, not retained :

HEADQUARTERS MILITARY DIVISION OF THE MISSISSIPPI,
IN THE FIELD, TUNNEL HILL, GEORGIA, *May* 11, 1864—*Morning.*

Major-General McPHERSON, *commanding Army of the Tennessee, Sugar Valley, Georgia.*

GENERAL : I received by courier (in the night) yours of 5 and 6.30 P. M. of yesterday.

You now have your twenty-three thousand men, and General Hooker is in close support, so that you can hold all of Jos. Johnston's army in check should he abandon Dalton. He cannot afford to abandon Dalton, for he has fixed it up on purpose to receive us, and he observes that we are close at hand, waiting for him to quit. He cannot afford a detachment strong enough to fight you, as his army will not admit of it.

Strengthen your position; fight any thing that comes; and threaten the safety of the railroad all the time. But, to tell the truth, I would rather the enemy would stay in Dalton two more days, when he may find in his rear a larger party than he expects in an open field. At all events, we can then choose our own ground, and he will be forced to move out of his works. I do not intend to put a column into Buzzard Roost-Gap at present.

See that you are in easy communication with me and with all head-quarters. After to-day the supplies will be at Ringgold. Yours,

W. T. SHERMAN, *Major-General commanding.*

HEADQUARTERS MILITARY DIVISION OF THE MISSISSIPPI, } IN THE FIELD, TUNNEL HILL, GEORGIA, *May* 11, 1864—*Evening.* }

General McPHERSON, *Sugar Valley.*

GENERAL: The indications are that Johnston is evacuating Dalton. In that event, Howard's corps and the cavalry will pursue; all the rest will follow your route. I will be down early in the morning.

Try to strike him if possible about the forks of the road.

Hooker must be with you now, and you may send General Garrard by Summerville to threaten Rome and that flank. I will cause all the lines to be felt at once.

W. T. SHERMAN, *Major-General commanding.*

McPherson had startled Johnston in his fancied security, but had not done the full measure of his work. He had in hand twenty-three thousand of the best men of the army, and could have walked into Resaca (then held only by a small brigade), or he could have placed his whole force astride the railroad above Resaca, and there have easily withstood the attack of all of Johnston's army, with the knowledge that Thomas and Scho-field were on his heels. Had he done so, I am certain that Johnston would not have ventured to attack him in position, but would have retreated eastward by Spring Place, and we should have captured half his army and all his artillery and wagons at the very beginning of the campaign.

Such an opportunity does not occur twice in a single life, but at the critical moment McPherson seems to have been a little timid. Still, he was perfectly justified by his orders, and fell back and assumed an unassailable defensive position in Sugar Valley, on the Resaca side of Snake-Creek Gap. As soon as informed of this, I determined to pass the whole army through Snake-Creek Gap, and to move on Resaca with the main army.

But during the 10th, the enemy showed no signs of evacu-ating Dalton, and I was waiting for the arrival of Garrard's and

Stoneman's cavalry, known to be near at hand, so as to secure the full advantages of victory, of which I felt certain. Hooker's Twentieth Corps was at once moved down to within easy supporting distance of McPherson; and on the 11th, perceiving signs of evacuation of Dalton, I gave all the orders for the general movement, leaving the Fourth Corps (Howard) and Stoneman's cavalry in observation in front of Buzzard-Roost Gap, and directing all the rest of the army to march through Snake-Creek Gap, straight on Resaca. The roads were only such as the country afforded, mere rough wagon-ways, and these converged to the single narrow track through Snake-Creek Gap; but during the 12th and 13th the bulk of Thomas's and Schofield's armies were got through, and deployed against Resaca, McPherson on the right, Thomas in the centre, and Schofield on the left. Johnston, as I anticipated, had abandoned all his well-prepared defenses at Dalton, and was found inside of Resaca with the bulk of his army, holding his divisions well in hand, acting purely on the defensive, and fighting well at all points of conflict. A complete line of intrenchments was found covering the place, and this was strongly manned at all points. On the 14th we closed in, enveloping the town on its north and west, and during the 15th we had a day of continual battle and skirmish. At the same time I caused two pontoon-bridges to be laid across the Oostenaula River at Lay's Ferry, about three miles below the town, by which we could threaten Calhoun, a station on the railroad seven miles below Resaca. At the same time, May 14th, I dispatched General Garrard, with his cavalry division, down the Oostenaula by the Rome road, with orders to cross over, if possible, and to attack or threaten the railroad at any point below Calhoun and above Kingston.

During the 15th, without attempting to assault the fortified works, we pressed at all points, and the sound of cannon and musketry rose all day to the dignity of a battle. Toward evening McPherson moved his whole line of battle forward, till he had gained a ridge overlooking the town, from which his field-artillery could reach the railroad-bridge across the Oostenaula. The enemy made several attempts to drive him away, repeating the sallies several times, and extending them into the night; but in every instance he was repulsed with bloody loss.

Hooker's corps had also some heavy and handsome fighting that afternoon and night on the left, where the Dalton road entered the intrenchments, capturing a four-gun intrenched battery, with its men and guns; and generally all our men showed the finest fighting qualities.

Howard's corps had followed Johnston down from Dalton, and was in line; Stoneman's division of cavalry had also got up, and was on the extreme left, beyond the Oostenaula.

On the night of May 15th Johnston got his army across the bridges, set them on fire, and we entered Resaca at daylight. Our loss up to that time was about six hundred dead and thirty-three hundred and seventy-five wounded—mostly light wounds that did not necessitate sending the men to the rear for treatment. That Johnston had deliberately designed in advance to give up such strong positions as Dalton and Resaca, for the purpose of drawing us farther south, is simply absurd. Had he remained in Dalton another hour, it would have been his total defeat, and he only evacuated Resaca because his safety demanded it. The movement by us through Snake-Creek Gap was a total surprise to him. My army about doubled his in size, but he had all the advantages of natural positions, of artificial forts and roads, and of concentrated action. We were compelled to grope our way through forests, across mountains, with a large army, necessarily more or less dispersed. Of course, I was disappointed not to have crippled his army more at that particular stage of the game; but, as it resulted, these rapid successes gave us the initiative, and the usual impulse of a conquering army.

Johnston having retreated in the night of May 15th, immediate pursuit was begun. A division of infantry (Jeff. C. Davis's) was at once dispatched down the valley toward Rome, to support Garrard's cavalry, and the whole army was ordered to pursue, McPherson by Lay's Ferry, on the right, Thomas directly by the railroad, and Schofield by the left, by the old road that crossed the Oostenaula above Echota or Newtown. We hastily repaired the railroad-bridge at Resaca, which had been partially burned, and built a temporary floating-bridge out of timber and materials found on the spot; so that Thomas got his advance corps over during the 16th, and marched as far as Calhoun, where he came into communication with McPherson's troops, which had crossed the Oostenaula at Lay's Ferry by our pontoon-bridges, previously laid. Inasmuch as the bridge at Resaca was overtaxed, Hooker's Twentieth Corps was also diverted to cross by the fords and ferries above Resaca, in the neighborhood of Echota.

On the 17th, toward evening, the head of Thomas's column, Newton's division, encountered the rear-guard of Johnston's army near Adairsville. I was near the head of column at the time, trying to get a view of the position of the enemy from an elevation in an open field. My party attracted the fire of a battery; a shell passed through the group of staff-officers and burst just beyond, which scattered us promptly. The next morning the enemy had disappeared, and our pursuit was continued to Kingston, which we reached during Sunday forenoon, the 19th.

From Resaca the railroad runs nearly due south, but at Kingston it makes junction with another railroad from Rome, and changes direction due east. At that time McPherson's head of column was about four miles to the west of Kingston, at a country place called "Woodlawn;" Schofield and Hooker were on the direct roads leading from Newtown to Cassville, diagonal to the route followed by Thomas. Thomas's head of column, which had followed the country roads alongside of the railroad, was about four miles east of Kingston, toward Cassville, when about noon I got a message from him that he had found the enemy, drawn up in line of battle, on some extensive, open ground, about half-way between Kingston and Cassville, and that appearances indicated a willingness and preparation for battle.

Hurriedly sending orders to McPherson to resume the march, to hasten forward by roads leading to the south of Kingston,

so as to leave for Thomas's troops and trains the use of the main
road, and to come up on his right, I rode forward rapidly, over
some rough gravel hills, and about six miles from Kingston
found General Thomas, with his troops deployed; but he reported that, the enemy had fallen back in echelon of divisions,
steadily and in superb order, into Cassville. I knew that the
roads by which Generals Hooker and Schofield were approaching would lead them to a seminary near Cassville, and that it
was all-important to secure the point of junction of these roads
with the main road along which we were marching. Therefore
I ordered General Thomas to push forward his deployed lines as
rapidly as possible; and, as night was approaching, I ordered
two field-batteries to close up at a gallop on some woods which
lay between us and the town of Cassville. We could not see
the town by reason of these woods, but a high range of hills
just back of the town was visible over the tree-tops. On these
hills could be seen fresh-made parapets, and the movements of
men, against whom I directed the artillery to fire at long range.
The stout resistance made by the enemy along our whole front of
a couple of miles indicated a purpose to fight at Cassville; and,
as the night was closing in, General Thomas and I were together,
along with our skirmish-lines near the seminary, on the edge of
the town, where musket-bullets from the enemy were cutting the
leaves of the trees pretty thickly about us. Either Thomas or I
remarked that that was not the place for the two senior officers of
a great army, and we personally went back to the battery, where
we passed the night on the ground. During the night I had
reports from McPherson, Hooker, and Schofield. The former
was about five miles to my right rear, near the "nitre-caves;"
Schofield was about six miles north, and Hooker between us,
within two miles. All were ordered to close down on Cassville at daylight, and to attack the enemy wherever found.
Skirmishing was kept up all night, but when day broke the next
morning, May 20th, the enemy was gone, and our cavalry was
sent in pursuit. These reported him beyond the Etowah River.
We were then well in advance of our railroad-trains, on which
we depended for supplies; so I determined to pause a few days

to repair the railroad, which had been damaged but little, except at the bridge at Resaca, and then to go on.

Nearly all the people of the country seemed to have fled with Johnston's army; yet some few families remained, and from one of them I procured the copy of an order which Johnston had made at Adairsville, in which he recited that he had retreated as far as strategy required, and that his army must be prepared for battle at Cassville. The newspapers of the South, many of which we found, were also loud in denunciation of Johnston's falling back before us without a serious battle, simply resisting by his skirmish-lines and by his rear-guard. But his friends proclaimed that it was all *strategic;* that he was deliberately drawing us farther and farther into the meshes, farther and farther away from our base of supplies, and that in due season he would not only halt for battle, but assume the bold offensive. Of course it was to my interest to bring him to battle as soon as possible, when our numerical superiority was at the greatest; for he was picking up his detachments as he fell back, whereas I was compelled to make similar and stronger detachments to repair the railroads as we advanced, and to guard them. I found at Cassville many evidences of preparation for a grand battle, among them a long line of fresh intrenchments on the hill beyond the town, extending nearly three miles to the south, embracing the railroad-crossing. I was also convinced that the whole of Polk's corps had joined Johnston from Mississippi, and that he had in hand three full corps, viz., Hood's, Polk's, and Hardee's, numbering about sixty thousand men, and could not then imagine why he had declined battle, and did not learn the real reason till after the war was over, and then from General Johnston himself.

In the autumn of 1865, when in command of the Military Division of the Missouri, I went from St. Louis to Little Rock, Arkansas, and afterward to Memphis. Taking a steamer for Cairo, I found as fellow-passengers Generals Johnston and Frank Blair. We were, of course, on the most friendly terms, and on our way up we talked over our battles again, played cards, and questioned each other as to particular parts of our mutual conduct in the game of war. I told Johnston that I had seen his order of preparation, in the nature of an address to his army, announcing his purpose to retreat no more, but to accept battle at Cassville. He answered that such was his purpose; that he had left Hardee's corps in the open fields to check Thomas, and gain time for his formation on the ridge, just behind Cassville; and it was this corps which General Thomas had seen deployed, and whose handsome movement in retreat he had reported in such complimentary terms. Johnston described how he had placed Hood's corps on the right, Polk's in the centre, and Hardee's on the left. He said he had ridden over the ground, given to each corps commander his position, and orders to throw up parapets during the night; that he was with Hardee on his extreme left as the night closed in, and as Hardee's troops fell back to the position assigned them for the intended battle of the next day; and that, after giving Hardee some general instructions, he and his staff rode back to Cassville. As he entered the town, or village, he met Generals Hood and Polk. Hood inquired of him if he had had any thing to eat, and he said no, that he was both hungry and tired, when Hood invited him to go and share a supper which had been prepared for him at a house close by. At the supper they discussed the chances of the impending battle, when Hood spoke of the ground assigned him as being enfiladed by our (Union) artillery, which Johnston disputed, when General Polk chimed in with the remark that General Hood was right; that the cannon-shots fired by us at nightfall had enfiladed their general line of battle, and that for this reason he feared they could not hold their men. General Johnston was surprised at this, for he understood General Hood to be one of those who professed to criticise his strategy, contending that, instead of retreating, he should have risked a battle. General Johnston said he was provoked, accused them of having been in conference, with being beaten before battle, and added that he was unwilling to engage in a critical battle with an army so superior to his own in numbers, with two of his three corps commanders dissatisfied with the ground and positions assigned them. He then and there made up his mind to retreat still farther south, to put the Etowah River and the Allatoona range between us; and he at once gave orders to resume the retrograde movement.

This was my recollection of the substance of the conversation, of which I made no note at the time; but, at a meeting of the Society of the Army of the Cumberland some years after, at Cleveland, Ohio, about 1868, in a short after-dinner speech, I related this conversation, and it got into print. Subsequently, in the spring of 1870, when I was at New Orleans, *en route* for Texas, General Hood called to see me at the St. Charles Hotel, explained that he had seen my speech reprinted in the newspapers and gave me his version of the same event, describing the halt at Cassville, the general orders for battle on that ground, and the meeting at supper with Generals Johnston and Polk, when the chances of the battle to be fought the next day were freely and fully discussed; and he stated that he had argued against fighting the battle purely on the defensive, but had asked General Johnston to permit him with his own corps and part of Polk's to quit their lines, and to march rapidly to attack and overwhelm Schofield, who was known to be separated from Thomas by an interval of nearly five miles, claiming that he could have defeated Schofield, and got back to his position in time to meet General Thomas's attack in front. He also stated that he had then contended with Johnston for the "offensive-defensive" game, instead of the "pure defensive," as proposed by General Johnston; and he said that it was at this time that General Johnston had taken offense, and that it was for this reason he had ordered the retreat that night. As subsequent events estranged these two officers, it is very natural they should now differ on this point; but it was sufficient for us that the rebel army did retreat that night, leaving us masters of all the country above the Etowah River.

For the purposes of rest, to give time for the repair of the railroads, and to replenish supplies, we lay by some few days in that quarter—Schofield with Stoneman's cavalry holding the ground at Cassville Depot, Cartersville, and the Etowah Bridge; Thomas holding his ground near Cassville, and Mc-

Pherson that near Kingston. The officer intrusted with the repair of the railroads was Colonel W. W. Wright, a railroad-engineer, who, with about two thousand men, was so industrious and skillful that the bridge at Resaca was rebuilt in three days, and cars loaded with stores came forward to Kingston on the 24th. The telegraph also brought us the news of the bloody and desperate battles of the Wilderness, in Virginia, and that General Grant was pushing his operations against Lee with ter-rific energy. I was therefore resolved to give my enemy no rest.

In early days (1844), when a lieutenant of the Third Artil-lery, I had been sent from Charleston, South Carolina, to Ma-rietta, Georgia, to assist Inspector-General Churchill to take tes-timony concerning certain losses of horses and accoutrements by the Georgia Volunteers during the Florida War; and after completing the work at Marietta we transferred our party over to Bellefonte, Alabama. I had ridden the distance on horse-back, and had noted well the topography of the country, es-pecially that about Kenesaw, Allatoona, and the Etowah River. On that occasion I had stopped some days with a Colonel Tum-lin, to see some remarkable Indian mounds on the Etowah River, usually called the "Hightower." I therefore knew that the Allatoona Pass was very strong, would be hard to force, and resolved not even to attempt it, but to turn the position, by moving from Kingston to Marietta *via* Dallas; accordingly I made orders on the 20th to get ready for the march to begin on the 23d. The Army of the Cumberland was ordered to march for Dallas, by Euharlee and Stilesboro'; Davis's division, then in Rome, by Van Wert; the Army of the Ohio to keep on the left of Thomas, by a place called Burnt Hickory; and the Army of the Tennessee to march for a position a little to the south, so as to be on the right of the general army, when grouped about Dallas.

The movement contemplated leaving our railroad, and to de-pend for twenty days on the contents of our wagons; and as the country was very obscure, mostly in a state of nature, dense-ly wooded, and with few roads, our movements were necessarily slow. We crossed the Etowah by several bridges and fords, and took as many roads as possible, keeping up communication by cross-roads, or by couriers through the woods. I personally joined General Thomas, who had the centre, and was consequently the main column, or " column of direction." The several columns followed generally the valley of the Euharlee, a tributary coming into the Etowah from the south, and gradually crossed over a ridge of mountains, parts of which had once been worked over for gold, and were consequently full of paths and unused wagon-roads or tracks. A cavalry picket of the enemy at Burnt Hickory was captured, and had on his person an order from General Johnston, dated at Allatoona, which showed that he had detected my purpose of turning his position, and it accordingly became necessary to use great caution, lest some of the minor columns should fall into ambush, but, luckily the enemy was not much more familiar with that part of the country than we were. On the other side of the Allatoona range, the Pumpkin-Vine Creek, also a tributary of the Etowah, flowed north and west; Dallas, the point aimed at, was a small town on the other or east side of this creek, and was the point of concentration of a great many roads that led in every direction. Its possession would be a threat to Marietta and Atlanta, but I could not then venture to attempt either, till I had regained the use of the railroad, at least as far down as its *débouché* from the Allatoona range of mountains. Therefore, the movement was chiefly designed to compel Johnston to give up Allatoona.

On the 25th all the columns were moving steadily on Dallas —McPherson and Davis away off to the right, near Van Wert; Thomas on the main road in the centre, with Hooker's Twentieth Corps ahead, toward Dallas; and Schofield to the left rear. For the convenience of march, Hooker had his three divisions on separate roads, all leading toward Dallas, when, in the afternoon, as he approached a bridge across Pumpkin-Vine Creek, he found it held by a cavalry force, which was driven off, but the bridge was on fire. This fire was extinguished, and Hooker's leading division (Geary's) followed the retreating

cavalry on a road leading due east toward Marietta, instead
of Dallas. This leading division, about four miles out from
the bridge, struck a heavy infantry force, which was moving down from Allatoona toward Dallas, and a sharp battle ensued. I came up in person soon after, and as my map showed
that we were near an important cross-road called " New Hope,"
from a Methodist meeting-house there of that name, I ordered
General Hooker to secure it if possible that night. He asked
for a short delay, till he could bring up his other two divisions,
viz., of Butterfield and Ward, but before these divisions had
got up and were deployed, the enemy had also gained corresponding strength. The woods were so dense, and the resistance so spirited, that Hooker could not carry the position,
though the battle was noisy, and prolonged far into the night.
This point, " New Hope," was the accidental intersection of the
road leading from Allatoona to Dallas with that from Van
Wert to Marietta, was four miles northeast of Dallas, and from
the bloody fighting there for the next week was called by the
soldiers " Hell-Hole."

The night was pitch-dark, it rained hard, and the conver-
gence of our columns toward Dallas produced much confusion. I am sure similar confusion existed in the army opposed to us, for we were all mixed up. I slept on the ground,
without cover, alongside of a log, got little sleep, resolved at
daylight to renew the battle, and to make a lodgment on the
Dallas and Allatoona road if possible, but the morning revealed
a strong line of intrenchments facing us, with a heavy force of
infantry and guns. The battle was renewed, and without success. McPherson reached Dallas that morning, viz., the 26th,
and deployed his troops to the southeast and east of the town,
placing Davis's division of the Fourteenth Corps, which had
joined him on the road from Rome, on his left; but this still
left a gap of at least three miles between Davis and Hooker.
Meantime, also, General Schofield was closing up on Thomas's
left.

Satisfied that Johnston in person was at New Hope with
all his army, and that it was so much nearer my " objective,"

the railroad, than Dallas, I concluded to draw McPherson from Dallas to Hooker's right, and gave orders accordingly; but McPherson also was confronted with a heavy force, and, as he began to withdraw according to his orders, on the morning of the 28th he was fiercely assailed on his right; a bloody battle ensued, in which he repulsed the attack, inflicting heavy loss on his assailants, and it was not until the 1st of June that he was enabled to withdraw from Dallas, and to effect a close junction with Hooker in front of New Hope. Meantime Thomas and Schofield were completing their deployments, gradually overlapping Johnston on his right, and thus extending our left nearer and nearer to the railroad, the nearest point of which was Acworth, about eight miles distant. All this time a continual battle was in progress by strong skirmish-lines, taking advantage of every species of cover, and both parties fortifying each night by rifle-trenches, with head-logs, many of which grew to be as formidable as first-class works of defense. Occasionally one party or the other would make a dash in the nature of a sally, but usually it sustained a repulse with great loss of life. I visited personally all parts of our lines nearly every day, was constantly within musket-range, and though the fire of musketry and cannon resounded day and night along the whole line, varying from six to ten miles, I rarely saw a dozen of the enemy at any one time; and these were always skirmishers dodging from tree to tree, or behind logs on the ground, or who occasionally showed their heads above the hastily-constructed but remarkably strong rifle-trenches. On the occasion of my visit to McPherson on the 30th of May, while standing with a group of officers, among whom were Generals McPherson, Logan, Barry, and Colonel Taylor, my former chief of artillery, a Minié-ball passed through Logan's coat-sleeve, scratching the skin, and struck Colonel Taylor square in the breast; luckily he had in his pocket a famous memorandum-book, in which he kept a sort of diary, about which we used to joke him a good deal; its thickness and size saved his life, breaking the force of the ball, so that after traversing th book it only penetrated the breast to the ribs, but it knoc' down and disabled him for the rest of the campaign. He was a most competent and worthy officer, and now lives in poverty in Chicago, sustained in part by his own labor, and in part by a pitiful pension recently granted.

On the 1st of June General McPherson closed in upon the right, and, without attempting further to carry the enemy's strong position at New Hope Church, I held our general right in close contact with it, gradually, carefully, and steadily working by the left, until our strong infantry-lines had reached and secured possession of all the wagon-roads between New Hope, Allatoona, and Acworth, when I dispatched Generals Garrard's and Stoneman's divisions of cavalry into Allatoona, the first around by the west end of the pass, and the latter by the direct road. Both reached their destination without opposition, and orders were at once given to repair the railroad forward from Kingston to Allatoona, embracing the bridge across the Etowah River. Thus the real object of my move on Dallas was accomplished, and on the 4th of June I was preparing to draw off from New Hope Church, and to take position on the railroad in front of Allatoona, when, General Johnston himself having evacuated his position, we effected the change without further battle, and moved to the railroad, occupying it from Allatoona and Acworth forward to Big Shanty, in sight of the famous Kenesaw Mountain.

Thus, substantially in the month of May, we had steadily driven our antagonist from the strong positions of Dalton, Resaca, Cassville, Allatoona, and Dallas; had advanced our lines in strong, compact order from Chattanooga to Big Shanty, nearly a hundred miles of as difficult country as was ever fought over by civilized armies; and thus stood prepared to go on, anxious to fight, and confident of success as soon as the railroad communications were complete to bring forward the necessary supplies. It is now impossible to state accurately our loss of life and men in any one separate battle; for the fighting was continuous, almost daily, among trees and bushes, on ground where one could rarely see a hundred yards ahead.

The aggregate loss in the several corps for the month of May is reported as follows in the usual monthly returns sent to the Adjutant-General's office, which are, therefore, official :

Casualties during the Month of May, 1864 *(Major-General* SHERMAN *commanding).*

ARMY OF THE CUMBERLAND (MAJOR-GENERAL THOMAS).

CORPS.	Killed and Missing.	Wounded.	Total.
Fourth (Howard)........................	576	1,910	2,486
Fourteenth (Palmer).................	147	655	802
Twentieth (Hooker)...................	571	2,997	3,568
Total............................	1,294	5,562	6,856

ARMY OF THE TENNESSEE (MAJOR-GENERAL MᶜPHERSON).

CORPS.	Killed and Missing.	Wounded.	Total.
Fifteenth (Logan)......................	122	624	746
Sixteenth (Dodge).....................	94	430	524
Seventeenth (Blair)...................	(Not yet up.)	1	1
Total............................	216	1,055	1,271

ARMY OF THE OHIO (MAJOR-GENERAL SCHOFIELD).

CORPS.	Killed and Missing.	Wounded.	Total.
Twenty-third (Schofield)..............	226	757	983
Cavalry.............................	127	62	189
Total............................	353	819	1,172
Grand aggregate.....................	1,863	7,436	9,299

General Joseph E. Johnston, in his "Narrative of his Military Operations," just published (March 27, 1874), gives the effective strength of his army at and about Dalton on the 1st of May, 1864 (page 302), as follows:

Infantry... 37,652
Artillery 2,812
Cavalry... 2,392

Total................................... 42,856

During May, and prior to reaching Cassville, he was further reënforced (page 352) :

Polk's corps of three divisions......................... 12,000
Martin's division of cavalry.......................... 3,500
Jackson's division of cavalry........................ 3,900

And at New Hope Church, May 26th :

Brigade of Quarles..................................... 2,200

Grand total.................................. 64,456

His losses during the month of May are stated by him, as taken from the report of Surgeon Foard (page 325) :

FROM DALTON TO CASSVILLE.

CORPS.	Killed.	Wounded.	Total.
Hardee's...............................	116	850	966
Hood's.................................	283	1,564	1,847
Polk's.................................	46	529	575
Total............................	445	2,943	3,388

AT NEW HOPE CHURCH (PAGE 335.)

CORPS.	Killed.	Wounded.	Total.
Hardee's	156	879	1,035
Hood's.................................	103	756	859
Polk's.................................	17	94	111
Total............................	276	1,729	2,005
Total killed and wounded during May..	721	4,672	5,393

These figures include only the killed and wounded, whereas my statement of losses embraces the " missing," which are usually " prisoners," and of these we captured, during the whole campaign of four and a half months, exactly 12,983, whose names, rank, and regiments, were officially reported to the Commissary-General of Prisoners ; and assuming a due proportion for the month of May, viz., one-fourth, makes 3,245 to be added to the killed and wounded given above, making an aggregate loss in

Johnston's army, from Dalton to New Hope, inclusive, of 8,638, against ours of 9,299.

Therefore General Johnston is greatly in error, in his estimates on page 357, in stating our loss, as compared with his, at six or ten to one.

I always estimated my force at about double his, and could afford to lose two to one without disturbing our relative proportion; but I also reckoned that, in the natural strength of the country, in the abundance of mountains, streams, and forests, he had a fair offset to our numerical superiority, and therefore endeavored to act with reasonable caution while moving on the vigorous " offensive."

With the drawn battle of New Hope Church, and our occupation of the natural fortress of Allatoona, terminated the month of May, and the first stage of the campaign.

CHAPTER XVI.

JUNE, 1864.

ON the 1st of June our three armies were well in hand, in the broken and densely-wooded country fronting the enemy intrenched at New Hope Church, about five miles north of Dallas. General Stoneman's division of cavalry had occupied Allatoona, on the railroad, and General Garrard's division was at the western end of the pass, about Stilesboro'. Colonel W. W. Wright, of the Engineers, was busily employed in repairing the railroad and rebuilding the bridge across the Etowah (or Hightower) River, which had been destroyed by the enemy on his retreat; and the armies were engaged in a general and constant skirmish along a front of about six miles—McPherson the right, Thomas the centre, and Schofield on the left. By gradually covering our front with parapet, and extending to the left, we approached the railroad toward Acworth and overlapped the enemy's right. By the 4th of June we had made such progress that Johnston evacuated his lines in the night, leaving us masters of the situation, when I deliberately shifted McPherson's army to the extreme left, at and in front of Acworth, with Thomas's about two miles on his right, and Schofield's on his right—all facing east. Heavy rains set in about the 1st of June, making the roads infamous; but our marches were short, as we needed time for the repair of the railroad, so as to bring supplies forward to Allatoona Station. On the 6th I rode back to Allatoona, seven miles, found it all that was expected, and gave orders for its fortification and preparation as a " secondary base."

General Blair arrived at Acworth on the 8th with his two divisions of the Seventeenth Corps—the same which had been on veteran furlough—had come up from Cairo by way of Clifton, on the Tennessee River, and had followed our general route to Allatoona, where he had left a garrison of about fifteen hundred men. His effective strength, as reported, was nine thousand. These, with new regiments and furloughed men who had joined early in the month of May, equaled our losses from battle, sickness, and by detachments; so that the three armies still aggregated about one hundred thousand effective men.

On the 10th of June the whole combined army moved forward six miles, to " Big Shanty," a station on the railroad, whence we had a good view of the enemy's position, which embraced three prominent hills, known as Kenesaw, Pine Mountain, and Lost Mountain. On each of these hills the enemy had signal-stations and fresh lines of parapets. Heavy masses of infantry could be distinctly seen with the naked eye, and it was manifest that Johnston had chosen his ground well, and with deliberation had prepared for battle; but his line was at least ten miles in extent—too long, in my judgment, to be held successfully by his force, then estimated at sixty thousand. As his position, however, gave him a perfect view over our field, we had to proceed with due caution. McPherson had the left, following the railroad, which curved around the north base of Kenesaw; Thomas the centre, obliqued to the right, deploying below Kenesaw and facing Pine Hill; and Schofield, somewhat refused, was on the general right, looking south, toward Lost Mountain.

On the 11th the Etowah bridge was done; the railroad was repaired up to our very skirmish-line, close to the base of Kenesaw, and a loaded train of cars came to Big Shanty. The locomotive, detached, was run forward to a water-tank within the range of the enemy's guns on Kenesaw, whence the enemy opened fire on the locomotive; but the engineer was not afraid, went on to the tank, got water, and returned safely to his train, answering the guns with the screams of his engine, heightened by the cheers and shouts of our men.

The rains continued to pour, and made our developments

slow and dilatory, for there were no roads, and these had to be improvised by each division for its own supply-train from the depot in Big Shanty to the camps. Meantime each army was deploying carefully before the enemy, intrenching every camp, ready as against a sally. The enemy's cavalry was also busy in our rear, compelling us to detach cavalry all the way back as far as Resaca, and to strengthen all the infantry posts as far as Nashville. Besides, there was great danger, always in my mind, that Forrest would collect a heavy cavalry command in Mississippi, cross the Tennessee River, and break up our railroad below Nashville. In anticipation of this very danger, I had sent General Sturgis to Memphis to take command of all the cavalry in that quarter, to go out toward Pontotoc, engage Forrest and defeat him; but on the 14th of June I learned that General Sturgis had himself been defeated on the 10th of June, and had been driven by Forrest back into Memphis in considerable confusion. I expected that this would soon be followed by a general raid on all our roads in Tennessee. General A. J. Smith, with the two divisions of the Sixteenth and Seventeenth Corps which had been with General Banks up Red River, had returned from that ill-fated expedition, and had been ordered to General Canby at New Orleans, who was making a diversion about Mobile; but, on hearing of General Sturgis's defeat, I ordered General Smith to go out from Memphis and renew the offensive, so as to keep Forrest off our roads. This he did finally, defeating Forrest at Tupelo, on the 13th, 14th, and 15th days of July; and he so stirred up matters in North Mississippi that Forrest could not leave for Tennessee. This, for a time, left me only the task of covering the roads against such minor detachments of cavalry as Johnston could spare from his immediate army, and I proposed to keep these too busy in their own defense to spare detachments.

By the 14th the rain slackened, and we occupied a continuous line of ten miles, intrenched, conforming to the irregular position of the enemy, when I reconnoitred, with a view to make a break in their line between Kenesaw and Pine Mountain. When abreast of Pine Mountain I noticed a rebel battery on its crest, with a continuous line of fresh rifle-trench about half-way down the hill. Our skirmishers were at the time engaged in the woods about the base of this hill between the lines, and I estimated the distance to the battery on the crest at about eight hundred yards. Near it, in plain view, stood a group of the enemy, evidently observing us with glasses. General Howard, commanding the Fourth Corps, was near by, and I called his attention to this group, and ordered him to compel it to keep behind its cover. He replied that his orders from General Thomas were to spare artillery-ammunition. This was right, according to the general policy, but I explained to him that we must keep up the *morale* of a bold offensive, that he must use his artillery, force the enemy to remain on the timid defensive, and ordered him to cause a battery close by to fire three volleys. I continued to ride down our line, and soon heard, in quick succession, the three volleys. The next division in order was Geary's, and I gave him similar orders. General Polk, in my opinion, was killed by the second volley fired from the first battery referred to.

In a conversation with General Johnston, after the war, he explained that on that day he had ridden in person from Marietta to Pine Mountain, held by Bates's division, and was accompanied by Generals Hardee and Polk. When on Pine Mountain, reconnoitring, quite a group of soldiers, belonging to the battery close by, clustered about him. He noticed the preparations of our battery to fire, and cautioned these men to scatter. They did so, and he likewise hurried behind the parapet, from which he had an equally good view of our position; but General Polk, who was dignified and corpulent, walked back slowly, not wishing to appear too hurried or cautious in the presence of the men, and was struck across the breast by an unexploded shell, which killed him instantly. This is my memory of the conversation, and it is confirmed by Johnston himself in his "Narrative," page 337, except that he calculated the distance of our battery at six hundred yards, and says that Polk was killed by the third shot; I know that our guns fired by volley, and believe that he was hit by a shot of the second volley. It has been asserted that I fired the gun which killed General Polk, and that I knew it was directed against that general. The fact is, at that distance we could not even tell that the group were officers at all; I was on horseback, a couple of hundred yards off, before my orders to fire were executed, had no idea that our shot had taken effect, and continued my ride down along the line to Schofield's extreme flank, returning late in the evening to my headquarters at Big Shanty, where I occupied an abandoned house. In a cotton-field back of that house was our signal-station, on the roof of an old gin-house. The signal-officer reported that by studying the enemy's signals he had learned the "key," and that he could read their signals. He explained to me that he had translated a signal about noon, from Pine Mountain to Marietta, "Send an ambulance for General Polk's body;" and later in the day another, "Why don't you send an ambulance for General Polk?" From this we inferred that General Polk had been killed, but how or where we knew not; and this inference was confirmed later in the same day by the report of some prisoners who had been captured.

On the 15th we advanced our general lines, intending to attack at any weak point discovered between Kenesaw and Pine Mountain; but Pine Mountain was found to be abandoned, and Johnston had contracted his front somewhat, on a direct line, connecting Kenesaw with Lost Mountain. Thomas and Schofield thereby gained about two miles of most difficult country, and McPherson's left lapped well around the north end of Kenesaw. We captured a good many prisoners, among them a whole infantry regiment, the Fourteenth Alabama, three hundred and twenty strong.

On the 16th the general movement was continued, when Lost Mountain was abandoned by the enemy. Our right naturally swung round, so as to threaten the railroad below Marietta, but Johnston had still further contracted and strengthened his lines, covering Marietta and all the roads below.

On the 17th and 18th the rain again fell in torrents, making army movements impossible, but we devoted the time to strengthening our positions, more especially the left and centre,

with a view gradually to draw from the left to add to the right;
and we had to hold our lines on the left extremely strong, to
guard against a sally from Kenesaw against our depot at Big
Shanty. Garrard's division of cavalry was kept busy on our
left, McPherson had gradually extended to his right, enabling
Thomas to do the same still farther; but the enemy's position
was so very strong, and everywhere it was covered by intrenchments, that we found it as dangerous to assault as a permanent
fort. We in like manner covered our lines of battle by similar
works, and even our skirmishers learned to cover their bodies
by the simplest and best forms of defensive works, such as rails
or logs, piled in the form of a simple lunette, covered on the
outside with earth thrown up at night.

The enemy and ourselves used the same form of rifle-trench,
varied according to the nature of the ground, viz.: the trees
and bushes were cut away for a hundred yards or more in front,
serving as an abatis or entanglement; the parapets varied from
four to six feet high, the dirt taken from a ditch outside and
from a covered way inside, and this parapet was surmounted by
a "head-log," composed of the trunk of a tree from twelve to
twenty inches at the butt, lying along the interior crest of the
parapet and resting in notches cut in other trunks which extended back, forming an inclined plane, in case the head-log
should be knocked inward by a cannon-shot. The men of both
armies became extremely skillful in the construction of these
works, because each man realized their value and importance to
himself, so that it required no orders for their construction. As
soon as a regiment or brigade gained a position within easy distance for a sally, it would set to work with a will, and would
construct such a parapet in a single night; but I endeavored to
spare the soldiers this hard labor by authorizing each division
commander to organize out of the freedmen who escaped to us
a pioneer corps of two hundred men, who were fed out of the
regular army supplies, and I promised them ten dollars a month,
under an existing act of Congress. These pioneer detachments
became very useful to us during the rest of the war, for they
could work at night while our men slept; they in turn were not

expected to fight, and could therefore sleep by day. Our enemies used their slaves for a similar purpose, but usually kept them out of the range of fire by employing them to fortify and strengthen the position to their rear *next* to be occupied in their general retrograde. During this campaign hundreds if not thousands of miles of similar intrenchments were built by both armies, and as a rule whichever party attacked one of them got the worst of it.

On the 19th of June the rebel army again fell back on its flanks, to such an extent that for a time I supposed it had retreated to the Chattahoochee River, fifteen miles distant; but as we pressed forward we were soon undeceived, for we found it still more concentrated, covering Marietta and the railroad. These successive contractions of the enemy's line encouraged us and discouraged him, but were doubtless justified by sound reasons. On the 20th Johnston's position was unusually strong. Kenesaw Mountain was his salient; his two flanks were refused and covered by parapets and by Noonday and Nose's Creeks. His left flank was his weak point, so long as he acted on the " defensive," whereas, had he designed to contract the extent of his line for the purpose of getting in reserve a force with which to strike " offensively " from his right, he would have done a wise act, and I was compelled to presume that such was his object. We were also so far from Nashville and Chattanooga that we were naturally sensitive for the safety of our railroad and depots, so that the left (McPherson) was held *very strong*.

About this time came reports that a large cavalry force of the enemy had passed around our left flank, evidently to strike this very railroad somewhere below Chattanooga. I therefore reënforced the cavalry stationed from Resaca to Cassville, and ordered forward from Huntsville, Alabama, the infantry division of General John E. Smith, to hold Kingston securely.

While we were thus engaged about Kenesaw, General Grant had his hands full with Lee, in Virginia. General Halleck was the chief of staff at Washington, and to him I communicated almost daily. I find from my letter-book that on the 21st of June I reported to him tersely and truly the condition of facts on that day: "This is the nineteenth day of rain, and the prospect of fair weather is as far off as ever. The roads are impassable; the fields and woods become quagmires after a few wagons have crossed over. Yet we are at work all the time. The left flank is across Noonday Creek, and the right is across Nose's Creek. The enemy still holds Kenesaw, a conical mountain, with Marietta behind it, and has his flanks retired, to cover that town and the railroad behind. I am all ready to attack the moment the weather and roads will permit troops and artillery to move with any thing like life."

The weather has a wonderful effect on troops: in action and on the march, rain is favorable; but in the woods, where all is blind and uncertain, it seems almost impossible for an army covering ten miles of front to act in concert during wet and stormy weather. Still I pressed operations with the utmost earnestness, aiming always to keep our fortified lines in absolute contact with the enemy, while with the surplus force we felt forward, from one flank or the other, for his line of communication and retreat. On the 22d of June I rode the whole line, and ordered General Thomas in person to advance his extreme right corps (Hooker's); and instructed General Schofield, by letter, to keep his entire army, viz., the Twenty-third Corps, as a strong right flank in close support of Hooker's deployed line. During this day the sun came out, with some promise of clear weather, and I had got back to my bivouac about dark, when a signal-message was received, dated—

KULP HOUSE, 5.30 P. M.

General SHERMAN:

We have repulsed two heavy attacks, and feel confident, our only apprehension being from our extreme right flank. Three entire corps are in front of us.

Major-General HOOKER.

Hooker's corps (the Twentieth) belonged to Thomas's army; Thomas's headquarters were two miles nearer to Hooker than mine; and Hooker, being an old army officer, knew that he should have reported this fact to Thomas and not to me; I was, moreover, specially disturbed by the assertion in his report that he was uneasy about his *right flank*, when Schofield had been specially ordered to protect that. I first inquired of my adjutant, Dayton, if he were certain that General Schofield had received his orders, and he answered that the envelope in which he had sent them was receipted by General Schofield himself. I knew, therefore, that General Schofield must be near by, in close support of Hooker's right flank. General Thomas had before this occasion complained to me of General Hooker's disposition to "switch off," leaving wide gaps in his line, so as to be independent, and to make *glory* on his own account. I therefore resolved not to overlook this breach of discipline and propriety. The rebel army was only composed of three corps; I had that very day ridden six miles of their lines, found them everywhere strongly occupied, and therefore Hooker could not have encountered "three entire corps." Both McPherson and Schofield had also complained to me of this same tendency of Hooker to widen the gap between his own corps and his proper army (Thomas's), so as to come into closer contact with one or other of the wings, asserting that he was the senior by commission to both McPherson and Schofield, and that in the event of battle he should assume command over them, by virtue of his older commission.

They appealed to me to protect them. I had heard during that day some cannonading and heavy firing down toward the "Kulp House," which was about five miles southeast of where I was, but this was nothing unusual, for at the same moment there was firing along our lines full ten miles in extent. Early the next day (23d) I rode down to the "Kulp House," which was on a road leading from Powder Springs to Marietta, about three miles distant from the latter. On the way I passed through General Butterfield's division of Hooker's corps, which I learned had not been engaged at all in the battle of the day before; then I rode along Geary's and Ward's divisions, which occupied the field of battle, and the men were engaged in burying the dead. I found General Schofield's corps on the Powder

Springs road, its head of column abreast of Hooker's right, therefore constituting "a strong right flank," and I met Generals Schofield and Hooker together. As rain was falling at the moment, we passed into a little church standing by the road-side, and I there showed General Schofield Hooker's signal-message of the day before. He was very angry, and pretty sharp words passed between them, Schofield saying that his head of column (Hascall's division) had been, at the time of the battle, actually in advance of Hooker's line; that the attack or sally of the enemy struck his troops before it did Hooker's; that General Hooker knew of it at the time ; and he offered to go out and show me that the dead men of his advance division (Hascall's) were lying farther out than any of Hooker's. General Hooker pretended not to have known this fact. I then asked him why he had called on me for help, until he had used all of his own troops; asserting that I had just seen Butterfield's division, and had learned from him that he had not been engaged the day before at all; and I asserted that the enemy's sally must have been made by one corps (Hood's), in place of three, and that it had fallen on Geary's and Ward's divisions, which had repulsed the attack handsomely. As we rode away from that church General Hooker was by my side, and I told him that such a thing must not occur again; in other words, I reproved him more gently than the occasion demanded, and from that time he began to sulk. General Hooker had come from the East with great fame as a "fighter," and at Chattanooga he was glorified by his "battle above the clouds," which I fear turned his head. He seemed jealous of all the army commanders, because in years, former rank, and experience, he thought he was our superior.

On the 23d of June I telegraphed to General Halleck this summary, which I cannot again better state:

We continue to press forward on the principle of an advance against fortified positions. The whole country is one vast fort, and Johnston must have at least fifty miles of connected trenches, with abatis and finished batteries. We gain ground daily, fighting all the time. On the 21st General Stanley gained a position near the south end of Kenesaw, from which the enemy attempted in vain to drive him; and the same day General T. J. Wood's division took a hill, which the enemy assaulted three times at night without success, leaving more than a hundred dead on the ground. Yesterday the extreme right (Hooker and Schofield) advanced on the Powder Springs road to within three miles of Marietta. The enemy made a strong effort to drive them away, but failed signally, leaving more than two hundred dead on the field. Our lines are now in close contact, and the fighting is incessant, with a good deal of artillery-fire. As fast as we gain one position the enemy has another all ready, but I think he will soon have to let go Kenesaw, which is the key to the whole country. The weather is now better, and the roads are drying up fast. Our losses are light, and, notwithstanding the repeated breaks of the road to our rear, supplies are ample.

During the 24th and 25th of June General Schofield extended his right as far as prudent, so as to compel the enemy to thin out his lines correspondingly, with the intention to make two strong assaults at points where success would give us the greatest advantage. I had consulted Generals Thomas, McPherson, and Schofield, and we all agreed that we could not with prudence stretch out any more, and therefore there was no alternative but to attack "fortified lines," a thing carefully avoided up to that time. I reasoned, if we could make a breach anywhere near the rebel centre, and thrust in a strong head of column, that with the one moiety of our army we could hold in check the corresponding wing of the enemy, and with the other sweep in flank and overwhelm the other half. The 27th of June was fixed as the day for the attempt, and in order to oversee the whole, and to be in close communication with all parts of the army, I had a place cleared on the top of a hill to the rear of Thomas's centre, and had the telegraph-wires laid to it. The points of attack were chosen, and the troops were all prepared with as little demonstration as possible. About 9 A. M. of the day appointed, the troops moved to the assault, and all along our lines for ten miles a furious fire of artillery and musketry was kept up. At all points the enemy met us with determined courage and in great force. McPherson's attacking column fought up the face of the lesser Kenesaw, but could not reach the summit. About a mile to the right (just below the Dallas road) Thomas's assaulting column reached the parapet, where Brigadier-General Harker was shot down mortally wounded, and Brigadier-General Daniel McCook (my old law-partner) was desperately wounded, from the effects of which he afterward died. By 11.30 the assault was in fact over, and had failed. We had not broken the rebel line at either point, but our assaulting columns held their ground within a few yards of the rebel trenches, and there covered themselves with parapet. McPherson lost about five hundred men and several valuable officers, and Thomas lost nearly two thousand men. This was the hardest fight of the campaign up to that date, and it is well described by Johnston in his "Narrative" (pages 342, 343), where he admits his loss in killed and wounded as—

	Men.
Hood's corps (not reported)............	...
Hardee's corps.........................	286
Loring's (Polk's)......................	522
Total................................	808

This, no doubt, is a true and fair statement; but, as usual, Johnston overestimates our loss, putting it at six thousand, whereas our entire loss was about twenty-five hundred, killed and wounded.

While the battle was in progress at the centre, Schofield crossed Olley's Creek on the right, and gained a position threatening Johnston's line of retreat; and, to increase the effect, I ordered Stoneman's cavalry to proceed rapidly still farther to the right, to Sweetwater. Satisfied of the bloody cost of attacking intrenched lines, I at once thought of moving the whole army to the railroad at a point (Fulton) about ten miles below Marietta, or to the Chattahoochee River itself, a movement similar to the one afterward so successfully practised at Atlanta. All the orders were issued to bring forward supplies enough to fill our wagons, intending to strip the railroad back to Allatoona, and leave that place as our depot, to be covered as well as possible by Garrard's cavalry. General Thomas, as usual, shook his head, deeming it risky to leave the railroad; but something had to be done, and I had resolved on this move, as reported in my dispatch to General Halleck on July 1st:

General Schofield is now south of Olley's Creek, and on the head of Nickajack. I have been hurrying down provisions and forage, and to-morrow night propose to move McPherson from the left to the extreme right, back of General Thomas. This will bring my right within three miles of the Chattahoochee River, and about five miles from the railroad. By this movement I think I can force Johnston to move his whole army down from Kenesaw to defend his railroad and the Chattahoochee, when I will (by the left flank) reach the railroad below Marietta; but in this I must cut loose from the railroad with ten days' supplies in wagons. Johnston may come out of his intrenchments to attack Thomas, which is exactly what I want, for General Thomas is well intrenched on a line parallel with the enemy south of Kenesaw. I think that Allatoona and the line of the Etowah are strong enough for me to venture on this move. The movement is substantially down the Sandtown road straight for Atlanta.

McPherson drew out of his lines during the night of July 2d, leaving Garrard's cavalry, dismounted, occupying his trenches, and moved to the rear of the Army of the Cumberland, stretching down the Nickajack; but Johnston detected the movement, and promptly abandoned Marietta and Kenesaw. I expected as much, for, by the earliest dawn of the 3d of July, I was up at a large spy-glass mounted on a tripod, which Colonel Poe, United States Engineers, had at his bivouac close by our camp. I directed the glass on Kenesaw, and saw some of our pickets crawling up the hill cautiously; soon they stood upon the very top, and I could plainly see their movements as they ran along the crest just abandoned by the enemy. In a minute I roused my staff, and started them off with orders in every direction for a pursuit by every possible road, hoping to catch Johnston in the confusion of retreat, especially at the crossing of the Chattahoochee River.

I must close this chapter here, so as to give the actual losses during June, which are compiled from the official returns by months. These losses, from June 1st to July 3d, were all substantially sustained about Kenesaw and Marietta, and it was really a continuous battle, lasting from the 10th day of June till the 3d of July, when the rebel army fell back from Marietta toward the Chattahoochee River. Our losses were:

ARMY OF THE CUMBERLAND.

CORPS.	Killed and Missing.	Wounded.	Total.
Fourth (Howard).....................	602	1,542	2,144
Fourteenth (Palmer)...................	353	1,466	1,819
Twentieth (Hooker).......	322	1,246	1,568
Total, Army of the Cumberland....	1,277	4,254	5,531

ARMY OF THE TENNESSEE.

CORPS.	Killed and Missing.	Wounded.	Total.
Fifteenth (Logan).....................	179	687	866
Sixteenth (Dodge).....................	52	157	209
Seventeenth (Blair)	47	212	259
Total, Army of the Tennessee.....	278	1,056	1,334

ARMY OF THE OHIO.

CORPS.	Killed and Missing.	Wounded.	Total.
Twenty-third (Schofield)	105	362	467
Cavalry...............................	130	68	198
Total, Army of the Ohio...........	235	430	665
Loss in June, aggregate..............	1,790	5,740	7,530

Johnston makes his statement of losses from the report of his surgeon Foard, for pretty much the same period, viz., from June 4th to July 4th (page 576):

CORPS.	Killed.	Wounded.	Total.
Hardee's	200	1,433	1,633
Hood's...............................	140	1,121	1,261
Polk's................................	128	926	1,054
Total.............................	468	3,480	3,948

In the tabular statement the "missing" embraces the prisoners; and, giving two thousand as a fair proportion of prisoners captured by us for the month of June (twelve thousand nine hundred and eighty-three in all the campaign), makes an aggregate loss in the rebel army of fifty-nine hundred and forty-eight, to ours of seventy-five hundred and thirty—a less proportion than in the relative strength of our two armies, viz., as six to ten, thus maintaining our relative superiority, which the desperate game of war justified.

CHAPTER XVII.

As before explained, on the 3d of July, by moving McPherson's entire army from the extreme left, at the base of Kenesaw to the right, below Olley's Creek, and stretching it down the Nickajack toward Turner's Ferry of the Chattahoochee, we forced Johnston to choose between a direct assault on Thomas's intrenched position, or to permit us to make a lodgment on his railroad below Marietta, or even to cross the Chattahoochee. Of course, he chose to let go Kenesaw and Marietta, and fall back on an intrenched camp prepared by his orders in advance on the north and west bank of the Chattahoochee, covering the railroad-crossing and his several pontoon-bridges. I confess I had not learned beforehand of the existence of this strong place, in the nature of a *tête-du-pont*, and had counted on striking him an effectual blow in the expected confusion of his crossing the Chattahoochee, a broad and deep river then to his rear. Ordering every part of the army to pursue vigorously on the morning of the 3d of July, I rode into Marietta, just quitted by the rebel rear-guard, and was terribly angry at the cautious pursuit by Garrard's cavalry, and even by the head of our infantry columns. But Johnston had in advance cleared and multiplied his roads, whereas ours had to cross at right angles from the direction of Powder Springs toward Marietta, producing delay and confusion. By night Thomas's head of column ran up against a strong rear-guard intrenched at Smyrna camp-ground, six miles below Marietta, and there on the next day we celebrated our Fourth of July, by a noisy but not a desperate battle, designed chiefly to hold the enemy there till Generals McPherson and Schofield could get well into position below him, near the Chattahoochee crossings.

It was here that General Noyes, late Governor of Ohio, lost his leg. I came very near being shot myself while reconnoitring in the second story of a house on our picket-line, which was struck several times by cannon-shot, and perfectly riddled with musket-balls.

During the night Johnston drew back all his army and trains inside the *tête-du-pont* at the Chattahoochee, which proved one of the strongest pieces of field-fortification I ever saw. We closed up against it, and were promptly met by a heavy and severe fire. Thomas was on the main road in immediate pursuit; next on his right was Schofield; and McPherson on the extreme right, reaching the Chattahoochee River below Turner's Ferry. Stoneman's cavalry was still farther to the right, along down the Chattahoochee River as far as opposite Sandtown; and on that day I ordered Garrard's division of cavalry up the river eighteen miles, to secure possession of the factories at Roswell, as well as to hold an important bridge and ford at that place.

About three miles out from the Chattahoochee the main road forked, the right branch following substantially the railroad, and the left one leading straight for Atlanta, *via* Paice's Ferry and Buckhead. We found the latter unoccupied and unguarded, and the Fourth Corps (Howard's) reached the river at Paice's Ferry. The right-hand road was perfectly covered by the *tête-du-pont* before described, where the resistance was very severe, and for some time deceived me, for I was pushing Thomas with orders to fiercely assault his enemy, supposing that he was merely opposing us to gain time to get his trains and troops across the Chattahoochee; but, on personally reconnoitring, I saw the abatis and the strong redoubts, which satisfied me of the preparations that had been made by Johnston in anticipation of this very event. While I was with General Jeff. C. Davis, a poor negro came out of the abatis, blanched with fright, said he had been hidden under a log all day, with a perfect storm of shot, shells, and musket-balls, passing over him, till a short lull had enabled him to creep out and make himself known to our skirmishers, who in turn had sent him back to where we were. This negro explained that he with about a thousand slaves had been at work a month or more on these very lines, which, as he explained, extended from the river about a mile above the railroad-bridge to Turner's Ferry below, being in extent from five to six miles.

Therefore, on the 5th of July we had driven our enemy to cover in the valley of the Chattahoochee, and we held possession of the river above for eighteen miles, as far as Roswell, and below ten miles to the mouth of the Sweetwater. Moreover, we held the high ground and could overlook his movements, instead of his looking down on us, as was the case at Kenesaw.

From a hill just back of Vining's Station I could see the houses in Atlanta, nine miles distant, and the whole intervening valley of the Chattahoochee; could observe the preparations for our reception on the other side, the camps of men and large trains of covered wagons; and supposed, as a matter of course, that Johnston had passed the river with the bulk of his army, and that he had only left on our side a corps to cover his bridges; but in fact he had only sent across his cavalry and trains. Between Howard's corps at Paice's Ferry and the rest of Thomas's army pressing up against this *tête-du-pont*, was a space concealed by dense woods, in crossing which I came near riding into a detachment of the enemy's cavalry; and later in the same day Colonel Frank Sherman, of Chicago, then on General Howard's staff, did actually ride straight into the enemy's camp, supposing that our lines were continuous. He was carried to Atlanta, and for some time the enemy supposed they were in possession of the commander-in-chief of the opposing army.

I knew that Johnston would not remain long on the west bank of the Chattahoochee, for I could easily practise on that ground to better advantage our former tactics of intrenching a moiety in his front, and with the rest of our army cross the river and threaten either his rear or the city of Atlanta itself, which city was of vital importance to the existence not only of his own army, but of the Confederacy itself. In my dispatch of July 6th to General Halleck, at Washington, I state that—

Johnston (in his retreat from Kenesaw) has left two breaks in the railroad—one above Marietta and one near Vining's Station. The former is already repaired, and Johnston's army has heard the sound of our locomotives. The telegraph is finished to Vining's Station, and the field-wire has just reached my bivouac, and will be ready to convey this message as soon as it is written and translated into cipher.

I propose to study the crossings of the Chattahoochee, and, when all is ready, to move quickly. As a beginning, I will keep the troops and wagons well back from the river, and only display to the enemy our picket-line, with a few field-batteries along at random. I have already shifted Schofield to a point in our left rear, whence he can in a single move reach the Chattahoochee at a point above the railroad-bridge, where there is a ford. At present the waters are turbid and swollen from recent rains; but if the present hot weather lasts, the water will run down very fast. We have pontoons enough for four bridges, but, as our crossing will be resisted, we must manœuvre some. All the regular crossing-places are covered by forts, apparently of long construction; but we shall cross in due time, and, instead of attacking Atlanta direct, or any of its forts, I propose to make a circuit, destroying all its railroads. This is a delicate movement, and must be done with caution. Our army is in good condition and full of confidence; but the weather is intensely hot, and a good many men have fallen with sunstroke. The country is high and healthy, and the sanitary condition of the army is good.

At this time Stoneman was very active on our extreme right, pretending to be searching the river below Turner's Ferry for a crossing, and was watched closely by the enemy's cavalry on the other side. McPherson, on the right, was equally demonstrative at and near Turner's Ferry. Thomas faced substantially the intrenched *tête-du-pont*, and had his left on the Chattahoochee River, at Paice's Ferry. Garrard's cavalry was up at Roswell, and McCook's small division of cavalry was intermediate, above Soap's Creek. Meantime, also, the railroad-construction party was hard at work, repairing the railroad up to our camp at Vining's Station.

Of course, I expected every possible resistance in crossing the Chattahoochee River, and had made up my mind to feign on the right, but actually to cross over by the left. We had already secured a crossing-place at Roswell, but one nearer was advisable; General Schofield had examined the river well, found a place just below the mouth of Soap's Creek which he deemed advantageous, and was instructed to effect an early crossing there, and to intrench a good position on the other side, viz., the east bank. But, preliminary thereto, I had ordered General Rousseau, at Nashville, to collect, out of the scattered detachments of cavalry in Tennessee, a force of a couple of thousand men, to rendezvous at Decatur, Alabama, thence to make a rapid march for Opelika, to break up the railroad-links between Georgia and Alabama, and then to make junction with me about Atlanta; or, if forced, to go on to Pensacola, or even to swing across to some of our posts in Mississippi. General Rousseau asked leave to command this expedition himself, to which I consented, and on the 6th of July he reported that he was all ready at Decatur, and I gave him orders to start. He moved promptly on the 9th, crossed the Coosa below the "Ten Islands" and the Tallapoosa below "Horseshoe Bend," having passed through Talladega. He struck the railroad west of Opelika, tore it up for twenty miles, then turned north and came to Marietta on the 22d of July, whence he reported to me. This expedition was in the nature of a raid, and must have disturbed the enemy somewhat; but, as usual, the cavalry did not work hard, and their destruction of the railroad was soon repaired. Rousseau, when he reported to me in person before Atlanta, on the 23d of July, stated his entire loss to have been only twelve killed and thirty wounded. He brought in four hundred captured mules and three hundred horses, and also told me a good story. He said he was far down in Alabama, below Talladega, one hot, dusty day, when the blue clothing of his men was gray with dust; he had halted his column along a road, and he in person, with his staff, had gone to the house of a planter, who met him kindly, on the front-porch. He asked for water, which was brought, and as the party sat on the porch in conversation he saw, in a stable-yard across the road, quite a number of good mules. He remarked to the planter, "My good sir, I fear I must take

some of your mules." The planter remonstrated, saying he had
already contributed liberally to the *good cause ;* that it was
only last week he had given to General Roddy ten mules.
Rousseau replied, "Well, in this war you should be at least
neutral—that is, you should be as liberal to us as to Roddy" (a
rebel cavalry general). "Well, ain't you on our side ?" "No,"
said Rousseau; "I am General Rousseau, and all these men you
see are Yanks." "Great God ! is it possible ? Are these
Yanks ? Who ever supposed they would come away down here
in Alabama ?" Of course, Rousseau took his ten mules.

Schofield effected his crossing at Soap's Creek very handsomely on the 9th, capturing the small guard that was watching
the crossing. By night he was on the high ground beyond,
strongly intrenched, with two good pontoon-bridges finished,
and was prepared, if necessary, for an assault by the whole Confederate army. The same day Garrard's cavalry also crossed
over at Roswell, drove away the cavalry-pickets, and held its
ground till relieved by Newton's division of Howard's corps,
which was sent up temporarily, till it in turn was relieved by
Dodge's corps (Sixteenth) of the Army of the Tennessee, which
was the advance of the whole of that army.

That night Johnston evacuated his trenches, crossed over the
Chattahoochee, burned the railroad-bridge and his pontoon and
trestle bridges, and left us in full possession of the north or west
bank—besides which, we had already secured possession of the
two good crossings at Roswell and Soap's Creek. I have always
thought Johnston neglected his opportunity there, for he had
lain comparatively idle while we got control of both banks of
the river above him.

On the 13th I ordered McPherson, with the Fifteenth Corps,
to move up to Roswell, to cross over, prepare good bridges, and
to make a strong *tête-du-pont* on the farther side. Stoneman
had been sent down to Campbellton, with orders to cross over
and to threaten the railroad below Atlanta, if he could do so
without too much risk ; and General Blair, with the Seventeenth
Corps, was to remain at Turner's Ferry, demonstrating as much
as possible, thus keeping up the feint below while we were actu-

ally crossing above. Thomas was also ordered to prepare his bridges at Powers's and Paice's Ferries. By crossing the Chattahoochee above the railroad-bridge, we were better placed to cover our railroad and depots than below, though a movement across the river below the railroad, to the south of Atlanta, might have been more decisive. But we were already so far from home, and would be compelled to accept battle whenever offered, with the Chattahoochee to *our* rear, that it became imperative for me to take all prudential measures the case admitted of, and I therefore determined to pass the river above the railroad-bridge—McPherson on the left, Schofield in the centre, and Thomas on the right.

On the 13th I reported to General Halleck as follows:

All is well. I have now accumulated stores at Allatoona and Marietta, both fortified and garrisoned points. Have also three places at which to cross the Chattahoochee in our possession, and only await General Stoneman's return from a trip down the river, to cross the army in force and move on Atlanta.

Stoneman is now out two days, and had orders to be back on the fourth or fifth day at furthest.

From the 10th to the 15th we were all busy in strengthening the several points for the proposed passage of the Chattahoochee, in increasing the number and capacity of the bridges, rearranging the garrisons to our rear, and in bringing forward supplies. On the 15th General Stoneman got back to Powder Springs, and was ordered to replace General Blair at Turner's Ferry, and Blair, with the Seventeenth Corps, was ordered up to Roswell to join McPherson.

On the 17th we began the general movement against Atlanta, Thomas crossing the Chattahoochee at Powers's and Paice's, by pontoon-bridges; Schofield moving out toward Cross Keys, and McPherson toward Stone Mountain. We encountered but little opposition except by cavalry. On the 18th all the armies moved on a general right wheel, Thomas to Buckhead, forming line of battle facing Peach-Tree Creek; Schofield was on his left, and McPherson well over toward the railroad between Stone Moun-

tain and Decatur, which he reached at 2 p. m. of that day, about
four miles from Stone Mountain, and seven miles east of Decatur, and there he turned toward Atlanta, breaking up the railroad as he progressed, his advance-guard reaching Decatur about
night, where he came into communication with Schofield's
troops, which had also reached Decatur. About 10 A. M. of that
day (July 18th), when the armies were all in motion, one of
General Thomas's staff-officers brought me a citizen, one of our
spies, who had just come out of Atlanta, and had brought a
newspaper of the same day, or of the day before, containing
Johnston's order relinquishing the command of the Confederate
forces in Atlanta, and Hood's order assuming the command.   I
immediately inquired of General Schofield, who was his class-
mate at West Point, about Hood, as to his general character,
etc., and learned that he was bold even to rashness, and coura-
geous in the extreme; I inferred that the change of commanders
meant "fight." Notice of this important change was at once
sent to all parts of the army, and every division commander was
cautioned to be always prepared for battle in any shape.   This
was just what we wanted, viz., to fight in open ground, on any
thing like equal terms, instead of being forced to run up against
prepared intrenchments ; but, at the same time, the enemy having Atlanta behind him, could choose the time and place of
attack, and could at pleasure mass a superior force on our weakest points.   Therefore, we had to be constantly ready for
sallies.

On the 19th the three armies were converging toward Atlanta, meeting such feeble resistance that I really thought the
enemy intended to evacuate the place.   McPherson was moving
astride of the railroad, near Decatur ; Schofield along a road
leading toward Atlanta, by Colonel Howard's house and the
distillery; and Thomas was crossing "Peach-Tree" in line of
battle, building bridges for nearly every division as deployed.
There was quite a gap between Thomas and Schofield, which I
endeavored to close by drawing two of Howard's divisions
nearer Schofield.   On the 20th I was with General Schofield
near the centre, and soon after noon heard heavy firing in front

of Thomas's right, which lasted an hour or so, and then ceased. I soon learned that the enemy had made a furious sally, the blow falling on Hooker's corps (the Twentieth), and partially on Johnson's division of the Fourteenth, and Newton's of the Fourth. The troops had crossed Peach-Tree Creek, were deployed, but at the time were resting for noon, when, without notice, the enemy came pouring out of their trenches down upon them, they became commingled, and fought in many places hand to hand. General Thomas happened to be near the rear of Newton's division, and got some field-batteries in a good position, on the north side of Peach-Tree Creek, from which he directed a furious fire on a mass of the enemy, which was passing around Newton's left and exposed flank. After a couple of hours of hard and close conflict, the enemy retired slowly within his trenches, leaving his dead and many wounded on the field. Johnson's and Newton's losses were light, for they had partially covered their fronts with light parapet; but Hooker's whole corps fought in open ground, and lost about fifteen hundred men. He reported four hundred rebel dead left on the ground, and that the rebel wounded would number four thousand; but this was conjectural, for most of them got back within their own lines. We had, however, met successfully a bold sally, had repelled it handsomely, and were also put on our guard; and the event illustrated the future tactics of our enemy. This sally came from the Peach-Tree line, which General Johnston had carefully prepared in advance, from which to fight us *outside* of Atlanta. We then advanced our lines in compact order, close up to these finished intrenchments, overlapping them on our left. From various parts of our lines the houses inside of Atlanta were plainly visible, though between us were the strong parapets, with ditch, *fraise, chevaux-de-frise*, and abatis, prepared long in advance by Colonel Jeremy F. Gilmer, formerly of the United States Engineers. McPherson had the Fifteenth Corps astride the Augusta Railroad, and the Seventeenth deployed on its left. Schofield was next on his right, then came Howard's, Hooker's, and Palmer's corps, on the extreme right. Each corps was deployed with strong reserves, and their trains were parked to their rear. McPherson's trains were in Decatur, guarded by a brigade commanded by Colonel Sprague of the Sixty-third Ohio. The Sixteenth Corps (Dodge's) was crowded out of position on the right of McPherson's line, by the contraction of the circle of investment; and, during the previous afternoon, the Seventeenth Corps (Blair's) had pushed its operations on the farther side of the Augusta Railroad, so as to secure possession of a hill, known as Leggett's Hill, because General Leggett's division had carried it by assault. Giles A. Smith's division was on Leggett's left, deployed with a weak left flank " in air," in military phraseology. It was in carrying this hill that General Gresham, a great favorite, was badly wounded; and there also Colonel Tom Reynolds, now of Madison, Wisconsin, was shot through the leg. When the surgeons were debating the propriety of amputating it in his hearing, he begged them to spare the leg, as it was very valuable, being an " imported leg." He was of Irish birth, and this well-timed piece of wit saved his leg, for the surgeons thought, if he could perpetrate a joke at such a time, they would trust to his vitality to save his limb.

During the night, I had full reports from all parts of our line, most of which was partially intrenched as against a sally, and finding that McPherson was stretching out too much on his left flank, I wrote him a note early in the morning not to extend so much by his left; for we had not troops enough to completely invest the place, and I intended to destroy utterly all parts of the Augusta Railroad to the east of Atlanta, then to withdraw from the left flank and add to the right. In that letter I ordered McPherson not to extend any farther to the left, but to employ General Dodge's corps (Sixteenth), then forced out of position, to destroy every rail and tie of the railroad, from Decatur up to his skirmish-line, and I wanted him (McPherson) to be ready, as soon as General Garrard returned from Covington (whither I had sent him), to move to the extreme right of Thomas, so as to reach if possible the railroad below Atlanta, viz., the Macon road. In the morning we found the strong line of parapet, " Peach-Tree line," to the front of Schofield and Thomas, abandoned, and our lines were advanced rapidly close up to Atlanta. For some moments I supposed the enemy intended to evacuate, and in person was on horseback at the head of Schofield's troops, who had advanced in front of the Howard House to some open ground, from which we could plainly see the whole rebel line of parapets, and I saw their men dragging up from the intervening valley, by the distillery, trees and saplings for abatis. Our skirmishers found the enemy down in this valley, and we could see the rebel main line strongly manned, with guns in position at intervals. Schofield was dressing forward his lines, and I could hear Thomas farther to the right engaged, when General McPherson and his staff rode up. We went back to the Howard House, a double frame-building with a porch, and sat on the steps, discussing the chances of battle, and of Hood's general character. McPherson had also been of the same class at West Point with Hood, Schofield, and Sheridan. We agreed that we ought to be unusually cautious and prepared at all times for sallies and for hard fighting, because Hood, though not deemed much of a scholar, or of great mental capacity, was undoubtedly a brave, determined, and rash man; and the change of commanders at that particular crisis argued the displeasure of the Confederate Government with the cautious but prudent conduct of General Jos. Johnston.

McPherson was in excellent spirits, well pleased at the progress of events so far, and had come over purposely to see me about the order I had given him to use Dodge's corps to break up the railroad, saying that the night before he had gained a position on Leggett's Hill from which he could look over the rebel parapet, and see the high smoke-stack of a large foundery in Atlanta; that before receiving my order he had diverted Dodge's two divisions (then in motion) from the main road, along a diagonal one that led to his extreme left flank, then held by Giles A. Smith's division (Seventeenth Corps), for the purpose of strengthening that flank; and that he had sent some intrenching-tools there, to erect some batteries from which he intended to knock down that foundery, and otherwise to damage the buildings inside of Atlanta. He said he could put all his pioneers to work, and do with them in the time indicated all I had proposed to do with General Dodge's two divisions. Of course I assented at once, and we walked down the road a short distance, sat down by the foot of a tree where I had my map, and on it pointed out to him Thomas's position and his own. I then explained minutely that, after we had sufficiently broken up the Augusta road, I wanted to shift his whole army around by the rear to Thomas's extreme right, and hoped thus to reach the other railroad at East Point. While we sat there we could hear lively skirmishing going on near us (down about the distillery), and occasionally round-shot from twelve or twenty-four pound guns came through the trees in reply to those of Schofield, and we could hear similar sounds all along down the lines of Thomas to our right, and his own to the left; but presently the firing appeared a little more brisk (especially over about Giles A. Smith's division), and then we heard an occasional gun back toward Decatur. I asked him what it meant. We took my pocket-compass (which I always carried), and by noting the direction of the sound, we became satisfied that the firing was too far to our left rear to be explained by known facts; and he hastily called for his horse, his staff, and his orderlies.

McPherson was then in his prime (about thirty-four years old), over six feet high, and a very handsome man in every way, was universally liked, and had many noble qualities. He had on his boots outside his pantaloons, gauntlets on his hands, had on his major-general's uniform, and wore a sword-belt, but no sword. He hastily gathered his papers (save one, which I now possess) into a pocket-book, put it in his breast-pocket, and jumped on his horse, saying he would hurry down his line and send me back word what these sounds meant. His adjutant-general, Clark, Inspector-General Strong, and his aides, Captains Steele and Gile, were with him. Although the sound of musketry on our left grew in volume, I was not so much disturbed by it as by the sound of artillery back toward Decatur. I ordered Schofield at once to send a brigade back to Decatur (some five miles) and was walking up and down the porch of the Howard House, listening, when one of McPherson's staff, with his horse covered with sweat, dashed up to the porch, and reported that General McPherson was either "killed or a prisoner." He explained that when they had left me a few minutes before, they had ridden rapidly across to the railroad, the sounds of battle increasing as they neared the position occupied by General Giles A. Smith's division, and that McPherson had sent first one, then another of his staff to bring some of the reserve brigades of the Fifteenth Corps over to the exposed left flank; that he had reached the head of Dodge's corps (marching by the flank on the diagonal road as described), and had ordered it to hurry forward to the same point; that then, almost if not entirely alone, he had followed this road leading across the wooded valley behind the Seventeenth Corps, and had disappeared in these woods, doubtless with a sense of absolute security. The sound of musketry was there heard, and McPherson's horse came back, bleeding, wounded, and riderless. I ordered the staff-officer who brought this message to return at once, to find General Logan (the senior officer present with the Army of the Tennessee), to report the same facts to him, and to instruct him to drive back this supposed small force, which had evidently got around the Seventeenth Corps through the blind woods in rear of our left flank. I soon dispatched one of my own staff (McCoy, I think) to General Logan with similar orders, telling him to refuse his left flank, and to fight the battle (holding fast to Leggett's Hill) with the Army of the Tennessee; that I would personally look to Decatur and to the safety of his rear, and would reënforce him if he needed it. I dispatched orders to General Thomas on our right, telling him of this strong sally, and my inference that the lines in his front had evidently been weakened by reason thereof, and that he ought to take advantage of the opportunity to make a lodgment in Atlanta, if possible.

Meantime the sounds of the battle rose on our extreme left more and more furious, extending to the place where I stood, at the Howard House. Within an hour an ambulance came in (attended by Colonels Clark and Strong, and Captains Steele and

Gile), bearing McPherson's body. I had it carried inside of the Howard House, and laid on a door wrenched from its hinges. Dr. Hewitt, of the army, was there, and I asked him to examine the wound. He opened the coat and shirt, saw where the ball had entered and where it came out, or rather lodged under the skin, and he reported that McPherson must have died in a few seconds after being hit; that the ball had ranged upward across his body, and passed near the heart. He was dressed just as he left me, with gauntlets and boots on, but his pocket-book was gone. On further inquiry I learned that his body must have been in possession of the enemy some minutes, during which time it was rifled of the pocket-book, and I was much concerned lest the letter I had written him that morning should have fallen into the hands of some one who could read and understand its meaning. Fortunately the spot in the woods where McPherson was shot was regained by our troops in a few minutes, and the pocket-book found in the haversack of a prisoner of war captured at the time, and it and its contents were secured by one of McPherson's staff.

While we were examining the body inside the house, the battle was progressing outside, and many shots struck the building, which I feared would take fire; so I ordered Captains Steele and Gile to carry the body to Marietta. They reached that place the same night, and, on application, I ordered his personal staff to go on and escort the body to his home, in Clyde, Ohio, where it was received with great honor, and it is now buried in a small cemetery, close by his mother's house, which cemetery is composed in part of the family orchard, in which he used to play when a boy. The foundation is ready laid for the equestrian monument now in progress, under the auspices of the Society of the Army of the Tennessee.

The reports that came to me from all parts of the field revealed clearly what was the game of my antagonist, and the ground somewhat favored him. The railroad and wagon-road from Decatur to Atlanta lie along the summit, from which the waters flow, by short, steep valleys, into the "Peach-Tree" and Chattahoochee, to the west, and by other valleys, of gentler declivity, toward the east (Ocmulgee). The ridges and level ground were mostly cleared, and had been cultivated as corn or cotton fields.; but where the valleys were broken, they were left in a state of nature—wooded, and full of undergrowth. McPherson's line of battle was across this railroad, along a general ridge, with a gentle but cleared valley to his front, between him and the defenses of Atlanta; and another valley, behind him, was clear of timber in part, but to his left rear the country was heavily wooded. Hood, during the night of July 21st, had withdrawn from his Peach-Tree line, had occupied the fortified line of Atlanta, facing north and east, with Stewart's—formerly Polk's—corps and part of Hardee's, and with G. W. Smith's division of militia. His own corps, and part of Hardee's, had marched out to the road leading from McDonough to Decatur, and had turned so as to strike the left and rear of McPherson's line "in air." At the same time he had sent Wheeler's division of cavalry against the trains parked in Decatur. Unluckily for us, I had sent away the whole of Garrard's division of cavalry during the night of the 20th, with orders to proceed to Covington, thirty miles east, to burn two important bridges across the Ulcofauhatchee and Yellow Rivers, to tear up the railroad, to damage it as much as possible from Stone Mountain eastward, and to be gone four days; so that McPherson had no cavalry in hand to guard that flank.

The enemy was therefore enabled, under cover of the forest, to approach quite near before he was discovered; indeed, his skirmish-line had worked through the timber and got into the field to the rear of Giles A. Smith's division of the Seventeenth Corps unseen, had captured Murray's battery of regular artillery, moving through these woods entirely unguarded, and had got possession of several of the hospital camps. The right of this rebel line struck Dodge's troops in motion; but, fortunately, this corps (Sixteenth) had only to halt, face to the left, and was in line of battle; and this corps not only held in check the enemy, but drove him back through the woods. About the same time this same force had struck General Giles A. Smith's left flank, doubled it back, captured four guns in position and the party engaged in building the very battery which was the spe-

cial object of McPherson's visit to me, and almost enveloped
the entire left flank. The men, however, were skillful and
brave, and fought for a time with their backs to Atlanta. They
gradually fell back, compressing their own line, and gaining
strength by making junction with Leggett's division of the
Seventeenth Corps, well and strongly posted on the hill. One
or two brigades of the Fifteenth Corps, ordered by McPherson,
came rapidly across the open field to the rear, from the direction of the railroad, filled up the gap from Blair's new left to
the head of Dodge's column—now facing to the general left—
thus forming a strong left flank, at right angles to the original
line of battle. The enemy attacked, boldly and repeatedly, the
whole of this flank, but met an equally fierce resistance; and
on that ground a bloody battle raged from little after noon till
into the night. A part of Hood's plan of action was to sally
from Atlanta at the same moment; but this sally was not, for
some reason, simultaneous, for the first attack on our extreme
left flank had been checked and repulsed before the sally came
from the direction of Atlanta. Meantime, Colonel Sprague, in
Decatur, had got his teams harnessed up, and safely conducted
his train to the rear of Schofield's position, holding in check
Wheeler's cavalry till he had got off all his trains, with the exception of three or four wagons. I remained near the Howard
House, receiving reports and sending orders, urging Generals
Thomas and Schofield to take advantage of the absence from
their front of so considerable a body as was evidently engaged
on our left, and, if possible, to make a lodgment in Atlanta
itself; but they reported that the lines to their front, at all
accessible points, were strong, by nature and by art, and were
fully manned. About 4 P. M. the expected sally came from
Atlanta, directed mainly against Leggett's Hill and along the
Decatur road. At Leggett's Hill they were met and bloodily repulsed. Along the railroad they were more successful. Sweeping over a small force with two guns, they reached our main
line, broke through it, and got possession of De Gres's battery
of four twenty-pound Parrotts, killing every horse, and turning
the guns against us. General Charles R. Wood's division of

the Fifteenth Corps was on the extreme right of the Army of
the Tennessee, between the railroad and the Howard House,
where he connected with Schofield's troops. He reported to
me in person that the line on his left had been swept back, and
that his connection with General Logan, on Leggett's Hill, was
broken. I ordered him to wheel his brigades to the left, to advance in echelon, and to catch the enemy in flank. General
Schofield brought forward all his available batteries, to the
number of twenty guns, to a position to the left front of the
Howard House, whence we could overlook the field of action,
and directed a heavy fire over the heads of General Wood's men
against the enemy ; and we saw Wood's troops advance and encounter the enemy, who had secured possession of the old line
of parapet which had been held by our men. His right crossed
this parapet, which he swept back, taking it in flank ; and, at
the same time, the division which had been driven back along
the railroad was rallied by General Logan in person, and fought
for their former ground. These combined forces drove the
enemy into Atlanta, recovering the twenty-pound Parrott guns
—but one of them was found "bursted " while in the possession
of the enemy. The two six-pounders farther in advance were,
however, lost, and had been hauled back by the enemy into
Atlanta. Poor Captain de Gres came to me in tears, lamenting
the loss of his favorite guns; when they were regained he had
only a few men left, and not a single horse. He asked an order
for a reëquipment, but I told him he must beg and borrow of
others till he could restore his battery, now reduced to three
guns. How he did so I do not know, but in a short time he
did get horses, men, and finally another gun, of the same special
pattern, and served them with splendid effect till the very close
of the war. This battery had also been with me from Shiloh
till that time.

The battle of July 22d is usually called the battle of Atlanta. It extended from the Howard House to General Giles
A. Smith's position, about a mile beyond the Augusta Railroad,
and then back toward Decatur, the whole extent of ground
being fully seven miles. In part the ground was clear and in

part densely wooded. I rode over the whole of it the next day, and it bore the marks of a bloody conflict. The enemy had retired during the night inside of Atlanta, and we remained masters of the situation outside. I purposely allowed the Army of the Tennessee to fight this battle almost unaided, save by demonstrations on the part of General Schofield and Thomas against the fortified lines to their immediate fronts, and by detaching, as described, one of Schofield's brigades to Decatur, because I knew that the attacking force could only be a part of Hood's army, and that, if any assistance were rendered by either of the other armies, the Army of the Tennessee would be jealous. Nobly did they do their work that day, and terrible was the slaughter done to our enemy, though at sad cost to ourselves, as shown by the following reports:

HEADQUARTERS MILITARY DIVISION OF THE MISSISSIPPI,
IN THE FIELD, NEAR ATLANTA, *July* 23, 1864.

General HALLECK, *Washington, D. C.*

Yesterday morning the enemy fell back to the intrenchments proper of the city of Atlanta, which are in a general circle, with a radius of one and a half miles, and we closed in. While we were forming our lines, and selecting positions for our batteries, the enemy appeared suddenly out of the dense woods in heavy masses on our extreme left, and struck the Seventeenth Corps (General Blair) in flank, and was forcing it back, when the Sixteenth Corps (General Dodge) came up and checked the movement, but the enemy's cavalry got well to our rear, and into Decatur, and for some hours our left flank was completely enveloped. The fight that resulted was continuous until night, with heavy loss on both sides. The enemy took one of our batteries (Murray's, of the Regular Army) that was marching in its place in column in the road, unconscious of danger. About 4 P. M. the enemy sallied against the division of General Morgan L. Smith, of the Fifteenth Corps, which occupied an abandoned line of rifle-trench near the railroad east of the city, and forced it back some four hundred yards, leaving in his hands for the time two batteries, but the ground and batteries were immediately after recovered by the same troops reënforced. I cannot well approximate our loss, which fell heavily on the Fifteenth and Seventeenth Corps, but count it as three thousand; I know that, being on the defensive, we have inflicted equally heavy loss on the enemy.

General McPherson, when arranging his troops about 11 A. M., and passing from one column to another, incautiously rode upon an ambuscade without apprehension, at some distance ahead of his staff and orderlies, and was shot dead.

W. T. SHERMAN, *Major-General commanding.*

HEADQUARTERS MILITARY DIVISION OF THE MISSISSIPPI,
IN THE FIELD, NEAR ATLANTA, GEORGIA, *July* 25, 1864—8 A. M.

Major-General HALLECK, *Washington, D. C.*

GENERAL: I find it difficult to make prompt report of results, coupled with some data or information, without occasionally making mistakes. McPherson's sudden death, and Logan succeeding to the command as it were in the midst of battle, made some confusion on our extreme left; but it soon recovered and made sad havoc with the enemy, who had practised one of his favorite games of attacking our left when in motion, and before it had time to cover its weak flank. After riding over the ground and hearing the varying statements of the actors, I directed General Logan to make an official report of the actual result, and I herewith inclose it.

Though the number of dead rebels seems excessive, I am disposed to give full credit to the report that our loss, though only thirty-five hundred and twenty-one killed, wounded, and missing, the enemy's dead alone on the field nearly equaled that number, viz., thirty-two hundred and twenty. Happening at that point of the line when a flag of truce was sent in to ask permission for each party to bury its dead, I gave General Logan authority to permit a temporary truce on that flank *alone*, while our labors and fighting proceeded at all others.

I also send you a copy of General Garrard's report of the breaking of the railroad toward Augusta. I am now grouping my command to attack the Macon road, and with that view will intrench a strong line of circumvallation with flanks, so as to have as large an infantry column as possible, with all the cavalry to swing round to the south and east, to strike that road at or below East Point.

I have the honor to be, your obedient servant,

W. T. SHERMAN, *Major-General commanding.*

HEADQUARTERS DEPARTMENT AND ARMY OF THE TENNESSEE,
BEFORE ATLANTA, GEORGIA, *July* 24, 1864.

Major-General W. T. SHERMAN, *commanding Military Division of the Mississippi.*

GENERAL: I have the honor to report the following general summary of the result of the attack of the enemy on this army on the 22d inst.

Total loss, killed, wounded, and missing, thirty-five hundred and twenty-one, and ten pieces of artillery.

We have buried and delivered to the enemy, under a flag of truce sent in by them, in front of the Third Division, Seventeenth Corps, one thousand of their killed.

The number of their dead in front of the Fourth Division of the same corps, including those on the ground not now occupied by our troops, General Blair reports, will swell the number of their dead on his front to two thousand.

The number of their dead buried in front of the Fifteenth Corps, up to this hour, is three hundred and sixty, and the commanding officer reports that at least as many more are yet unburied, burying-parties being still at work.

The number of dead buried in front of the Sixteenth Corps is four hundred and twenty-two. We have over one thousand of their wounded in our hands, the larger number of the wounded being carried off during the night, after the engagement, by them.

We captured eighteen stands of colors, and have them now. We also captured five thousand stands of arms.

The attack was made on our lines seven times, and was seven times repulsed. Hood's and Hardee's corps and Wheeler's cavalry engaged us.

We have sent to the rear one thousand prisoners, including thirty-three commissioned officers of high rank.

We still occupy the field, and the troops are in fine spirits. A detailed and full report will be furnished as soon as completed.

Recapitulation.

Our total loss.. 3,521
Enemy's dead, thus far reported, buried, and delivered
  to them...................................... 3,220
Total prisoners sent North........................... 1,017
Total prisoners, wounded, in our hands.............. 1,000
Estimated loss of the enemy, at least............... 10,000

Very respectfully, your obedient servant,

JOHN A. LOGAN, *Major-General.*

On the 22d of July General Rousseau reached Marietta, having returned from his raid on the Alabama road at Opelika, and on the next day General Garrard also returned from Covington, both having been measurably successful. The former was about twenty-five hundred strong, the latter about four thousand, and both reported that their horses were jaded and tired, needing shoes and rest. But, about this time, I was advised by General Grant (then investing Richmond) that the rebel Government had become aroused to the critical condition of things about Atlanta, and that I must look out for Hood being greatly reënforced. I therefore was resolved to push matters, and at once set about the original purpose of transferring the whole of the Army of the Tennessee to our right flank, leaving Schofield to stretch out so as to rest his left on the Augusta road, then torn up for thirty miles eastward; and, as auxiliary thereto, I ordered all the cavalry to be ready to pass around Atlanta on both flanks, to break up the Macon road at some point below, so as to cut off all supplies to the rebel army inside, and thus to force it to evacuate, or come out and fight us on equal terms.

But it first became necessary to settle the important question of who should succeed General McPherson? General Logan had taken command of the Army of the Tennessee by virtue of his seniority, and had done well; but I did not consider him equal to the command of three corps. Between him and General Blair there existed a natural rivalry. Both were men of great courage and talent, but were politicians by nature and experience, and it may be that for this reason they were mistrusted by regular officers like Generals Schofield, Thomas, and myself. It was all-important that there should exist a perfect understanding among the army commanders, and at a conference with General George H. Thomas at the headquarters of General Thomas J. Woods, commanding a division in the Fourth Corps, he (Thomas) remonstrated warmly against my recommending that General Logan should be regularly assigned to the command of the Army of the Tennessee by reason of his accidental seniority. We discussed fully the merits and qualities of every officer of high rank in the army, and finally settled on Major-General O. O. Howard as the best officer who was present and available for the purpose; on the 24th of July I telegraphed to General Halleck this preference, and it was promptly ratified by the President. General Howard's place in command of the Fourth Corps was filled by General Stanley, one of his division commanders, on the recommendation of General Thomas. All these promotions happened to fall upon West-Pointers, and doubtless Logan and Blair had some reason to believe that we intended to monopolize the higher honors of the war for the regular officers. I remember well my own thoughts and feelings at the time, and feel sure that I was not intentionally partial to any class. I wanted to succeed in taking Atlanta, and needed commanders who were purely and technically soldiers, men who would obey orders and execute them promptly and on time; for I knew that we would have to execute some most delicate manœuvres, requiring the utmost skill, nicety, and precision. I believed that General Howard would do all these faithfully and well, and I think the result has justified my choice. I regarded both Generals Logan and Blair as " volunteers," that looked to personal fame and glory as auxiliary and secondary to their political ambition, and not as professional soldiers.

As soon as it was known that General Howard had been chosen to command the Army of the Tennessee, General Hooker applied to General Thomas to be relieved of the command of the Twentieth Corps, and General Thomas forwarded his application to me approved and *heartily* recommended. I at once telegraphed to General Halleck, recommending General Slocum (then at Vicksburg) to be his successor, because Slocum had been displaced from the command of his corps at the time when the Eleventh and Twelfth were united and made the Twentieth.

General Hooker was offended because he was not chosen to succeed McPherson; but his chances were not even considered; indeed, I had never been satisfied with him since his affair at the Kulp House, and had been more than once disposed to relieve him of his corps, because of his repeated attempts to interfere with Generals McPherson and Schofield. I am told that he says that Thomas and I were jealous of him; but this is hardly probable, for we on the spot did not rate his fighting qualities as high as he did, and I am, moreover, convinced that both he and General Butterfield went to the rear for personal reasons. We were then two hundred and fifty miles in advance of our base, dependent on a single line of railroad for our daily food. We had a bold, determined foe in our immediate front, strongly

intrenched, with communication open to his rear for supplies and
reënforcements, and every soldier realized that we had plenty
of hard fighting ahead, and that all honors had to be fairly
earned.   General Hooker, moreover, when he got back to
Cincinnati, reported (I was told) that we had run up against a
rock at Atlanta, and that the country ought to be prepared to
hear of disaster from that quarter.

Until General Slocum joined (in the latter part of August),
the Twentieth Corps was commanded by General A. S. Williams,
the senior division commander present.   On the 25th of July the
army, therefore, stood thus : the Army of the Tennessee (General
O. O. Howard commanding) was on the left, pretty much on the
same ground it had occupied during the battle of the 22d, all
ready to move rapidly by the rear to the extreme right beyond
Proctor's Creek ; the Army of the Ohio (General Schofield)
was next in order, with its left flank reaching the Augusta
Railroad ; next in order, conforming closely with the rebel intrenchments of Atlanta, was General Thomas's Army of the
Cumberland, in the order of—the Fourth Corps (Stanley's),
the Twentieth Corps (Williams's), and the Fourteenth Corps
(Palmer's).   Palmer's right division (Jefferson C. Davis's) was
strongly refused along Proctor's Creek.   This line was about five
miles long, and was intrenched as against a sally about as strong
as was our enemy.   The cavalry was assembled in two strong
divisions; that of McCook (including the brigade of Harrison
which had been brought in from Opelika by General Rousseau)
numbered about thirty-five hundred effective cavalry, and was
posted to our right rear, at Turner's Ferry, where we had
a good pontoon-bridge; and to our left rear, at and about
Decatur, were the two cavalry divisions of Stoneman, twenty-
five hundred, and Garrard, four thousand, united for the time
and occasion under the command of Major-General George
Stoneman, a cavalry-officer of high repute.   My plan of action
was to move the Army of the Tennessee to the right rapidly
and boldly against the railroad below Atlanta, and at the same
time to send all the cavalry around· by the right and left to
make a lodgment on the Macon road about Jonesboro'.

All the orders were given, and the morning of the 27th was fixed for commencing the movement. On the 26th I received from General Stoneman a note asking permission (after having accomplished his orders to break up the railroad at Jonesboro') to go on to Macon to rescue our prisoners of war known to be held there, and then to push on to Andersonville, where was the great depot of Union prisoners, in which were penned at one time as many as twenty-three thousand of our men, badly fed and harshly treated. I wrote him an answer consenting substantially to his proposition, only modifying it by requiring him to send back General Garrard's division to its position on our left flank after he had broken up the railroad at Jonesboro'. Promptly, and on time, all got off, and General Dodge's corps (the Sixteenth, of the Army of the Tennessee) reached its position across Proctor's Creek the same evening, and early the next morning (the 28th) Blair's corps (the Seventeenth) deployed on his right, both corps covering their front with the usual parapet; the Fifteenth Corps (General Logan's) came up that morning on the right of Blair, strongly refused, and began to prepare the usual cover. As General Jeff. C. Davis's division was, as it were, left out of line, I ordered it on the evening before to march down toward Turner's Ferry, and then to take a road laid down on our maps which led from there toward East Point, ready to engage any enemy that might attack our general right flank, after the same manner as had been done to the left flank on the 22d.

Personally on the morning of the 28th I followed the movement, and rode to the extreme right, where we could hear some skirmishing and an occasional cannon-shot. As we approached the ground held by the Fifteenth Corps, a cannon-ball passed over my shoulder and killed the horse of an orderly behind; and seeing that this gun enfiladed the road by which we were riding, we turned out of it and rode down into a valley, where we left our horses and walked up to the hill held by Morgan L. Smith's division of the Fifteenth Corps. Near a house I met Generals Howard and Logan, who explained that there was an intrenched battery to their front, with the appearance of a strong infantry support. I then walked up to the ridge, where I found General Morgan L. Smith. His men were deployed and engaged in rolling logs and fence-rails, preparing a hasty cover. From this ridge we could overlook the open fields near a meeting-house known as "Ezra Church," close by the Poor-House. We could see the fresh earth of a parapet covering some guns (that fired an occasional shot), and there was also an appearance of activity beyond. General Smith was in the act of sending forward a regiment from his right flank to feel the position of the enemy, when I explained to him and to Generals Logan and Howard that they must look out for General Jeff. C. Davis's division, which was coming up from the direction of Turner's Ferry.

As the skirmish-fire warmed up along the front of Blair's corps, as well as along the Fifteenth Corps (Logan's), I became convinced that Hood designed to attack this right flank, to prevent, if possible, the extension of our line in that direction. I regained my horse, and rode rapidly back to see that Davis's division had been dispatched as ordered. I found General Davis in person, who was unwell, and had sent his division that morning early, under the command of his senior brigadier, Morgan; but, as I attached great importance to the movement, he mounted his horse, and rode away to overtake and to hurry forward the movement, so as to come up on the left rear of the enemy, during the expected battle.

By this time the sound of cannon and musketry denoted a severe battle as in progress, which began seriously at 11½ A. M., and ended substantially by 4 P. M. It was a fierce attack by the enemy on our extreme right flank, well posted and partially covered. The most authentic account of the battle is given by General Logan, who commanded the Fifteenth Corps, in his official report to the Adjutant-General of the Army of the Tennessee, thus:

HEADQUARTERS FIFTEENTH ARMY CORPS,
BEFORE ATLANTA, GEORGIA, <i>July</i> 29, 1864. }</div>

Lieutenant-Colonel WILLIAM T. CLARK, *Assistant Adjutant-General, Army of the Tennessee, present.*

COLONEL: I have the honor to report that, in pursuance of orders, I moved my command into position on the right of the Seventeenth Corps, which was the extreme right of the army in the field, during the night of the 27th and morning of the 28th; and, while advancing in line of battle to a more favorable position, we were met by the rebel infantry of Hardee's and Lee's corps, who made a determined and desperate attack on us at $11\frac{1}{2}$ A. M. of the 28th (yesterday).

My lines were only protected by logs and rails, hastily thrown up in front of them.

The first onset was received and checked, and the battle commenced and lasted until about three o'clock in the evening. During that time six successive charges were made, which were six times gallantly repulsed, each time with fearful loss to the enemy.

Later in the evening my lines were several times assaulted vigorously, but each time with like result.

The worst of the fighting occurred on General Harrow's and Morgan L. Smith's fronts, which formed the centre and right of the corps.

The troops could not have displayed greater courage, nor greater determination not to give ground; had they shown less, they would have been driven from their position.

Brigadier-Generals C. R. Woods, Harrow, and Morgan L. Smith, division commanders, are entitled to equal credit for gallant conduct and skill in repelling the assault.

My thanks are due to Major-Generals Blair and Dodge for sending me reënforcements at a time when they were much needed.

My losses were fifty killed, four hundred and forty-nine wounded, and seventy-three missing: aggregate, five hundred and seventy-two.

The division of General Harrow captured five battle-flags. There were about fifteen hundred or two thousand muskets left on the ground. One hundred and six prisoners were captured, exclusive of seventy-three wounded, who were sent to our hospital, and are being cared for by our surgeons.

Five hundred and sixty-five rebels have up to this time been buried, and about two hundred are supposed to be yet unburied.

A large number of their wounded were undoubtedly carried away in the night, as the enemy did not withdraw till near daylight. The enemy's loss could not have been less than six or seven thousand men.

A more detailed report will hereafter be made.

I am, very respectfully,

Your obedient servant,

JOHN A. LOGAN,
Major-General, commanding Fifteenth Army Corps.

General Howard, in transmitting this report, added:

I wish to express my high gratification with the conduct of the troops engaged. I never saw better conduct in battle. General Logan, though ill and much worn out, was indefatigable, and the success of the day is as much attributable to him as to any one man.

This was, of course, the first fight in which General Howard had commanded the Army of the Tennessee, and he evidently aimed to reconcile General Logan in his disappointment, and to gain the heart of his army, to which he was a stranger. He very properly left General Logan to fight his own corps, but exposed himself freely; and, after the firing had ceased, in the afternoon he walked the lines; the men, as reported to me, gathered about him in the most affectionate way, and he at once gained their respect and confidence. To this fact I at the time attached much importance, for it put me at ease as to the future conduct of that most important army.

At no instant of time did I feel the least uneasiness about the result on the 28th, but wanted to reap fuller results, hoping that Davis's division would come up at the instant of defeat, and catch the enemy in flank; but the woods were dense, the roads obscure, and as usual this division got on the wrong road, and did not come into position until about dark. In like manner, I thought that Hood had greatly weakened his main lines inside of Atlanta, and accordingly sent repeated orders to Schofield and Thomas to make an attempt to break in; but both reported that they found the parapets very strong and full manned.

Our men were unusually encouraged by this day's work, for they realized that we could compel Hood to come out from behind his fortified lines to attack us at a disadvantage. In conversation with me, the soldiers of the Fifteenth Corps, with whom I was on the most familiar terms, spoke of the affair of the 28th as the easiest thing in the world; that, in fact, it was a common slaughter of the enemy; they pointed out where the rebel lines had been, and how they themselves had fired deliberately, had shot down their antagonists, whose bodies still lay unburied, and marked plainly their lines of battle, which must have halted within easy musket-range of our men, who were partially protected by their improvised line of logs and fence-rails. All bore willing testimony to the courage and spirit of the foe, who, though repeatedly repulsed, came back with increased determination some six or more times.

The next morning the Fifteenth Corps wheeled forward to the left over the battle-field of the day before, and Davis's division still farther prolonged the line, which reached nearly to the ever-to-be-remembered "Sandtown road."

Then, by further thinning out Thomas's line, which was well intrenched, I drew another division of Palmer's corps (Ward's) around to the right, to further strengthen that flank. I was impatient to hear from the cavalry raid, then four days out, and was watching for its effect, ready to make a bold push for the possession of East Point. General Garrard's division returned to Decatur on the 31st, and reported that General Stoneman had posted him at Flat Rock, while he (Stoneman) went on. The month of July therefore closed with our infantry line strongly intrenched, but drawn out from the Augusta road on the left to the Sandtown road on the right, a distance of full ten measured miles.

The enemy, though evidently somewhat intimidated by the results of their defeats on the 22d and 28th, still presented a bold front at all points, with fortified lines that defied a direct assault. Our railroad was done to the rear of our camps, Colonel W. W. Wright having reconstructed the bridge across the Chattahoochee in six days; and our garrisons and detachments to the rear had so effectually guarded the railroad that the trains from Nashville arrived daily, and our substantial wants were well supplied.

The month, though hot in the extreme, had been one of constant conflict, without intermission, and on four several occasions—viz., July 4th, 20th, 22d, and 28th—these affairs had amounted to real battles, with casualty lists by the thousands. Assuming the correctness of the rebel surgeon Foard's report, on page 577 of Johnston's "Narrative," commencing with July 4th and terminating with July 31st, we have:

CORPS.	Killed.	Wounded.	Total.
Hardee's.............................	523	2,774	3,297
Lee's................................	351	2,408	2,759
Stewart's	436	2,141	2,577
Wheeler's Cavalry	29	156	185
Engineers...........................	2	21	23
Total...........................	1,341	7,500	8,841

To these I add as prisoners, at least................ 2,000
Aggregate loss of the enemy in July, 1864............ 10,841

Our losses, as compiled from the official returns for July, 1864, are:

ARMY OF THE CUMBERLAND.

CORPS.	Killed and Missing.	Wounded.	Total.
Fourth	116	432	548
Fourteenth..........................	317	1,084	1,401
Twentieth...........................	541	1,480	2,021
Total, Army of the Cumberland....	974	2,996	3,970

ARMY OF THE TENNESSEE.

CORPS.	Killed and Missing.	Wounded.	Total.
Fifteenth.............	590	797	1,387
Sixteenth...........................	289	721	1,010
Seventeenth ....,....................	1,361	1,203	2,564
Total, Army of the Tennessee......	2,240	2,721	4,961

ARMY OF THE OHIO.

CORPS.	Killed and Missing.	Wounded.	Total.
Twenty-third.........................	95	167	262
Cavalry.............................	495	31	526
Total, Army of the Ohio...........	590	198	788
Aggregate loss for July............	3,804	5,915	9,719

In this table the column of "killed and missing" embraces the prisoners that fell into the hands of the enemy, mostly lost in the Seventeenth Corps, on the 22d of July, and does not embrace the losses in the cavalry divisions of Garrard and McCook, which, however, were small for July. In all other respects the statement is absolutely correct. I am satisfied, however, that Surgeon Foard could not have been in possession of data sufficiently accurate to enable him to report the losses in actual battle of men who never saw the hospital. During the whole campaign I had rendered to me tri-monthly statements of " effective strength," from which I carefully eliminated the figures not essential for my conduct, so that at all times I knew the exact fighting-strength of each corps, division, and brigade, of the whole army, and also endeavored to bear in mind our losses both on the several fields of battle and by sickness, and well remember that I always estimated that during the month of July we had inflicted heavier loss on the enemy than we had sustained ourselves, and the above figures prove it conclusively. Before closing this chapter, I must record one or two minor events that occurred about this time, that may prove of interest.

On the 24th of July I received a dispatch from Inspector-General James A. Hardie, then on duty at the War Department in Washington, to the effect that Generals Osterhaus and Alvan P. Hovey had been appointed major-generals. Both of these had begun the campaign with us in command of divisions, but had gone to the rear—the former by reason of sickness, and the latter dissatisfied with General Schofield and myself about the composition of his division of the Twenty-third Corps. Both were esteemed as first-class officers, who had gained special distinction in the Vicksburg campaign. But up to that time, when the newspapers announced daily promotions elsewhere, no prominent officers serving with me had been advanced a peg, and I felt hurt. I answered Hardie on the 25th, in a dispatch which has been made public, closing with this language: " If the rear be the post of honor, then we had better all change front on Washington." To my amazement, in a few days I received from President Lincoln himself an answer, in which he caught me fairly. I have not preserved a copy of that dispatch, and suppose it was burned up in the Chicago fire; but it was characteristic of Mr. Lincoln, and was dated the 26th or 27th day of July, contained unequivocal expressions of respect for those who were fighting hard and unselfishly, offering us a full share of the honors and rewards of the war, and saying that, in the cases of Hovey and Osterhaus, he was influenced mainly by the recommendations of Generals Grant and Sherman.   On the 27th I replied direct, apologizing somewhat for my message to General Hardie, saying that I did not suppose such messages ever reached him personally, explaining that General Grant's and Sherman's recommendations for Hovey and Osterhaus had been made when the events of the Vicksburg campaign were fresh with us, and that my dispatch of the 25th to General Hardie had reflected chiefly the feelings of the officers then present with me before Atlanta.   The result of all this, however, was good, for another dispatch from General Hardie, of the 28th, called on me to nominate eight colonels for promotion as brigadier-generals.   I at once sent a circular note to the army-commanders to nominate two colonels from the Army of the Ohio and three from each of the others; and the result was, that on the 29th of July I telegraphed the names of —Colonel William Gross, Thirty-sixth Indiana; Colonel Charles C. Walcutt, Forty-sixth Ohio; Colonel James W. Riley, One Hundred and Fourth Ohio; Colonel L. P. Bradley, Fifty-first Illinois; Colonel J. W. Sprague, Sixty-third Ohio; Colonel Joseph A. Cooper, Sixth East Tennessee; Colonel John T. Croxton, Fourth Kentucky; Colonel William W. Belknap, Fifteenth Iowa.   These were promptly appointed brigadier-generals, were already in command of brigades or divisions; and I doubt if eight promotions were ever made fairer, or were more honestly earned, during the whole war.

CHAPTER XVIII.

AUGUST AND SEPTEMBER, 1864.

THE month of August opened hot and sultry, but our position before Atlanta was healthy, with ample supply of wood, water, and provisions. The troops had become habituated to the slow and steady progress of the siege; the skirmish-lines were held close up to the enemy, were covered by rifle-trenches or logs, and kept up a continuous clatter of musketry. The main lines were held farther back, adapted to the shape of the ground, with muskets loaded and stacked for instant use. The field-batteries were in select positions, covered by handsome parapets, and occasional shots from them gave life and animation to the scene. The men loitered about the trenches carelessly, or busied themselves in constructing ingenious huts out of the abundant timber, and seemed as snug, comfortable, and happy, as though they were at home. General Schofield was still on the extreme left, Thomas in the centre, and Howard on the right. Two divisions of the Fourteenth Corps (Baird's and Jeff. C. Davis's) were detached to the right rear, and held in reserve.

I thus awaited the effect of the cavalry movement against the railroad about Jonesboro', and had heard from General Garrard that Stoneman had gone on to Macon; during that day (August 1st) Colonel Brownlow, of a Tennessee cavalry regiment, came in to Marietta from General McCook, and reported that McCook's whole division had been overwhelmed, defeated, and captured at Newnan. Of course, I was disturbed by this wild report, though I discredited it, but made all possible preparations to strengthen our guards along the railroad to the rear, on the theory that the force of cavalry which had defeated McCook would at once be on the railroad about Marietta. At the same time Garrard was ordered to occupy the trenches on our left, while Schofield's whole army moved to the extreme right, and extended the line toward East Point. Thomas was also ordered still further to thin out his lines, so as to set free the other division (Johnson's) of the Fourteenth Corps (Palmer's), which was moved to the extreme right rear, and held in reserve ready to make a bold push from that flank to secure a footing on the Macon Railroad at or below East Point.

These changes were effected during the 2d and 3d days of August, when General McCook came in and reported the actual results of his cavalry expedition. He had crossed the Chattahoochee River below Campbellton, by his pontoon-bridge; had then marched rapidly across to the Macon Railroad at Lovejoy's Station, where he had reason to expect General Stoneman; but, not hearing of him, he set to work, tore up two miles of track, burned two trains of cars, and cut away five miles of telegraph-wire. He also found the wagon-train belonging to the rebel army in Atlanta, burned five hundred wagons, killed eight hundred mules, and captured seventy-two officers and three hundred and fifty men. Finding his progress eastward, toward McDonough, barred by a superior force, he turned back to Newnan, where he found himself completely surrounded by infantry and cavalry. He had to drop his prisoners and fight his way out, losing about six hundred men in killed and captured, and then returned with the remainder to his position at Turner's Ferry. This was bad enough, but not so bad as had been reported by Colonel Brownlow. Meantime, rumors came that General Stoneman was down about Macon, on the east bank of the Ocmulgee. On the 4th of August Colonel Adams got to Marietta with his small brigade of nine hundred men belonging to Stoneman's cavalry, reporting, as usual, all the rest lost, and this was partially confirmed by a report which came to me all the way round by General Grant's headquarters before Richmond. A few days afterward Colonel Capron also got in, with another small brigade perfectly demoralized, and confirmed the report that General Stoneman had covered the escape of these two small brigades, himself standing with a reserve of seven hundred men, with which he surrendered to a Colonel Iverson. Thus another of my cavalry divisions was badly damaged, and out of the fragments we hastily reorganized three small divisions under Brigadier-Generals Garrard, McCook, and Kilpatrick.

Stoneman had not obeyed his orders to attack the railroad *first* before going to Macon and Andersonville, but had crossed the Ocmulgee River high up near Covington, and had gone down that river on the east bank. He reached Clinton, and sent out detachments which struck the railroad leading from Macon to Savannah at Griswold Station, where they found and destroyed seventeen locomotives and over a hundred cars; then went on and burned the bridge across the Oconee, and reunited the division before Macon. Stoneman shelled the town across the river, but could not cross over by the bridge, and returned to Clinton, where he found his retreat obstructed, as he supposed, by a superior force. There he became bewildered, and sacrificed himself for the safety of his command. He occupied the attention of his enemy by a small force of seven hundred men, giving Colonels Adams and Capron leave, with their brigades, to cut their way back to me at Atlanta. The former reached us entire, but the latter was struck and scattered at some place farther north, and came in by detachments. Stoneman surrendered, and remained a prisoner until he was exchanged some time after, late in September, at Rough and Ready.

I now became satisfied that cavalry could not, or would not, make a sufficient lodgment on the railroad below Atlanta, and that nothing would suffice but for us to reach it with the main army. Therefore the most urgent efforts to that end were made, and to Schofield, on the right, was committed the charge of this special object. He had his own corps (the Twenty-third), composed of eleven thousand and seventy-five infantry and eight hundred and eighty-five artillery, with McCook's broken division of cavalry, seventeen hundred and fifty-four men and horses. For this purpose I also placed the Fourteenth Corps (Palmer) under his orders. This corps numbered at the time seventeen thousand two hundred and eighty-eight infantry and eight hundred and twenty-six artillery; but General Palmer claimed to rank General Schofield in the date of his commission as major-general, and denied the latter's right to exercise command over him. General Palmer was a man of ability, but was not enterprising. His three divisions were compact and strong, well commanded, admirable on the defensive, but slow to move or to act on the offensive. His corps (the Fourteenth) had sustained, up to that time, fewer hard knocks than any other corps in the whole army, and I was anxious to give it a chance. I always expected to have a desperate fight to get possession of the Macon road, which was then the vital objective of the campaign. Its possession by us would, in my judgment, result in the capture of Atlanta, and give us the fruits of victory, although the destruction of Hood's army was the real object to be desired. Yet Atlanta was known as the " Gate-City of the South," was full of founderies, arsenals, and machine-shops, and I knew that its capture would be the death-knell of the Southern Confederacy.

On the 4th of August I ordered General Schofield to make a bold attack on the railroad, anywhere about East Point, and ordered General Palmer to report to him for duty. He at once denied General Schofield's right to command him; but, after examining the dates of their respective commissions, and hearing their arguments, I wrote to General Palmer.

August 4th—10.45 P. M.

From the statements made by yourself and General Schofield to-day, my decision is, that he ranks you as a major-general, being of the same date of present commission, by reason of his previous superior rank as *brigadier-general.* The movements of to-morrow are so important that the orders of the superior on that flank must be regarded as military orders, and not in the nature of coöperation. I did hope that there would be no necessity for my making this decision; but it is better for all parties interested that no question of rank should occur in actual battle. The Sandtown road, and the railroad, if possible, must be gained to-morrow, if it costs half your command. I regard the loss of time this afternoon as equal to the loss of two thousand men.

I also communicated the substance of this to General Thomas, to whose army Palmer's corps belonged, who replied on the 5th :

I regret to hear that Palmer has taken the course he has, and I know that he intends to offer his resignation as soon as he can properly do so. I recommend that his application be granted.

And on the 5th I again wrote to General Palmer, arguing the point with him, advising him, as a friend, not to resign at that crisis lest his motives might be misconstrued, and because it might damage his future career in civil life; but, at the same time, I felt it my duty to say to him that the operations on that flank, during the 4th and 5th, had not been satisfactory—not imputing to him, however, any want of energy or skill, but insisting that "the events did not keep pace with my desires." General Schofield had reported to me that night:

I am compelled to acknowledge that I have totally failed to make any aggressive movement with the Fourteenth Corps. I have ordered General Johnson's division to replace General Hascall's this evening, and I propose to-morrow to take my own troops (Twenty-third Corps) to the right, and try to recover what has been lost by two days' delay. The force may likely be too small.

I sanctioned the movement, and ordered two of Palmer's divisions—Davis's and Baird's—to follow *en échelon* in support of Schofield, and summoned General Palmer to meet me in person. He came on the 6th to my headquarters, and insisted on his resignation being accepted, for which formal act I referred him to General Thomas. He then rode to General Thomas's camp, where he made a written resignation of his office as commander of the Fourteenth Corps, and was granted the usual leave of absence to go to his home in Illinois, there to await further orders. General Thomas recommended that the resignation be accepted; that Johnson, the senior division commander of the corps, should be ordered back to Nashville as chief of cavalry, and that Brigadier-General Jefferson C. Davis, the next in order, should be promoted major-general, and assigned to command the corps. These changes had to be referred to the President, in Washington, and were, in due time, approved and executed; and thenceforward I had no reason to complain of the slowness or inactivity of that splendid corps. It had been originally formed by General George H. Thomas, had been commanded by him in person, and had imbibed somewhat his personal character, viz., steadiness, good order, and deliberation—nothing hasty or rash, but always safe, " slow, and sure."

On August 7th I telegraphed to General Halleck :

Have received to-day the dispatches of the Secretary of War and of General Grant, which are very satisfactory. We keep hammering away all the time, and there is no peace, inside or outside of Atlanta. To-day General Schofield got round the line which was assaulted yesterday by General Reilly's brigade, turned it and gained the ground where the assault had been made, and got possession of all our dead and wounded. He continued to press on that flank, and brought on a noisy but not a bloody battle. He drove the enemy behind his main breastworks, which cover the railroad from Atlanta to East Point, and captured a good many of the skirmishers, who are of his best troops—for the militia hug the breastworks close. I do not deem it prudent to extend any more to the right, but will push forward daily by parallels, and make the inside of Atlanta too hot to be endured. I have sent back to Chattanooga for two thirty-pound Parrotts, with which we can pick out almost any house in town. I am too impatient for a siege, and don't know but this is as good a place to fight it out on, as farther inland. One thing is certain, whether we get inside of Atlanta or not, it will be a used-up community when we are done with it.

In Schofield's extension on the 5th, General Reilly's brigade had struck an outwork, which he promptly attacked, but, as usual, got entangled in the trees and bushes which had been felled, and lost about five hundred men, in killed and wounded; but, as above reported, this outwork was found abandoned the next day, and we could see from it that the rebels were extending their lines, parallel with the railroad, about as fast as we could add to our line of investment. On the 10th of August

the Parrott thirty-pounders were received and placed in position; for a couple of days we kept up a sharp fire from all
our batteries converging on Atlanta, and at every available point
we advanced our infantry-lines, thereby shortening and strengthening the investment; but I was not willing to order a direct
assault, unless some accident or positive neglect on the part of
our antagonist should reveal an opening.   However, it was
manifest that no such opening was intended by Hood, who felt
secure behind his strong defenses.   He had repelled our cavalry
attacks on his railroad, and had damaged us seriously thereby,
so I expected that he would attempt the same game against our
rear.   Therefore I made extraordinary exertions to recompose
our cavalry divisions, which were so essential, both for defense
and offense.   Kilpatrick was given that on our right rear, in
support of Schofield's exposed flank; Garrard retained that on
our general left; and McCook's division was held somewhat in
reserve, about Marietta and the railroad.   On the 10th, having
occasion to telegraph to General Grant, then in Washington, I
used this language:

Since July 28th Hood has not attempted to meet us outside his parapets.
In order to possess and destroy effectually his communications, I may have
to leave a corps at the railroad-bridge, well intrenched, and cut loose with
the balance to make a circle of desolation around Atlanta. I do not propose to assault the works, which are too strong, nor to proceed by regular
approaches. I have lost a good many regiments, and will lose more, by the
expiration of service; and this is the only reason why I want reënforcements. We have killed, crippled, and captured more of the enemy than
we have lost by his acts.

On the 12th of August I heard of the success of Admiral
Farragut in entering Mobile Bay, which was regarded as a most
valuable auxiliary to our operations at Atlanta; and learned that
I had been commissioned a major-general in the regular army,
which was unexpected, and not desired until successful in the
capture of Atlanta.   These did not change the fact that we were
held in check by the stubborn defense of the place, and a conviction was forced on my mind that our enemy would hold fast,
even though every house in the town should be battered down

by our artillery. It was evident that we must decoy him out to fight us on something like equal terms, or else, with the whole army, raise the siege and attack his communications. Accordingly, on the 13th of August, I gave general orders for the Twentieth Corps to draw back to the railroad-bridge at the Chattahoochee, to protect our trains, hospitals, spare artillery, and the railroad-depot, while the rest of the army should move bodily to some point on the Macon Railroad below East Point.

Luckily, I learned just then that the enemy's cavalry, under General Wheeler, had made a wide circuit around our left flank, and had actually reached our railroad at Tilton Station, above Resaca, captured a drove of one thousand of our beef-cattle, and was strong enough to appear before Dalton, and demand of its commander, Colonel Raum, the surrender of the place. General John E. Smith, who was at Kingston, collected together a couple of thousand men, and proceeded in cars to the relief of Dalton, when Wheeler retreated northward toward Cleveland. On the 16th another detachment of the enemy's cavalry appeared in force about Allatoona and the Etowah bridge, when I became fully convinced that Hood had sent *all* of his cavalry to raid upon our railroads. For some days our communication with Nashville was interrupted by the destruction of the telegraph-lines, as well as railroad. I at once ordered strong reconnoissances forward from our flanks on the left by Garrard, and on the right by Kilpatrick. The former moved with so much caution that I was displeased; but Kilpatrick, on the contrary, displayed so much zeal and activity that I was attracted to him at once. He reached Fairburn Station, on the West Point road, and tore it up, returning safely to his position on our right flank. I summoned him to me, and was so pleased with his spirit and confidence, that I concluded to suspend the general movement of the main army, and to send him with his small division of cavalry to break up the Macon road about Jonesboro', in the hopes that it would force Hood to evacuate Atlanta, and that I should thereby not only secure possession of the city itself, but probably could catch Hood in the confusion of retreat; and, further to increase the chances of success,

I ordered General Thomas to detach two brigades of Garrard's division of cavalry from the left to the right rear, to act as a reserve in support of General Kilpatrick. Meantime, also, the utmost activity was ordered along our whole front by the infantry and artillery. Kilpatrick got off during the night of the 18th, and returned to us on the 22d, having made the complete circuit of Atlanta. He reported that he had destroyed three miles of the railroad about Jonesboro', which he reckoned would take ten days to repair; that he had encountered a division of infantry and a brigade of cavalry (Ross's); that he had captured a battery and destroyed three of its guns, bringing one in as a trophy, and he also brought in three battle-flags and seventy prisoners. On the 23d, however, we saw trains coming into Atlanta from the south, when I became more than ever convinced that cavalry could not or would not work hard enough to disable a railroad properly, and therefore resolved at once to proceed to the execution of my original plan. Meantime, the damage done to our own railroad and telegraph by Wheeler, about Resaca and Dalton, had been repaired, and Wheeler himself was too far away to be of any service to his own army, and where he could not do us much harm, viz., up about the Hiawassee. On the 24th I rode down to the Chattahoochee bridge, to see in person that it could be properly defended by the single corps proposed to be left there for that purpose, and found that the rebel works, which had been built by Johnston to resist us, could be easily utilized against themselves; and on returning to my camp, at 7.15 P. M. that same evening, I telegraphed to General Halleck as follows:

Heavy fires in Atlanta all day, caused by our artillery. I will be all ready, and will commence the movement around Atlanta by the south, to-morrow night, and for some time you will hear little of us. I will keep open a courier line back to the Chattahoochee bridge, by way of Sandtown. The Twentieth Corps will hold the railroad-bridge, and I will move with the balance of the army, provisioned for twenty days.

Meantime General Dodge (commanding the Sixteenth Corps) had been wounded in the forehead, had gone to the rear, and his two divisions were distributed to the Fifteenth and Seventeenth Corps. The real movement commenced on the 25th, at night. The Twentieth Corps drew back and took post at the railroad-bridge, and the Fourth Corps (Stanley) moved to his right rear, closing up with the Fourteenth Corps (Jeff. C. Davis) near Utoy Creek; at the same time Garrard's cavalry, leaving their horses out of sight, occupied the vacant trenches, so that the enemy did not detect the change at all. The next night (26th) the Fifteenth and Seventeenth Corps, composing the Army of the Tennessee (Howard), drew out of their trenches, made a wide circuit, and came up on the extreme right of the Fourth and Fourteenth Corps of the Army of the Cumberland (Thomas) along Utoy Creek, facing south. The enemy seemed to suspect something that night, using his artillery pretty freely; but I think he supposed we were going to retreat altogether. An artillery-shot, fired at random, killed one man and wounded another, and the next morning some of his infantry came out of Atlanta and found our camps abandoned. It was afterward related that there was great rejoicing in Atlanta "that the Yankees were gone;" the fact was telegraphed all over the South, and several trains of cars (with ladies) came up from Macon to assist in the celebration of their grand victory.

On the 28th (making a general left-wheel, pivoting on Scho-field) both Thomas and Howard reached the West Point Railroad, extending from East Point to Red-Oak Station and Fairburn, where we spent the next day (29th) in breaking it up thoroughly. The track was heaved up in sections the length of a regiment, then separated rail by rail; bonfires were made of the ties and of fence-rails on which the rails were heated, carried to trees or telegraph-poles, wrapped around and left to cool. Such rails could not be used again; and, to be still more certain, we filled up many deep cuts with trees, brush, and earth, and commingled with them loaded shells, so arranged that they would explode on an attempt to haul out the bushes. The explosion of one such shell would have demoralized a gang of negroes, and thus would have prevented even the attempt to clear the road.

Meantime Schofield, with the Twenty-third Corps, presented

a bold front toward East Point, daring and inviting the enemy to sally out to attack him in position. His first movement was on the 30th, to Mount Gilead Church, then to Morrow's Mills, facing Rough and Ready. Thomas was on his right, within easy support, moving by cross-roads from Red Oak to the Fayetteville road, extending from Couch's to Renfrew's; and Howard was aiming for Jonesboro'.

I was with General Thomas that day, which was hot but otherwise very pleasant. We stopped for a short noon-rest near a little church (marked on our maps as Shoal-Creek Church), which stood back about a hundred yards from the road, in a grove of native oaks. The infantry column had halted in the road, stacked their arms, and the men were scattered about— some lying in the shade of the trees, and others were bringing corn-stalks from a large corn-field across the road to feed our horses, while still others had arms full of the roasting-ears, then in their prime. Hundreds of fires were soon started with the fence-rails, and the men were busy roasting the ears. Thomas and I were walking up and down the road which led to the church, discussing the chances of the movement, which he thought were extra-hazardous, and our path carried us by a fire at which a soldier was roasting his corn. The fire was built artistically; the man was stripping the ears of their husks, standing them in front of his fire, watching them carefully, and turning each ear little by little, so as to roast it nicely. He was down on his knees intent on his business, paying little heed to the stately and serious deliberations of his leaders. Thomas's mind was running on the fact that we had cut loose from our base of supplies, and that seventy thousand men were then dependent for their food on the chance supplies of the country (already impoverished by the requisitions of the enemy), and on the contents of our wagons. Between Thomas and his men there existed a most kindly relation, and he frequently talked with them in the most familiar way. Pausing awhile, and watching the operations of this man roasting his corn, he said, "What are you doing?" The man looked up smilingly: "Why, general, I am laying in a supply of provisions." "That is right, my man, but don't waste your provisions." As we resumed our walk, the man remarked, in a sort of musing way, but loud enough for me to hear: "There he goes, there goes the old man, economizing as usual." "Economizing" with corn, which cost only the labor of gathering and roasting!

As we walked, we could hear General Howard's guns at intervals, away off to our right front, but an ominous silence continued toward our left, where I was expecting at each moment to hear the sound of battle. That night we reached Renfrew's, and had reports from left to right (from General Schofield, about Morrow's Mills, to General Howard, within a couple of miles of Jonesboro'). The next morning (August 31st) all moved straight for the railroad. Schofield reached it near Rough and Ready, and Thomas at two points between there and Jonesboro'. Howard found an intrenched foe (Hardee's corps) covering Jonesboro', and his men began at once to dig their accustomed rifle-pits. Orders were sent to Generals Thomas and Schofield to turn straight for Jonesboro', tearing up the railroad-track as they advanced. About 3 P. M. the enemy sallied from Jonesboro' against the Fifteenth corps, but was easily repulsed, and driven back within his lines. All hands were kept busy tearing up the railroad, and it was not until toward evening of the 1st day of September that the Fourteenth Corps (Davis) closed down on the north front of Jonesboro', connecting on his right with Howard, and his left reaching the railroad, along which General Stanley was moving, followed by Schofield. General Davis formed his divisions in line about 4 P. M., swept forward over some old cotton-fields in full view, and went over the rebel parapet handsomely, capturing the whole of Govan's brigade, with two field-batteries of ten guns. Being on the spot, I checked Davis's movement, and ordered General Howard to send the two divisions of the Seventeenth Corps (Blair) round by his right rear, to get below Jonesboro', and to reach the railroad, so as to cut off retreat in that direction. I also dispatched orders after orders to hurry forward Stanley, so as to lap around Jonesboro' on the east, hoping thus to capture the whole of Hardee's corps. I sent first Captain Audenried (aide-de-camp), then Colonel Poe, of the Engineers, and lastly General Thomas himself (and that is the only time during the campaign I can recall seeing General Thomas urge his horse into a gallop). Night was approaching, and the country on the farther side of the railroad was densely wooded. General Stanley had come up on the left of Davis, and was deploying, though there could not have been on his front more than a skirmish-line. Had he moved straight on by the flank, or by a slight circuit to his left, he would have inclosed the whole ground occupied by Hardee's corps, and that corps could not have escaped us; but night came on, and Hardee did escape.

Meantime General Slocum had reached his corps (the Twentieth), stationed at the Chattahoochee bridge, had relieved General A. S. Williams in command, and orders had been sent back to him to feel forward occasionally toward Atlanta, to observe the effect when we had reached the railroad. That night I was so restless and impatient that I could not sleep, and about midnight there arose toward Atlanta sounds of shells exploding, and other sound like that of musketry. I walked to the house of a farmer close by my bivouac, called him out to listen to the reverberations which came from the direction of Atlanta (twenty miles to the north of us), and inquired of him if he had resided there long. He said he had, and that these sounds were just like those of a battle. An interval of quiet then ensued, when again, about 4 A. M., arose other similar explosions, but I still remained in doubt whether the enemy was engaged in blowing up his own magazines, or whether General Slocum had not felt forward, and become engaged in a real battle.

The next morning General Hardee was gone, and we all pushed forward along the railroad south, in close pursuit, till we ran up against his lines at a point just above Lovejoy's Station. While bringing forward troops and feeling the new position of our adversary, rumors came from the rear that the enemy had evacuated Atlanta, and that General Slocum was in the city. Later in the day I received a note in Slocum's own handwriting, stating that he had heard during the night the very sounds that I have referred to; that he had moved rapidly up from the bridge about daylight, and had entered Atlanta unopposed. His letter was dated inside the city, so there was no doubt of the fact. General Thomas's bivouac was but a short distance from mine, and, before giving notice to the army in general orders, I sent one of my staff-officers to show him the note. In a few minutes the officer returned, soon followed by Thomas himself, who again examined the note, so as to be perfectly certain that it was genuine. The news seemed to him too good to be true. He snapped his fingers, whistled, and almost danced, and, as the news spread to the army, the shouts that arose from our men, the wild hallooing and glorious laughter, were to us a full recompense for the labor and toils and hardships through which we had passed in the previous three months.

A courier-line was at once organized, messages were sent back and forth from our camp at Lovejoy's to Atlanta, and to our telegraph-station at the Chattahoochee bridge. Of course, the glad tidings flew on the wings of electricity to all parts of the North, where the people had patiently awaited news of their husbands, sons, and brothers, away down in " Dixie Land ; " and congratulations came pouring back full of good-will and patriotism. This victory was most opportune ; Mr. Lincoln himself told me afterward that even he had previously felt in doubt, for the summer was fast passing away ; that General Grant seemed to be checkmated about Richmond and Petersburg, and my army seemed to have run up against an impassable barrier, when, suddenly and unexpectedly, came the news that " Atlanta was ours, and fairly won." On this text many a fine speech was made, but none more eloquent than that by Edward Everett, in Boston. A presidential election then agitated the North. Mr. Lincoln represented the national cause, and General McClellan had accepted the nomination of the Democratic party, whose platform was that the war was a failure, and that it was better to allow the South to go free to establish a separate government, whose corner-stone should be slavery. Success to our arms at that instant was therefore a political necessity ; and it was all-important that something startling in our interest should occur before the election in November. The brilliant success at Atlanta filled that requirement, and made the election of Mr. Lincoln certain. Among the many letters of congratulation received, those of Mr. Lincoln and General Grant seem most important :

EXECUTIVE MANSION,
WASHINGTON, D. C., *September* 3, 1864.

The national thanks are rendered by the President to Major-General W. T. Sherman and the gallant officers and soldiers of his command before Atlanta, for the distinguished ability and perseverance displayed in the campaign in Georgia, which, under Divine favor, has resulted in the capture of Atlanta. The marches, battles, sieges, and other military operations, that have signalized the campaign, must render it famous in the annals of war, and have entitled those who have participated therein to the applause and thanks of the nation.   ABRAHAM LINCOLN,
President of the United States.

CITY POINT, VIRGINIA, *September* 4, 1864—9 P. M.
Major-General SHERMAN :

I have just received your dispatch announcing the capture of Atlanta. In honor of your great victory, I have ordered a salute to be fired with *shotted* guns from every battery bearing upon the enemy. The salute will be fired within an hour, amid great rejoicing.

U. S. GRANT, *Lieutenant-General.*

These dispatches were communicated to the army in general orders, and we all felt duly encouraged and elated by the praise of those competent to bestow it.

The army still remained where the news of success had first found us, viz., Lovejoy's ; but, after due reflection, I resolved not to attempt at that time a further pursuit of Hood's army, but slowly and deliberately to move back, occupy Atlanta, enjoy a short period of rest, and to think well over the next step required in the progress of events. Orders for this movement were made on the 5th September, and three days were given for each army to reach the place assigned it, viz.: the Army of the Cumberland in and about Atlanta ; the Army of the Tennessee at East Point; and the Army of the Ohio at Decatur.

Personally I rode back to Jonesboro' on the 6th, and there inspected the rebel hospital, full of wounded officers and men left by Hardee in his retreat. The next night we stopped at

Rough and Ready, and on the 8th of September we rode into Atlanta, then occupied by the Twentieth Corps (General Slocum). In the Court-House Square was encamped a brigade, embracing the Massachusetts Second and Thirty-third Regiments, which had two of the finest bands of the army, and their music was to us all a source of infinite pleasure during our sojourn in that city. I took up my headquarters in the house of Judge Lyons, which stood opposite one corner of the Court-House Square, and at once set about a measure already ordered, of which I had thought much and long, viz., to remove the entire civil population, and to deny to all civilians from the rear the expected profits of civil trade. Hundreds of sutlers and traders were waiting at Nashville and Chattanooga, greedy to reach Atlanta with their wares and goods, with which to drive a profitable trade with the inhabitants. I gave positive orders that none of these traders, except three (one for each separate army), should be permitted to come nearer than Chattanooga; and, moreover, I peremptorily required that all the citizens and families resident in Atlanta should go away, giving to each the option to go south or north, as their interests or feelings dictated. I was resolved to make Atlanta a pure military garrison or depot, with no civil population to influence military measures. I had seen Memphis, Vicksburg, Natchez, and New Orleans, all captured from the enemy, and each at once was garrisoned by a full division of troops, if not more; so that success was actually crippling our armies in the field by detachments to guard and protect the interests of a hostile population.

I gave notice of this purpose, as early as the 4th of September, to General Halleck, in a letter concluding with these words:

If the people raise a howl against my barbarity and cruelty, I will answer that war is war, and not popularity-seeking. If they want peace, they and their relatives must stop the war.

I knew, of course, that such a measure would be strongly criticised, but made up my mind to do it with the absolute certainty of its justness, and that time would sanction its wisdom. I knew that the people of the South would read in this measure two important conclusions: one, that we were in earnest; and the other, if they were sincere in their common and popular clamor "to die in the last ditch," that the opportunity would soon come.

Soon after our reaching Atlanta, General Hood had sent in by a flag of truce a proposition, offering a general exchange of prisoners, saying that he was authorized to make such an exchange by the Richmond authorities, out of the vast number of our men then held captive at Andersonville, the same whom General Stoneman had hoped to rescue at the time of his raid. Some of these prisoners had already escaped and got in, had described the pitiable condition of the remainder, and, although I felt a sympathy for their hardships and sufferings as deeply as any man could, yet as nearly all the prisoners who had been captured by us during the campaign had been sent, as fast as taken, to the usual depots North, they were then beyond my control. There were still about two thousand, mostly captured at Jonesboro', who had been sent back by cars, but had not passed Chattanooga. These I ordered back, and offered General Hood to exchange them for Stoneman, Buell, and such of my own army as would make up the equivalent; but I would not exchange for his prisoners *generally*, because I knew these would have to be sent to their own regiments, away from my army, whereas all we could give him could at once be put to duty in his immediate army. Quite an angry correspondence grew up between us, which was published at the time in the newspapers, but it is not to be found in any book of which I have present knowledge, and therefore is given here, as illustrative of the events referred to, and of the feelings of the actors in the game of war at that particular crisis, together with certain other original letters of Generals Grant and Halleck, never hitherto published.

HEADQUARTERS ARMIES OF THE UNITED STATES, }
CITY POINT, VIRGINIA, *September* 12, 1864. }

Major-General W. T. SHERMAN, *commanding Military Division of the Mississippi.*

GENERAL: I send Lieutenant-Colonel Horace Porter, of my staff, with this. Colonel Porter will explain to you the exact condition of affairs here, better than I can do in the limits of a letter. Although I feel myself strong enough now for offensive operations, I am holding on quietly, to get advantage of recruits and convalescents, who are coming forward very rapidly. My lines are necessarily very long, extending from Deep Bottom, north of the James, across the peninsula formed by the Appomattox and the James, and south of the Appomattox to the Weldon road. This line is very strongly fortified, and can be held with comparatively few men; but, from its great length, necessarily takes many in the aggregate. I propose, when I do move, to extend my left so as to control what is known as the Southside, or Lynchburg & Petersburg road; then, if possible, to keep the Danville road cut. At the same time this move is made, I want to send a force of from six to ten thousand men against Wilmington. The way I propose to do this is to land the men north of Fort Fisher, and hold that point. At the same time a large naval fleet will be assembled there, and the iron-clads will run the batteries as they did at Mobile. This will give us the same control of the harbor of Wilmington that we now have of the harbor of Mobile. What you are to do with the forces at your command, I do not exactly see. The difficulties of supplying your army, except when they are constantly moving beyond where you are, I plainly see. If it had not been for Price's movement, Canby could have sent twelve thousand more men to Mobile. From your command on the Mississippi, an equal number could have been taken. With these forces, my idea would have been to divide them, sending one-half to Mobile, and the other half to Savannah. You could then move as proposed in your telegram, so as to threaten Macon and Augusta equally. Whichever one should be abandoned by the enemy, you could take and open up a new base of supplies. My object now in sending a staff-officer to you is not so much to suggest operations for you as to get your views, and to have plans matured by the time every thing can be got ready. It would probably be the 5th of October before any of the plans here indicated will be executed. If you have any promotions to recommend, send the names forward, and I will approve them.

In conclusion, it is hardly necessary for me to say that I feel you have accomplished the most gigantic undertaking given to any general in this war, and with a skill and ability that will be acknowledged in history as unsurpassed, if not unequaled. It gives me as much pleasure to record this in your favor as it would in favor of any living man, myself included.

Truly yours,   U. S. GRANT, *Lieutenant-General.*

HEADQUARTERS MILITARY DIVISION OF THE MISSISSIPPI, }
IN THE FIELD, ATLANTA, GEORGIA, *September* 20, 1864. }

Lieutenant-General U. S. GRANT, *Commander-in-Chief, City Point, Virginia.*

GENERAL: I have the honor to acknowledge, at the hands of Lieutenant-

Colonel Porter, of your staff, your letter of September 12th, and accept with thanks the honorable and kindly mention of the services of this army in the great cause in which we are all engaged.

I send by Colonel Porter all official reports which are completed, and will in a few days submit a list of names which are deemed worthy of promotion.

I think we owe it to the President to save him the invidious task of selection among the vast number of worthy applicants, and have ordered my army commanders to prepare their lists with great care, and to express their preferences, based upon claims of actual capacity and services rendered.

These I will consolidate, and submit in such a form that, if mistakes are made, they will at least be sanctioned by the best contemporaneous evidence of merit, for I know that vacancies do not exist equal in number to that of the officers who really deserve promotion.

As to the future, I am pleased to know that your army is being steadily reënforced by a good class of men, and I hope it will go on until you have a force that is numerically double that of your antagonist, so that with one part you can watch him, and with the other push out boldly from your left flank, occupy the Southside Railroad, compel him to attack you in position, or accept battle on your own terms.

We ought to ask our country for the largest possible armies that can be raised, as so important a thing as the self-existence of a great nation should not be left to the fickle chances of war.

Now that Mobile is shut out to the commerce of our enemy, it calls for no further effort on our part, unless the capture of the city can be followed by the occupation of the Alabama River and the railroad to Columbus, Georgia, when that place would be a magnificent auxiliary to my further progress into Georgia; but, until General Canby is much reënforced, and until he can more thoroughly subdue the scattered armies west of the Mississippi, I suppose that much cannot be attempted by him against the Alabama River and Columbus, Georgia.

The utter destruction of Wilmington, North Carolina, is of importance only in connection with the necessity of cutting off all foreign trade to our enemy, and if Admiral Farragut can get across the bar, and move quickly, I suppose he will succeed. From my knowledge of the mouth of Cape Fear River, I anticipate more difficulty in getting the heavy ships across the bar than in reaching the town of Wilmington; but, of course, the soundings of the channel are well known at Washington, as well as the draught of his iron-clads, so that it must be demonstrated to be feasible, or else it would not be attempted. If successful, I suppose that Fort Caswell will be occupied, and the fleet at once sent to the Savannah River. Then the reduction of that city is the next question. It once in our possession, and the river open to us, I would not hesitate to cross the State of Georgia with sixty thousand men, hauling some stores, and depending on the country for the balance. Where a million of people find subsistence, my army won't starve; but, as you know, in a country like Georgia, with few roads and innumerable streams, an inferior force can so delay an army and harass it, that it would not be a formidable object; but if the enemy knew that we had our boats in the Savannah River I could rapidly move to Milledgeville, where there is abundance of corn and meat, and could so threaten Macon and Augusta that the enemy would doubtless give up Macon for Augusta; then I would move so as to interpose between Augusta and Savannah, and force him to give us Augusta, with the only powder-mills and factories remaining in the South, or let us have the use of the Savannah River. Either horn of the dilemma will be worth a battle. I would prefer his holding Augusta (as the probabilities are); for then, with the Savannah River in our possession, the taking of Augusta would be a mere matter of time. This campaign can be made in the winter.

But the more I study the game, the more am I convinced that it would be wrong for us to penetrate farther into Georgia without an objective beyond. It would not be productive of much good. I can start east and make a circuit south and back, doing vast damage to the State, but resulting in no permanent good; and by mere threatening to do so, I hold a rod over the Georgians, who are not over-loyal to the South. I will therefore give it as my opinion that your army and Canby's should be reënforced to the maximum; that, after you get Wilmington, you should strike for Savannah and its river; that General Canby should hold the Mississippi River, and send a force to take Columbus, Georgia, either by way of the Alabama or Appalachicola River; that I should keep Hood employed and put my army in fine order for a march on Augusta, Columbia, and Charleston; and start as soon as Wilmington is sealed to commerce, and the city of Savannah is in our possession.

I think it will be found that the movements of Price and Shelby, west of the Mississippi, are mere diversions. They cannot hope to enter Missouri except as raiders; and the truth is, that General Rosecrans should be ashamed to take my troops for such a purpose. If you will secure Wilmington and the city of Savannah from your centre, and let General Canby have command over the Mississippi River and country west of it, I will send a force to the Alabama and Appalachicola, provided you give me one hundred thousand of the drafted men to fill up my old regiments; and if you will fix a day to be in Savannah, I will insure our possession of Macon and a point on the river below Augusta. The possession of the Savannah River is more than fatal to the possibility of Southern independence. They may stand the fall of Richmond, but not of all Georgia.

I will have a long talk with Colonel Porter, and tell him every thing that may occur to me of interest to you.

In the mean time, know that I admire your dogged perseverance and pluck more than ever. If you can whip Lee and I can march to the Atlantic, I think Uncle Abe will give us a twenty days' leave of absence to see the young folks. Yours as ever,

W. T. SHERMAN, *Major-General.*

HEADQUARTERS OF THE ARMY, }
WASHINGTON, *September* 16, 1864. }

General W. T. SHERMAN, *Atlanta, Georgia.*

MY DEAR GENERAL: Your very interesting letter of the 4th is just received. Its perusal has given me the greatest pleasure. I have not written before to congratulate you on the capture of Atlanta, the objective point of your brilliant campaign, for the reason that I have been suffering from my annual attack of "coryza," or hay-cold. It affects my eyes so much that I can scarcely see to write. As you suppose, I have watched your movements most attentively and critically, and I do not hesitate to say that your campaign has been the most brilliant of the war. Its results are less striking and less complete than those of General Grant at Vicksburg, but then you have had greater difficulties to encounter, a longer line of communications to keep up, and a longer and more continuous strain upon yourself and upon your army.

You must have been very considerably annoyed by the State negro recruiting-agents. Your letter was a capital one, and did much good. The law was a ridiculous one; it was opposed by the War Department, but passed through the influence of Eastern manufacturers, who hoped to escape the draft in that way. They were making immense fortunes out of the war, and could well afford to *purchase* negro recruits, and thus save their employés at home.

I fully agree with you in regard to the policy of a stringent draft; but, unfortunately, political influences are against us, and I fear it will not amount to much. Mr. Seward's speech at Auburn, again prophesying, for the twentieth time, that the rebellion would be crushed in a few months, and saying that there would be no draft, as we now had enough soldiers to end the war, etc., has done much harm, in a military point of view. I have seen enough of politics here to last me for life. You are right in avoiding them. McClellan may possibly reach the White House, but he will lose the respect of all honest, high-minded patriots, by his affiliation with such traitors and Copperheads as B——, V——, W——, S——, & Co. He would not stand upon the traitorous Chicago platform, but he had not the manliness to oppose it. A major-general in the United States Army, and yet not one word to utter against rebels or the rebellion! I had much respect for McClellan before he became a politician, but very little after reading his letter accepting the nomination.

Hooker certainly made a mistake in leaving before the capture of Atlanta. I understand that, when here, he said that you would fail; your army was discouraged and dissatisfied, etc., etc. He is most unmeasured in his abuse of me. I inclose you a specimen of what he publishes in Northern papers, wherever he goes. They are dictated by himself and written by W. B. and such worthies. The funny part of the business is, that I had nothing whatever to do with his being relieved on either occasion. Moreover, I have never said any thing to the President or Secretary of War to injure him in the slightest degree, and he knows that perfectly well. His animosity arises from another source. He is aware that I know some things about his character and conduct in California, and, fearing that I may use that information against him, he seeks to ward off its effect by making it appear that I am his personal enemy, am jealous of him, etc. I know of no other reason for his hostility to me. He is welcome to abuse me as much as he pleases; I don't think it will do him much good, or me much harm. I know very little of General Howard, but believe him to be a true, honorable man. Thomas is also a noble old war-horse. It is true, as you say, that he is slow, but he is always sure.

I have not seen General Grant since the fall of Atlanta, and do not know what instructions he has sent you. I fear that Canby has not the means to do much by way of Mobile. The military effects of Banks's disaster are now showing themselves by the threatened operations of Price & Co. toward Missouri, thus keeping in check our armies west of the Mississippi.

With many thanks for your kind letter, and wishes for your future success, yours truly,   H. W. HALLECK.

HEADQUARTERS MILITARY DIVISION OF THE MISSISSIPPI, }
ATLANTA, GEORGIA, *September* 20, 1864.   }

Major-General HALLECK, *Chief of Staff, Washington, D. C.*

GENERAL: I have the honor herewith to submit copies of a correspondence between General Hood, of the Confederate Army, the Mayor of Atlanta, and myself, touching the removal of the inhabitants of Atlanta.

In explanation of the tone which marks some of these letters, I will only call your attention to the fact that, after I had announced my determination, General Hood took upon himself to question my motives. I could not tamely submit to such impertinence; and I have also seen that, in violation of all official usage, he has published in the Macon newspapers such parts of the correspondence as suited his purpose. This could have had no other object than to create a feeling on the part of the people; but if he expects to resort to such artifices, I think I can meet him there too.

It is sufficient for my Government to know that the removal of the inhabitants has been made with liberality and fairness, that it has been attended with no force, and that no women or children have suffered, unless for want of provisions by their natural protectors and friends.

My real reasons for this step were:

We want all the houses of Atlanta for military storage and occupation.

We want to contract the lines of defense, so as to diminish the garrison to the limit necessary to defend its narrow and vital parts, instead of embracing, as the lines now do, the vast suburbs. This contraction of the lines, with the necessary citadels and redoubts, will make it necessary to destroy the very houses used by families as residences.

Atlanta is a fortified town, was stubbornly defended, and fairly captured. As captors, we have a right to it.

The residence here of a poor population would compel us, sooner or later, to feed them or to see them starve under our eyes.

The residence here of the families of our enemies would be a temptation and a means to keep up a correspondence dangerous and hurtful to our cause; a civil population calls for provost-guards, and absorbs the attention of officers in listening to everlasting complaints and special grievances that are not military.

These are my reasons; and, if satisfactory to the Government of the United States, it makes no difference whether it pleases General Hood and *his* people or not. I am, with respect, your obedient servant,

W. T. SHERMAN, *Major-General commanding.*

HEADQUARTERS MILITARY DIVISION OF THE MISSISSIPPI, }
IN THE FIELD, ATLANTA, GEORGIA, *September* 7, 1864. }

General HOOD, *commanding Confederate Army.*

GENERAL: I have deemed it to the interest of the United States that the citizens now residing in Atlanta should remove, those who prefer it to go south, and the rest north. For the latter I can provide food and transportation to points of their election in Tennessee, Kentucky, or farther north. For the former I can provide transportation by cars as far as Rough and Ready, and also wagons; but, that their removal may be made with as little discomfort as possible, it will be necessary for you to help the familes from Rough and Ready to the cars at Lovejoy's. If you consent, I will undertake to remove all the families in Atlanta who prefer to go south to Rough and Ready, with all their movable effects, viz., clothing, trunks, reasonable furniture, bedding, etc., with their servants, white and black, with the proviso that no force shall be used toward the blacks, one way or the other. If they want to go with their masters or mistresses, they may do so; otherwise they will be sent away, unless they be men, when they may be employed by our quartermaster. Atlanta is no place for families or non-combatants, and I have no desire to send them north if you will assist in conveying them south. If this proposition meets your views, I will consent to a truce in the neighborhood of Rough and Ready, stipulating that any wagons, horses, animals, or persons sent there for the purposes herein stated, shall in no manner be harmed or molested; you in your turn agreeing that any cars, wagons, or carriages, persons or animals sent to the same point, shall not be interfered with. Each of us might send a guard of, say, one hundred men, to maintain order, and limit the truce to, say, two days after a certain time appointed.

I have authorized the mayor to choose two citizens to convey to you this letter, with such documents as the mayor may forward in explanation, and shall await your reply. I have the honor to be your obedient servant,

W. T. SHERMAN, *Major-General commanding.*

HEADQUARTERS ARMY OF TENNESSEE,
OFFICE CHIEF OF STAFF, *September* 9, 1864.

Major-General W. T. SHERMAN, *commanding United States Forces in Georgia.*

GENERAL : Your letter of yesterday's date, borne by James M. Ball and James R. Crew, citizens of Atlanta, is received. You say therein, "I deem it to be to the interest of the United States that the citizens now residing in Atlanta should remove," etc. I do not consider that I have any alternative in this matter. I therefore accept your proposition to declare a truce of two days, or such time as may be necessary to accomplish the purpose mentioned, and shall render all assistance in my power to expedite the transportation of citizens in this direction. I suggest that a staff-officer be appointed by you to superintend the removal from the city to Rough and Ready, while I appoint a like officer to control their removal farther south; that a guard of one hundred men be sent by either party as you propose, to maintain order at that place, and that the removal begin on Monday next.

And now, sir, permit me to say that the unprecedented measure you propose transcends, in studied and ingenious cruelty, all acts ever before brought to my attention in the dark history of war.

In the name of God and humanity, I protest, believing that you will find that you are expelling from their homes and firesides the wives and children of a brave people. I am, general, very respectfully, your obedient servant,

J. B. HOOD, *General.*

HEADQUARTERS MILITARY DIVISION OF THE MISSISSIPPI,
IN THE FIELD, ATLANTA, GEORGIA, *September* 10, 1864.

General J. B. HOOD, *commanding Army of Tennessee, Confederate Army.*

GENERAL : I have the honor to acknowledge the receipt of your letter of this date, at the hands of Messrs. Ball and Crew, consenting to the arrangements I had proposed to facilitate the removal south of the people of

Atlanta, who prefer to go in that direction. I inclose you a copy of my orders, which will, I am satisfied, accomplish my purpose perfectly.

You style the measures proposed "unprecedented," and appeal to the dark history of war for a parallel, as an act of "studied and ingenious cruelty." It is not unprecedented; for General Johnston himself very wisely and properly removed the families all the way from Dalton down, and I see no reason why Atlanta should be excepted. Nor is it necessary to appeal to the dark history of war, when recent and modern examples are so handy. You yourself burned dwelling-houses along your parapet, and I have seen to-day fifty houses that you have rendered uninhabitable because they stood in the way of your forts and men. You defended Atlanta on a line so close to town that every cannon-shot and many musket-shots from our line of investment, that overshot their mark, went into the habitations of women and children. General Hardee did the same at Jonesboro', and General Johnston did the same, last summer, at Jackson, Mississippi. I have not accused you of heartless cruelty, but merely instance these cases of very recent occurrence, and could go on and enumerate hundreds of others, and challenge any fair man to judge which of us has the heart of pity for the families of a "brave people."

I say that it is kindness to these families of Atlanta to remove them now, at once, from scenes that women and children should not be exposed to, and the "brave people" should scorn to commit their wives and children to the rude barbarians who thus, as you say, violate the laws of war, as illustrated in the pages of its dark history.

In the name of common-sense, I ask you not to appeal to a just God in such a sacrilegious manner. You who, in the midst of peace and prosperity, have plunged a nation into war—dark and cruel war—who dared and badgered us to battle, insulted our flag, seized our arsenals and forts that were left in the honorable custody of peaceful ordnance-sergeants, seized and made "prisoners of war" the very garrisons sent to protect your people against negroes and Indians, long before any overt act was committed by the (to you) hated Lincoln Government; tried to force Kentucky and Missouri into rebellion, spite of themselves; falsified the vote of Louisiana; turned loose your privateers to plunder unarmed ships; expelled Union families by the thousands, burned their houses, and declared, by an act of your Congress, the confiscation of all debts due Northern men for goods had and received! Talk thus to the marines, but not to me, who have seen these things, and who will this day make as much sacrifice for the peace and honor of the South as the best-born Southerner among you! If we must be enemies, let us be men, and fight it out as we propose to do, and not deal in such hypocritical appeals to God and humanity. God will judge us in due time, and he will pronounce whether it be more humane to fight with a town full of women and the families of a brave people at our back, or to remove them in time to places of safety among their own friends and people. I am, very respectfully, your obedient servant,

W. T. SHERMAN, *Major-General commanding.*

HEADQUARTERS ARMY OF TENNESSEE, }
September 12, 1864.   }

Major-General W. T. SHERMAN, *commanding Military Division of the Mississippi.*

GENERAL: I have the honor to acknowledge the receipt of your letter of the 9th inst., with its inclosure in reference to the women, children, and others, whom you have thought proper to expel from their homes in the city of Atlanta. Had you seen proper to let the matter rest there, I would gladly have allowed your letter to close this correspondence, and, without your expressing it in words, would have been willing to believe that, while "the interests of the United States," in your opinion, compelled you to an act of barbarous cruelty, you regretted the necessity, and we would have dropped the subject; but you have chosen to indulge in statements which I feel compelled to notice, at least so far as to signify my dissent, and not allow silence in regard to them to be construed as acquiescence.

I see nothing in your communication which induces me to modify the language of condemnation with which I characterized your order. It but strengthens me in the opinion that it stands "preëminent in the dark history of war for studied and ingenious cruelty." Your original order was stripped of all pretenses; you announced the edict for the sole reason that it was " to the interest of the United States." This alone you offered to us and the civilized world as an all-sufficient reason for disregarding the laws of God and man. You say that " General Johnston himself very wisely and properly removed the families all the way from Dalton down." It is due to that gallant soldier and gentleman to say that no act of his distinguished career gives the least color to your unfounded aspersions upon his conduct. He depopulated no villages, nor towns, nor cities, either friendly or hostile. He offered and extended friendly aid to his unfortunate fellow-citizens who desired to flee from your fraternal embraces. You are equally unfortunate in your attempt to find a justification for this act of cruelty, either in the defense of Jonesboro', by General Hardee, or of Atlanta, by myself. General Hardee defended his position in front of Jonesboro' at the expense of injury to the houses; an ordinary, proper, and justifiable act of war. I defended Atlanta at the same risk and cost. If there was any fault in either case, it was your own, in not giving notice, especially in the case of Atlanta, of your purpose to shell the town, which is usual in war among civilized nations. No inhabitant was expelled from his home and fireside by the orders of General Hardee or myself, and therefore your recent order can find no support from the conduct of either of us. I feel no other emotion

other than pain in reading that portion of your letter which attempts to justify your shelling Atlanta without notice under pretense that I defended Atlanta upon a line so close to town that every cannon-shot and many musket-balls from your line of investment, that overshot their mark, went into
the habitations of women and children. I made no complaint of your firing
into Atlanta in any way you thought proper. I make none now, but there
are a hundred thousand witnesses that you fired into the habitations of
women and children for weeks, firing far above and miles beyond my line
of defense. I have too good an opinion, founded both upon observation
and experience, of the skill of your artillerists, to credit the insinuation
that they for several weeks unintentionally fired too high for my modest
field-works, and slaughtered women and children by accident and want of
skill.

The residue of your letter is rather discussion. It opens a wide field for
the discussion of questions which I do not feel are committed to me. I am
only a general of one of the armies of the Confederate States, charged with
military operations in the field, under the direction of my superior officers,
and I am not called upon to discuss with you the causes of the present war,
or the political questions which led to or resulted from it. These grave and
important questions have been committed to far abler hands than mine,
and I shall only refer to them so far as to repel any unjust conclusion which
might be drawn from my silence. You charge my country with "daring
and badgering you to battle." The truth is, we sent commissioners to you,
respectfully offering a peaceful separation, before the first gun was fired on
either side. You say we insulted your flag. The truth is, we fired upon
it, and those who fought under it, when you came to our doors upon the
mission of subjugation. You say we seized upon your forts and arsenals,
and made prisoners of the garrisons sent to protect us against negroes and
Indians. The truth is, we, by force of arms, drove out insolent intruders
and took possession of our own forts and arsenals, to resist your claims to
dominion over masters, slaves, and Indians, all of whom are to this day,
with a unanimity unexampled in the history of the world, warring against
your attempts to become their masters. You say that we tried to force
Missouri and Kentucky into rebellion in spite of themselves. The truth is,
my Government, from the beginning of this struggle to this hour, has again
and again offered, before the whole world, to leave it to the unbiased will
of these States, and all others, to determine for themselves whether they
will cast their destiny with your Government or ours; and your Government
has resisted this fundamental principle of free institutions with the bayonet, and labors daily, by force and fraud, to fasten its hateful tyranny upon
the unfortunate freemen of these States. You say we falsified the vote of
Louisiana. The truth is, Louisiana not only separated herself from your
Government by nearly a unanimous vote of her people, but has vindicated

the act upon every battle-field from Gettysburg to the Sabine, and has exhibited an heroic devotion to her decision which challenges the admiration and respect of every man capable of feeling sympathy for the oppressed or admiration for heroic valor. You say that we turned loose pirates to plunder your unarmed ships. The truth is, when you robbed us of our part of the navy, we built and bought a few vessels, hoisted the flag of our country, and swept the seas, in defiance of your navy, around the whole circumference of the globe. You say we have expelled Union families by thousands. The truth is, not a single family has been expelled from the Confederate States, that I am aware of; but, on the contrary, the moderation of our Government toward traitors has been a fruitful theme of denunciation by its enemies and well-meaning friends of our cause. You say my Government, by acts of Congress, has confiscated "all debts due Northern men for goods sold and delivered." The truth is, our Congress gave due and ample time to your merchants and traders to depart from our shores with their ships, goods, and effects, and only sequestrated the property of our enemies in retaliation for their acts—declaring us traitors, and confiscating our property wherever their power extended, either in their country or our own. Such are your accusations, and such are the facts known of all men to be true.

You order into exile the whole population of a city; drive men, women, and children from their homes at the point of the bayonet, under the plea that it is to the interest of your Government, and on the claim that it is an act of "kindness to these families of Atlanta." Butler only banished from New Orleans the registered enemies of his Government, and acknowledged that he did it as a punishment. You issue a sweeping edict, covering all the inhabitants of a city, and add insult to the injury heaped upon the defenseless by assuming that you have done them a kindness. This you follow by the assertion that you will "make as much sacrifice for the peace and honor of the South as the best-born Southerner." And, because I characterize what you call a kindness as being real cruelty, you presume to sit in judgment between me and my God; and you decide that my earnest prayer to the Almighty Father to save our women and children from what you call kindness, is a " sacrilegious, hypocritical appeal."

You came into our country with your army, avowedly for the purpose of subjugating free white men, women, and children, and not only intend to rule over them, but you make negroes your allies, and desire to place over us an inferior race, which we have raised from barbarism to its present position, which is the highest ever attained by that race, in any country, in all time. I must, therefore, decline to accept your statements in reference to your kindness toward the people of Atlanta, and your willingness to sacrifice every thing for the peace and honor of the South, and refuse to be governed by your decision in regard to matters between myself, my country, and my God.

You say, "Let us fight it out like men." To this my reply is—for myself, and I believe for all the true men, ay, and women and children, in my country—we will fight you to the death! Better die a thousand deaths than submit to live under you or your Government and your negro allies!

Having answered the points forced upon me by your letter of the 9th of September, I close this correspondence with you; and, notwithstanding your comments upon my appeal to God in the cause of humanity, I again humbly and reverently invoke his almighty aid in defense of justice and right. Respectfully, your obedient servant,

J. B. Hood, *General.*

ATLANTA, GEORGIA, *September* 11, 1864.

Major-General W. T. SHERMAN.

SIR: We the undersigned, Mayor and two of the Council for the city of Atlanta, for the time being the only legal organ of the people of the said city, to express their wants and wishes, ask leave most earnestly but respectfully to petition you to reconsider the order requiring them to leave Atlanta.

At first view, it struck us that the measure would involve extraordinary hardship and loss, but since we have seen the practical execution of it so far as it has progressed, and the individual condition of the people, and heard their statements as to the inconveniences, loss, and suffering attending it, we are satisfied that the amount of it will involve in the aggregate consequences appalling and heart-rending.

Many poor women are in advanced state of pregnancy, others now having young children, and whose husbands for the greater part are either in the army, prisoners, or dead. Some say: "I have such a one sick at my house; who will wait on them when I am gone?" Others say: "What are we to do? We have no house to go to, and no means to buy, build, or rent any; no parents, relatives, or friends, to go to." Another says: "I will try and take this or that article of property, but such and such things I must leave behind, though I need them much." We reply to them: "General Sherman will carry your property to Rough and Ready, and General Hood will take it thence on." And they will reply to that: "But I want to leave the railroad at such a place, and cannot get conveyance from there on."

We only refer to a few facts, to try to illustrate in part how this measure will operate in practice. As you advanced, the people north of this fell back; and before your arrival here, a large portion of the people had retired south, so that the country south of this is already crowded, and without houses enough to accommodate the people, and we are informed that many are now staying in churches and other out-buildings.

This being so, how is it possible for the people still here (mostly women and children) to find any shelter? And how can they live through the winter in the woods—no shelter or subsistence, in the midst of strangers who know them not, and without the power to assist them much, if they were willing to do so?

This is but a feeble picture of the consequences of this measure. You know the woe, the horrors, and the suffering, cannot be described by words; imagination can only conceive of it, and we ask you to take these things into consideration.

We know your mind and time are constantly occupied with the duties of your command, which almost deters us from asking your attention to this matter, but thought it might be that you had not considered this subject in all of its awful consequences, and that on more reflection you, we hope, would not make this people an exception to all mankind, for we know of no such instance ever having occurred—surely never in the United States—and what has this *helpless* people done, that they should be driven from their homes, to wander strangers and outcasts, and exiles, and to subsist on charity?

We do not know as yet the number of people still here; of those who are here, we are satisfied a respectable number, if allowed to remain at home, could subsist for several months without assistance, and a respectable number for a much longer time, and who might not need assistance at any time.

In conclusion, we most earnestly and solemnly petition you to reconsider this order, or modify it, and suffer this unfortunate people to remain at home, and enjoy what little means they have.

Respectfully submitted:

JAMES M. CALHOUN, *Mayor.*
E. E. RAWSON, *Councilman.*
S. C. WELLS, *Councilman.*

HEADQUARTERS MILITARY DIVISION OF THE MISSISSIPPI, ⎫
IN THE FIELD, ATLANTA, GEORGIA, *September* 12, 1864. ⎭

JAMES M. CALHOUN, *Mayor,* E. E. RAWSON *and* S. C. WELLS, *representing City Council of Atlanta.*

GENTLEMEN: I have your letter of the 11th, in the nature of a petition to revoke my orders removing all the inhabitants from Atlanta. I have read it carefully, and give full credit to your statements of the distress that will be occasioned, and yet shall not revoke my orders, because they were not designed to meet the humanities of the case, but to prepare for the future struggles in which millions of good people outside of Atlanta have a deep interest. We must have peace, not only at Atlanta, but in all America. To secure this, we must stop the war that now desolates our once happy and favored country. To stop war, we must defeat the rebel armies which are arrayed against the laws and Constitution that all must respect and obey. To defeat those armies, we must prepare the way to reach them in their recesses, provided with the arms and instruments which enable us to accomplish our purpose. Now, I know the vindictive nature of our enemy, that we may have many years of military operations from this quarter; and, therefore, deem it wise and prudent to prepare in time. The use of Atlanta for warlike purposes is inconsistent with its character as a home for families. There will be no manufactures, commerce, or agriculture here, for the maintenance of families, and sooner or later want will compel the inhabitants to go. Why not go now, when all the arrangements are completed for the transfer, instead of waiting till the plunging shot of contending armies will renew the scenes of the past month? Of course, I do not apprehend any such thing at this moment, but you do not suppose this army will be here until the war is over. I cannot discuss this subject with you fairly, because I cannot impart to you what we propose to do, but I assert that our military plans make it necessary for the inhabitants to go away, and I can only renew my offer of services to make their exodus in any direction as easy and comfortable as possible.

You cannot qualify war in harsher terms than I will. War is cruelty, and you cannot refine it; and those who brought war into our country deserve all the curses and maledictions a people can pour out. I know I had no hand in making this war, and I know I will make more sacrifices to-day than any of you to secure peace. But you cannot have peace and a division of our country. If the United States submits to a division now, it will not stop, but will go on until we reap the fate of Mexico, which is eternal war. The United States does and must assert its authority, wherever it once had power; for, if it relaxes one bit to pressure, it is gone, and I believe that such is the national feeling. This feeling assumes various shapes, but always comes back to that of Union. Once admit the Union, once more acknowledge the authority of the national Government, and, instead of devoting your houses and streets and roads to the dread uses of war, I and this army become at once your protectors and supporters, shielding you from danger, let it come from what quarter it may. I know that a few individuals cannot resist a torrent of error and passion, such as swept the South into rebellion, but you can point out, so that we may know those who desire a government, and those who insist on war and its desolation.

You might as well appeal against the thunder-storm as against these terrible hardships of war. They are inevitable, and the only way the people of Atlanta can hope once more to live in peace and quiet at home, is to stop the war, which can only be done by admitting that it began in error and is perpetuated in pride.

We don't want your negroes, or your horses, or your houses, or your lands, or any thing you have, but we do want and will have a just obedience to the laws of the United States. That we will have, and, if it involves the destruction of your improvements, we cannot help it.

You have heretofore read public sentiment in your newspapers, that live by falsehood and excitement; and the quicker you seek for truth in other quarters, the better. I repeat then that, by the original compact of Government, the United States had certain rights in Georgia, which have never been relinquished and never will be; that the South began war by seizing forts, arsenals, mints, custom-houses, etc., etc., long before Mr. Lincoln was installed, and before the South had one jot or tittle of provocation. I myself have seen in Missouri, Kentucky, Tennessee, and Mississippi, hundreds and thousands of women and children fleeing from your armies and desperadoes, hungry and with bleeding feet. In Memphis, Vicksburg, and Mississippi, we fed thousands upon thousands of the families of rebel soldiers left on our hands, and whom we could not see starve. Now that war comes home to you, you feel very different. You deprecate its horrors, but did not feel them when you sent car-loads of soldiers and ammunition, and moulded shells and shot, to carry war into Kentucky and Tennessee, to desolate the homes of hundreds and thousands of good people who only asked to live in peace at their old homes, and under the Government of their inheritance. But these comparisons are idle. I want peace, and believe it can only be reached through union and war, and I will ever conduct war with a view to perfect and early success.

But, my dear sirs, when peace does come, you may call on me for any thing. Then will I share with you the last cracker, and watch with you to shield your homes and families against danger from every quarter.

Now you must go, and take with you the old and feeble, feed and nurse them, and build for them, in more quiet places, proper habitations to shield them against the weather until the mad passions of men cool down, and allow the Union and peace once more to settle over your old homes at Atlanta. Yours in haste,

W. T. SHERMAN, *Major-General commanding.*

HEADQUARTERS MILITARY DIVISION OF THE MISSISSIPPI, }
IN THE FIELD, ATLANTA, GEORGIA, *September* 14, 1864. }

General J. B. HOOD, *commanding Army of the Tennessee, Confederate Army.*

GENERAL: Yours of September 12th is received, and has been carefully perused. I agree with you that this discussion by two soldiers is out of place, and profitless; but you must admit that you began the controversy by characterizing an official act of mine in unfair and improper terms. I reiterate my former answer, and to the only new matter contained in your rejoinder add: We have no "negro allies" in this army; not a single negro soldier left Chattanooga with this army, or is with it now. There are a few guarding Chattanooga, which General Steedman sent at one time to drive Wheeler out of Dalton.

I was not bound by the laws of war to give notice of the shelling of Atlanta, a "fortified town, with magazines, arsenals, founderies, and public stores;" you were bound to take notice. See the books.

This is the conclusion of our correspondence, which I did not begin, and terminate with satisfaction. I am, with respect, your obedient servant,

W. T. SHERMAN, *Major-General commanding.*

HEADQUARTERS OF THE ARMY, }
WASHINGTON, *September* 28, 1864, }

Major-General SHERMAN, *Atlanta, Georgia.*

GENERAL: Your communications of the 20th in regard to the removal of families from Atlanta, and the exchange of prisoners, and also the official report of your campaign, are just received. I have not had time as yet to examine your report. The course which you have pursued in removing rebel families from Atlanta, and in the exchange of prisoners, is fully approved by the War Department. Not only are you justified by the laws and usages of war in removing these people, but I think it was your duty to your own army to do so. Moreover, I am fully of opinion that the nature of your position, the character of the war, the conduct of the enemy (and especially of non-combatants and women of the territory which we have heretofore conquered and occupied), will justify you in gathering up all the forage and provisions which your army may require, both for a siege of Atlanta and for your supply in your march farther into the enemy's country. Let the disloyal families of the country, thus stripped, go to their husbands, fathers, and natural protectors, in the rebel ranks; we have tried three years of conciliation and kindness without any reciprocation; on the contrary, those thus treated have acted as spies and guerrillas in our rear and within our lines. The safety of our armies, and a proper regard for the lives of our soldiers, require that we apply to our inexorable foes the severe rules of war. We certainly are not required to treat the so-called non-combatant rebels better than they themselves treat each other. Even here in Virginia, within fifty miles of Washington, they strip their own families of provisions, leaving them, as our army advances, to be fed by us, or to starve within our lines. We have fed this class of people long enough. Let them go with their husbands and fathers in the rebel ranks; and if they won't go, we must send them to their friends and natural protectors. I would destroy every mill and factory within reach which I did not want for my own use. This the rebels have done, not only in Maryland and Pennsylvania, but also in Virginia and other rebel States, when compelled to fall back before our armies. In many sections of the country they have not left a mill to grind grain for their own suffering families, lest we might use them to supply our armies. We must do the same.

I have endeavored to impress these views upon our commanders for the last two years. You are almost the only one who has properly applied them. I do not approve of General Hunter's course in burning private houses or uselessly destroying private property. That is barbarous. But I approve of taking or destroying whatever may serve as supplies to us or to the enemy's army.

Very respectfully, your obedient servant,

H. W. HALLECK, *Major-General, Chief of Staff.*

In order to effect the exchange of prisoners, to facilitate the exodus of the people of Atlanta, and to keep open communication with the South, we established a neutral camp, at and about the railroad-station next south of Atlanta, known as "Rough and Ready," to which point I dispatched Lieutenant-Colonel Willard Warner, of my staff, with a guard of one hundred men, and General Hood sent Colonel Clare, of his staff, with a similar guard; these officers and men harmonized perfectly, and parted good friends when their work was done. In the mean time I also had reconnoitred the entire rebel lines about Atlanta, which were well built, but were entirely too extensive to be held by a single corps or division of troops, so I instructed Colonel Poe, United States Engineers, on my staff, to lay off an inner and shorter line, susceptible of defense by a smaller garrison.

By the middle of September all these matters were in progress, the reports of the past campaign were written up and dispatched to Washington, and our thoughts began to turn toward the future. Admiral Farragut had boldly and successfully run the forts at the entrance to Mobile Bay, which resulted in the capture of Fort Morgan, so that General Canby was enabled to begin his regular operations against Mobile City, with a view to open the Alabama River to navigation. My first thoughts were to concert operations with him, either by way of Montgomery, Alabama, or by the Appalachicola; but so long a line, to be used as a base for further operations eastward, was not advisable, and I concluded to await the initiative of the enemy, supposing that he would be forced to resort to some desperate campaign by the clamor raised at the South on account of the great loss to them of the city of Atlanta.

General Thomas occupied a house on Marietta Street, which had a veranda with high pillars. We were sitting there one evening, talking about things generally, when General Thomas asked leave to send his trains back to Chattanooga, for the convenience and economy of forage. I inquired of him if he supposed we would be allowed much rest at Atlanta, and he said he thought we would, or that at all events it would not be prudent for us to go much farther into Georgia because of our already long line of communication, viz., three hundred miles from Nashville. This was true; but there we were, and we could not afford to remain on the defensive, simply holding Atlanta and fighting for the safety of its railroad. I insisted on his retaining all trains, and on keeping all his divisions ready to move at a moment's warning. All the army, officers and men, seemed to relax more or less, and sink into a condition of idleness. General Schofield was permitted to go to Knoxville, to look after matters in his Department of the Ohio; and Generals Blair and Logan went home to look after politics. Many of the regiments were entitled to, and claimed, their discharge, by reason of the expiration of their term of service; so that with victory and success came also many causes of disintegration.

The rebel General Wheeler was still in Middle Tennessee, threatening our railroads, and rumors came that Forrest was on his way from Mississippi to the same theatre, for the avowed purpose of breaking up our railroads and compelling us to fall back from our conquest. To prepare for this, or any other emergency, I ordered Newton's division of the Fourth Corps back to Chattanooga, and Corse's division of the Seventeenth Corps to Rome, and instructed General Rousseau at Nashville, Granger at Decatur, and Steadman at Chattanooga, to adopt the most active measures to protect and insure the safety of our roads.

Hood still remained about Lovejoy's Station, and, up to the 15th of September, had given no signs of his future plans; so that with this date I close the campaign of Atlanta, with the following review of our relative losses during the months of

August and September, with a summary of those for the whole campaign, beginning May 6 and ending September 15, 1864. The losses for August and September are added together, so as to include those about Jonesboro':

ARMY OF THE CUMBERLAND—(MAJOR-GENERAL THOMAS.)

CORPS.	Killed and Missing.	Wounded.	Total.
Fourth (Stanley)......................	166	416	582
Fourteenth (Davis, Palmer)...........	444	1,809	2,253
Twentieth (Williams, Slocum)	71	189	260
Total..........................	681	2,414	3,095

ARMY OF THE TENNESSEE—(MAJOR-GENERAL O. O. HOWARD.)

CORPS.	Killed and Missing.	Wounded.	Total.
Fifteenth (Logan).....................	143	430	573
Sixteenth (Dodge).....................	40	217	257
Seventeenth (Blair)	102	258	360
Total..........................	285	905	1,190

ARMY OF THE OHIO—(MAJOR-GENERAL SCHOFIELD.)

CORPS.	Killed and Missing.	Wounded.	Total.
Twenty-third (Cox)....................	146	279	425
Cavalry (Garrard, McCook, Kilpatrick)..	296	133	429
Total..........................	442	412	854
Grand Aggregate.................	1,408	3,731	5,139

Hood's losses, as reported for the same period, page 577, Johnston's "Narrative:"

CORPS.	Killed.	Wounded.	Total.
Hardee's.............................	141	1,018	1,159
Lee's................................	248	1,631	1,879
Stewart's............................	98	574	667
Total..........................	482	3,223	3,705

To which should be added:

Prisoners captured by us........................... 3,738

Giving his total loss......................... 7,443

On recapitulating the entire losses of each army during the entire campaign, from May to September, inclusive, we have, in the Union army, as per table appended:

Killed 4,423
Wounded 22,822
Missing.. 4,442

Aggregate loss............................. 31,687

In the Southern army, according to the reports of Surgeon Foard (pp. 576, 577, Johnston's "Narrative"):

Killed (Johnston)................................. 1,221
  "   (Hood) 1,823

Total killed................................. 3,044
Wounded (Johnston)............................. 8,229
  "   (Hood) 10,723

Total killed and wounded.................... 21,996
Add prisoners captured by us, and officially reported
at the time (*see* table)......................... 12,983

Aggregate loss to Southern army............. 34,979

The foregoing figures are official, and are very nearly correct. I see no room for error save in the cavalry, which was very much scattered, and whose reports are much less reliable than of the infantry and artillery; but as Surgeon Foard's tables do not embrace Wheeler's, Jackson's, and Martin's divisions of cavalry, I infer that the comparison, as to cavalry losses, is a "stand-off."

I have no doubt that the Southern officers flattered themselves that they had killed and crippled of us two and even six to one, as stated by Johnston; but they were simply mistaken, and I herewith submit official tabular statements made up from the archives of the War Department, in proof thereof:

Statement showing the Losses sustained in Battle by the Army under Command of General W. T. Sherman, from May to September, 1864, inclusive.

COMMANDS.	MAY. Killed or Missing.	MAY. Wounded.	JUNE. Killed or Missing.	JUNE. Wounded.	JULY. Killed or Missing.	JULY. Wounded.	AUGUST. Killed or Missing.	AUGUST. Wounded.	SEPTEMBER. Killed or Missing.	SEPTEMBER. Wounded.	Total Killed or Missing.	Total Wounded.	Aggregate.	REMARKS.
Fourth Corps...........	576	1,910	602	1,542	116	492	106	152	60	264	1,460	4,300	5,760	
Fourteenth Corps.......	147	655	353	1,466	817	1,084	180	801	264	1,008	1,261	5,014	6,275	
Twentieth Corps........	571	2,997	322	1,246	341	1,480	70	189	1	......	1,505	5,912	7,417	
Total—Army of the Cumberland.	1,294	5,562	1,277	4,254	974	2,996	356	1,142	325	1,272	4,226	15,226	19,452	
Fifteenth Corps........	122	624	179	687	590	797	108	867	85	63	1,084	2,588	3,672	
Sixteenth Corps........	a 94	a 480	a 52	a 157	a 289	a 721	a 40	a 217	......	......	475	1,525	2,000	Left wing broken up September, 1864, and troops transferred to Fifteenth and Seventeenth Corps.
	b 40	b 209	c 20	c 102	d 26	d 146	......	e 3	......	......	*86	*460	*546	
Seventeenth Corps......	......	1	47	212	1,861	1,208	74	212	28	46	1,510	1,674	3,184	
Total—Army of the Tennessee..	256	1,264	298	1,158	2,266	2,867	222	799	63	109	3,105	6,197	9,302	
Twenty-third Corps.....	226	757	105	862	95	167	142	270	4	9	572	1,565	2,187	
Cavalry................	127	62	180	63	495	81	199	110	97	23	1,048	294	1,342	
Grand Total........	1,903	7,645	1,810	5,842	3,830	6,061	919	2,321	489	1,418	*8,951	*23,282	*32,233	

a Left wing in Atlanta campaign.   b Right wing on Red River expedition.   c Right wing at Lake Chicot, La.   d Right wing at Tupelo, Miss.   e Right wing skirmishes in Mississippi.

* These figures have been obtained principally from the monthly returns of the several army corps, and are believed to be approximately correct. The killed and missing, being reported in the same column on the returns, cannot be shown separately in this table, but from another source of information (Regimental Rolls and Returns) the aggregate number of missing during the period in question is found to have been 4,442. Deducting this number from the 8,951 of both classes would give 4,508 as the number killed. Then subtracting the casualties (86 killed and 460 wounded) of the right wing, Sixteenth Army Corps, not engaged in the Atlanta campaign, would give the losses of General Sherman's immediate command from Chattanooga to Atlanta as follows: Killed, 4,428; wounded, 22,822; missing, 4,442—total 31,657.

E. D. TOWNSEND, Adjutant-General.

HEADQUARTERS MILITARY DIVISION OF THE MISSISSIPPI, ⎱
IN THE FIELD, ATLANTA, GEORGIA, *September* 15, 1864. ⎰

Prisoners and Deserters taken by "Army in the Field," Military Division of the Mississippi, during May, June, July, and August, 1864.

COMMANDS.	PRISONERS.		DESERTERS.		Aggregate.
	Commissioned Officers.	Enlisted Men.	Commissioned Officers.	Enlisted Men.	
Army of the Cumberland.......	121	3,888	21	1,543	5,523
Army of the Tennessee........	133	2,591	5	576	3,305
Army of the Ohio.............	16	781	1	292	1,090
Total..................	270	7,210	27	2,411	9,918

To which add the prisoners and deserters taken by the
Army of the Cumberland, September 1st to 20th.. 3,065

Making aggregate.............. 12,983

Reports from armies of the Tennessee and Ohio include the whole campaign, to September 15, 1864.

W. T. SHERMAN,
Major-General United States Army commanding.

I have also had a careful tabular statement compiled from official records in the adjutant-general's office, giving the " effective strength " of the army under my command for each of the months of May, June, July, August, and September, 1864, which enumerate every man (infantry, artillery, and cavalry) for duty. The recapitulation clearly exhibits the actual truth. We opened the campaign with 98,797 (ninety-eight thousand seven hundred and ninety-seven) men. Blair's two divisions joined us early in June, giving 112,819 (one hundred and twelve thousand eight hundred and nineteen), which number gradually became reduced to 106,070 (one hundred and six thousand and seventy men), 91,675 (ninety-one thousand six hundred and seventy-five), and 81,758 (eighty-one thousand seven hundred and fifty-eight) at the end of the campaign. This gradual reduction was not altogether owing to death and wounds, but to the expiration of service, or by detachments sent to points at the rear.

Statement showing the Effective Strength of the Army under General W. T. Sherman, during the Campaign against Atlanta, Georgia, 1864.

COMMANDS.	JUNE 1. Infantry Comm. Officers	Enlisted Men	Cavalry Comm. Officers	Enlisted Men	Artillery Comm. Officers	Enlisted Men	JULY 1. Infantry Comm. Officers	Enlisted Men	Cavalry Comm. Officers	Enlisted Men	Artillery Comm. Officers	Enlisted Men	AUGUST 1. Infantry Comm. Officers	Enlisted Men	Cavalry Comm. Officers	Enlisted Men	Artillery Comm. Officers	Enlisted Men	SEPTEMBER 1. Infantry Comm. Officers	Enlisted Men	Cavalry Comm. Officers	Enlisted Men	Artillery Comm. Officers	Enlisted Men
Fourth Army Corps	999	15,453	....	....	21	754	878	13,388	....	....	16	724	827	11,887	....	....	20	835	736	10,678	....	....	22	682
Fourteenth Army Corps	1,007	21,618	....	....	21	802	906	17,900	....	....	21	780	847	16,441	....	....	19	707	720	18,788	....	....	22	774
Twentieth Army Corps	808	15,071	3	68	25	826	734	13,057	3	68	24	786	645	11,112	8	40	27	751	649	10,955	3	35	31	740
Total—A'y of the Cmbr'ld	2,814	52,142	3	68	67	2,382	2,518	44,295	3	68	61	2,290	2,319	39,390	8	40	66	2,293	2,105	35,866	3	35	75	2,196
Fifteenth Army Corps	636	11,044	....	....	25	792	612	10,896	4	38	23	757	508	8,083	....	....	14	578	528	7,691	....	....	9	447
Sixteenth A. C. (left wing)	408	9,053	26	322	12	540	441	9,025	9	91	16	620	402	8,111	29	370	11	422	322	7,054	3	27	11	401
Seventeenth Army Corps	387	8,380	4	68	17	904	380	7,812	....	....	23	947	280	5,541	5	29	22	923	225	4,962	4	23	16	705
Total—Army of the Tenn.	1,481	28,477	30	405	54	2,236	1,433	27,833	13	129	62	2,324	1,190	21,685	34	399	47	1,923	1,070	19,707	7	50	36	1,553
Twenty-third Army Corps	406	9,040	200	4,822	20	505	498	11,509	180	4,047	24	875	490	10,555	179	8,699	25	860	407	9,019	....	....	15	540
Garrard's Cavalry	....	....	188	2,758	8	180	....	....	128	2,580	8	122	....	....	96	1,803	8	111	....	....	166	2,911	3	104
Stoneman's Cavalry	....	....	152	2,570	....	....	....	....	161	2,169	....	....	....	....	120	1,634	....	....	....	....	101	1,835	....	....
McCook's Cavalry	....	....	59	1,678	8	79	....	....	128	2,458	8	75	....	....	144	2,366	3	60	....	....	182	1,720	3	73
Kilpatrick's Cavalry	....	....	....	....	5	117	....	....	....	....	4	102	....	....	....	....	4	104	....	....	166	2,268	4	88
Grand Aggregate	4,651	89,659	612	12,296	152	5,449	4,449	83,637	618	11,426	157	5,788	3,999	71,660	676	9,941	148	5,351	3,582	64,092	575	8,819	186	4,554

RECAPITULATION—ATLANTA CAMPAIGN.

ARM.	June 1.	July 1.	August 1.	September 1.
Infantry....................	94,810	88,086	75,659	67,674
Cavalry	12,908	12,089	10,517	9,394
Artillery....................	5,601	5,945	5,499	4,690
Aggregate.............	112,819	106,070	91,675	81,758

CHAPTER XIX.

By the middle of September, matters and things had settled down in Atlanta, so that we felt perfectly at home. The telegraph and railroads were repaired, and we had uninterrupted communication to the rear. The trains arrived with regularity and dispatch, and brought us ample supplies. General Wheeler had been driven out of Middle Tennessee, escaping south across the Tennessee River at Bainbridge; and things looked as though we were to have a period of repose.

One day, two citizens, Messrs. Hill and Nelson, came into our lines at Decatur, and were sent to my headquarters. They represented themselves as former members of Congress, and particular friends of my brother John Sherman; that Mr. Hill had a son killed in the rebel army as it fell back before us somewhere near Cassville, and they wanted to obtain the body, having learned from a comrade where it was buried. I gave them permission to go by rail to the rear, with a note to the commanding officer, General John E. Smith, at Cartersville, requiring him to furnish them an escort and an ambulance for the purpose. I invited them to take dinner with our mess, and we naturally ran into a general conversation about politics and the devastation and ruin caused by the war. They had seen a part of the country over which the army had passed, and could easily apply its measure of desolation to the remainder of the State, if necessity should compel us to go ahead.

Mr. Hill resided at Madison, on the main road to Augusta, and seemed to realize fully the danger ; said that further resistance on the part of the South was madness, that he hoped Governor Brown, of Georgia, would so proclaim it, and withdraw his people from the rebellion, in pursuance of what was known as the policy of " separate State action." I told him, if he saw Governor Brown, to describe to him fully what he had seen, and to say that if he remained inert, I would be compelled to go ahead, devastating the State in its whole length and breadth; that there was no adequate force to stop us, etc.; but if he would issue his proclamation withdrawing his State troops from the armies of the Confederacy, I would spare the State, and in our passage across it confine the troops to the main roads, and would, moreover, pay for all the corn and food we needed. I also told Mr. Hill that he might, in my name, invite Governor Brown to visit Atlanta; that I would give him a safeguard, and that if he wanted to make a speech, I would guarantee him as full and respectable an audience as any he had ever spoken to. I believe that Mr. Hill, after reaching his home at Madison, went to Milledgeville, the capital of the State, and delivered the message to Governor Brown. I had also sent similar messages by Judge Wright of Rome, Georgia, and by Mr. King, of Marietta. On the 15th of September I telegraphed to General Halleck as follows:

My report is done, and will be forwarded as soon as I get in a few more of the subordinate reports. I am awaiting a courier from General Grant. All well; the troops are in good, healthy camps, and supplies are coming forward finely. Governor Brown has disbanded his militia, to gather the corn and sorghum of the State. I have reason to believe that he and Stephens want to visit me, and have sent them a hearty invitation. I will exchange two thousand prisoners with Hood, but no more.

Governor Brown's action at that time is fully explained by the following letter, since made public, which was then only known to us in part by hearsay:

EXECUTIVE DEPARTMENT,
MILLEDGEVILLE, GEORGIA, *September* 10, 1864.

General J. B. HOOD, *commanding Army of Tennessee.*

GENERAL: As the militia of the State were called out for the defense of

Atlanta during the campaign against it, which has terminated by the fall of the city into the hands of the enemy, and as many of these left their homes without preparation (expecting to be gone but a few weeks), who have remained in service over three months (most of the time in the trenches), justice requires that they be permitted, while the enemy are preparing for the winter campaign, to return to their homes, and look for a time after important interests, and prepare themselves for such service as may be required when another campaign commences against other important points in the State. I therefore hereby withdraw said organization from your command. . . .   JOSEPH C. BROWN.

This militia had composed a division under command of Major-General Gustavus W. Smith, and were thus dispersed to their homes, to gather the corn and sorghum, then ripe and ready for the harvesters.

On the 17th I received by telegraph from President Lincoln this dispatch :

WASHINGTON, D. C., *September* 17, 1864—10 A. M.

Major-General SHERMAN :

I feel great interest in the subjects of your dispatch, mentioning corn and sorghum, and the contemplated visit to you.

A. LINCOLN, *President of the United States.*

I replied at once :

HEADQUARTERS MILITARY DIVISION OF THE MISSISSIPPI,
IN THE FIELD, ATLANTA, GEORGIA, *September* 17, 1864.

President LINCOLN, *Washington, D. C.:*

I will keep the department fully advised of all developments connected with the subject in which you feel interested.

Mr. Wright, former member of Congress from Rome, Georgia, and Mr. King, of Marietta, are now going between Governor Brown and myself. I have said to them that some of the people of Georgia are engaged in rebellion, begun in error and perpetuated in pride, but that Georgia can now save herself from the devastations of war preparing for her, only by withdrawing her quota out of the Confederate Army, and aiding me to expel Hood from the borders of the State ; in which event, instead of desolating the land as we progress, I will keep our men to the high-roads and commons, and pay for the corn and meat we need and take.

I am fully conscious of the delicate nature of such assertions, but it would be a magnificent stroke of policy if we could, without surrendering principle or a foot of ground, arouse the latent enmity of Georgia against Davis.

The people do not hesitate to say that Mr. Stephens was and is a Union man at heart; and they say that Davis will not trust him or let him have a share in his Government.   W. T. Sherman, *Major-General.*

I have not the least doubt that Governor Brown, at that time, seriously entertained the proposition; but he hardly felt ready to act, and simply gave a furlough to the militia, and called a special session of the Legislature, to meet at Milledgeville, to take into consideration the critical condition of affairs in the State.

On the 20th of September Colonel Horace Porter arrived from General Grant, at City Point, bringing me the letter of September 12th, asking my general views as to what should next be done. He staid several days at Atlanta, and on his return carried back to Washington my full reports of the past campaign, and my letter of September 20th to General Grant in answer to his of the 12th.

About this time we detected signs of activity on the part of the enemy. On the 21st Hood shifted his army across from the Macon road, at Lovejoy's, to the West Point road, at Palmetto Station, and his cavalry appeared on the west side of the Chattahoochee, toward Powder Springs; thus, as it were, stepping aside, and opening wide the door for us to enter Central Georgia. I inferred, however, that his real purpose was to assume the offensive against our railroads, and on the 24th a heavy force of cavalry from Mississippi, under General Forrest, made its appearance at Athens, Alabama, and captured its garrison.

General Newton's division (of the Fourth Corps), and Corse's (of the Seventeenth), were sent back by rail, the former to Chattanooga, and the latter to Rome. On the 25th I telegraphed to General Halleck:

Hood seems to be moving, as it were, to the Alabama line, leaving open the road to Macon, as also to Augusta; but his cavalry is busy on all our roads. A force, number estimated as high as eight thousand, are reported to have captured Athens, Alabama; and a regiment of three hundred and fifty men sent to its relief. I have sent Newton's division up to Chattanooga in cars, and will send another division to Rome. If I were sure that Savannah would soon be in our possession, I should be tempted to march for Milledgeville and Augusta; but I must first secure what I have. Jeff. Davis is at Macon. W. T. SHERMAN, *Major-General*.

On the next day I telegraphed further that Jeff. Davis was with Hood at Palmetto Station. One of our spies was there at the time, who came in the next night, and reported to me the substance of his speech to the soldiers. It was a repetition of those he had made at Columbia, South Carolina, and Macon, Georgia, on his way out, which I had seen in the newspapers. Davis seemed to be perfectly upset by the fall of Atlanta, and to have lost all sense and reason. He denounced General Jos. Johnston and Governor Brown as little better than traitors; attributed to them personally the many misfortunes which had befallen their cause, and informed the soldiers that now the tables were to be turned; that General Forrest was already on our roads in Middle Tennessee; and that Hood's army would soon be there. He asserted that the Yankee army would have to retreat or starve, and that the retreat would prove more disastrous than was that of Napoleon from Moscow. He promised his Tennessee and Kentucky soldiers that their feet should soon tread their "native soil," etc., etc. He made no concealment of these vainglorious boasts, and thus gave us the full key to his future designs. To be forewarned was to be forearmed, and I think we took full advantage of the occasion.

On the 26th I received this dispatch:

CITY POINT, VIRGINIA, *September* 26, 1864—10 A. M.

Major-General SHERMAN, *Atlanta:*

It will be better to drive Forrest out of Middle Tennessee as a first step, and do any thing else you may feel your force sufficient for. When a movement is made on any part of the sea-coast, I will advise you. If Hood goes to the Alabama line, will it not be impossible for him to subsist his army?

U. S. GRANT, *Lieutenant-General*.

Answer:

HEADQUARTERS MILITARY DIVISION OF THE MISSISSIPPI, }
IN THE FIELD, ATLANTA, GEORGIA, *September* 26, 1864. }

GENERAL: I have your dispatch of to-day. I have already sent one division (Newton's) to Chattanooga, and another (Corse's) to Rome.

Our armies are much reduced, and if I send back any more, I will not be able to threaten Georgia much. There are men enough to the rear to whip Forrest, but they are necessarily scattered to defend the roads.

Can you expedite the sending to Nashville of the recruits that are in Indiana and Ohio? They could occupy the forts.

Hood is now on the West Point road, twenty-four miles south of this, and draws his supplies by that road. Jefferson Davis is there to-day, and superhuman efforts will be made to break my road.

Forrest is now lieutenant-general, and commands all the enemy's cavalry.   W. T. SHERMAN, *Major-General.*

General Grant first thought I was in error in supposing that Jeff. Davis was at Macon and Palmetto, but on the 27th I received a printed copy of his speech made at Macon on the 22d, which was so significant that I ordered it to be telegraphed entire as far as Louisville, to be sent thence by mail to Washington, and on the same day received this dispatch:

WASHINGTON, D. C., *September* 27, 1864—9 A. M.
Major-General SHERMAN, *Atlanta:*

You say Jeff. Davis is on a visit to General Hood. I judge that Brown and Stephens are the objects of his visit.
A. LINCOLN, *President of the United States.*

To which I replied:

HEADQUARTERS MILITARY DIVISION OF THE MISSISSIPPI, }
IN THE FIELD, ATLANTA, GEORGIA, *September* 28, 1864. }
President LINCOLN, *Washington, D. C.:*

I have positive knowledge that Mr. Davis made a speech at Macon, on the 22d, which I mailed to General Halleck yesterday. It was bitter against General Jos. Johnston and Governor Brown. The militia are on furlough. Brown is at Milledgeville, trying to get a Legislature to meet next month, but he is afraid to act unless in concert with other Governors. Judge Wright, of Rome, has been here, and Messrs. Hill and Nelson, former members of Congress, are here now, and will go to meet Wright at Rome, and then go back to Madison and Milledgeville.

Great efforts are being made to reënforce Hood's army, and to break up my railroads, and I should have at once a good reserve force at Nashville. It would have a bad effect, if I were forced to send back any considerable part of my army to guard roads, so as to weaken me to an extent that I could not act offensively if the occasion calls for it.
W. T. SHERMAN, *Major-General.*

All this time Hood and I were carrying on the foregoing correspondence relating to the exchange of prisoners, the removal of the people from Atlanta, and the relief of our prisoners of war at Andersonville. Notwithstanding the severity of their imprisonment, some of these men escaped from Andersonville, and got to me at Atlanta. They described their sad condition: more than twenty-five thousand prisoners confined in a stockade designed for only ten thousand; debarred the privilege of gathering wood out of which to make huts; deprived of sufficient healthy food, and the little stream that ran through their prison-pen poisoned and polluted by the offal from their cooking and butchering houses above. On the 22d of September I wrote to General Hood, describing the condition of our men at Andersonville, purposely refraining from casting odium on him or his associates for the treatment of these men, but asking his consent for me to procure from our generous friends at the North the articles of clothing and comfort which they wanted, viz., under-clothing, soap, combs, scissors, etc.—all needed to keep them in health—and to send these stores with a train, and an officer to issue them. General Hood, on the 24th, promptly consented, and I telegraphed to my friend Mr. James E. Yeatman, Vice-President of the Sanitary Commission at St. Louis, to send us all the under-clothing and soap he could spare, specifying twelve hundred fine-tooth combs, and four hundred pairs of shears to cut hair. These articles indicate the plague that most afflicted our prisoners at Andersonville.

Mr. Yeatman promptly responded to my request, expressed the articles, but they did not reach Andersonville in time, for the prisoners were soon after removed; these supplies did, however, finally overtake them at Jacksonville, Florida, just before the war closed.

On the 28th I received from General Grant two dispatches:

CITY POINT, VIRGINIA, *September* 27, 1864—8.30 A. M.

Major-General SHERMAN:

It is evident, from the tone of the Richmond press and from other sources of information, that the enemy intend making a desperate effort to drive you from where you are. I have directed all new troops from the West, and from the East too, if necessary, in case none are ready in the West, to be sent to you. If General Burbridge is not too far on his way to Abingdon, I think he had better be recalled and his surplus troops sent into Tennessee. U. S. GRANT, *Lieutenant-General.*

CITY POINT, VIRGINIA, *September* 27, 1864—10.30 A. M.
Major-General SHERMAN:

I have directed all recruits and new troops from all the Western States to be sent to Nashville, to receive their further orders from you. I was mistaken about Jeff. Davis being in Richmond on Thursday last. He was then on his way to Macon. U. S. GRANT, *Lieutenant-General.*

Forrest having already made his appearance in Middle Tennessee, and Hood evidently edging off in that direction, satisfied me that the general movement against our roads had begun. I therefore determined to send General Thomas back to Chattanooga, with another division (Morgan's, of the Fourteenth Corps), to meet the danger in Tennessee. General Thomas went up on the 29th, and Morgan's division followed the same day, also by rail. And I telegraphed to General Halleck:

I take it for granted that Forrest will cut our road, but think we can prevent him from making a serious lodgment. His cavalry will travel a hundred miles where ours will ten. I have sent two divisions up to Chattanooga and one to Rome, and General Thomas started to-day to drive Forrest out of Tennessee. Our roads should be watched from the rear, and I am glad that General Grant has ordered reserves to Nashville. I prefer for the future to make the movement on Milledgeville, Millen, and Savannah. Hood now rests twenty-four miles south, on the Chattahoochee, with his right on the West Point road. He is removing the iron of the Macon road. I can whip his infantry, but his cavalry is to be feared.

There was great difficulty in obtaining correct information about Hood's movements from Palmetto Station. I could not get spies to penetrate his camps, but on the 1st of October I was satisfied that the bulk of his infantry was at and across the Chattahoochee River, near Campbellton, and that his cavalry was on the west side, at Powder Springs. On that day I telegraphed to General Grant:

Hood is evidently across the Chattahoochee, below Sweetwater. If he tries to get on our road, this side of the Etowah, I shall attack him; but if he goes to the Selma & Talladega road, why will it not do to leave Tennessee to the forces which Thomas has, and the reserves soon to come to Nashville, and for me to destroy Atlanta and march across Georgia to Savannah or Charleston, breaking roads and doing irreparable damage? We cannot remain on the defensive.

The Selma & Talladega road herein referred to was an unfinished railroad from Selma, Alabama, through Talladega, to Blue Mountain, a terminus sixty-five miles southwest of Rome and about fifteen miles southeast of Gadsden, where the rebel army could be supplied from the direction of Montgomery and Mobile, and from which point Hood could easily threaten Middle Tennessee. My first impression was, that Hood would make for that point; but by the 3d of October the indications were that he would strike our railroad nearer us, viz., about Kingston or Marietta.

Orders were at once made for the Twentieth Corps (Slocum's) to hold Atlanta and the bridges of the Chattahoochee, and the other corps were put in motion for Marietta.

The army had undergone many changes since the capture of Atlanta. General Schofield had gone to the rear, leaving General J. D. Cox in command of the Army of the Ohio (Twenty-third Corps). General Thomas, also, had been dispatched to Chattanooga, with Newton's division of the Fourth Corps and Morgan's of the Fourteenth Corps, leaving General D. S. Stanley, the senior major-general of the two corps of his Army of the Cumberland, remaining and available for this movement, viz., the Fourth and Fourteenth, commanded by himself and Major-General Jeff. C. Davis; and after General Dodge was wounded, his corps (the Sixteenth) had been broken up, and its two divisions were added to the Fifteenth and Seventeenth Corps, constituting the Army of the Tennessee, commanded by Major-General O. O. Howard. Generals Logan and Blair had gone home to assist in the political canvass, leaving their corps, viz., the Fifteenth and Seventeenth, under the command of Major-Generals Osterhaus and T. E. G. Ransom.

These five corps were very much reduced in strength, by detachments and by discharges, so that for the purpose of fighting Hood I had only about sixty thousand infantry and artillery, with two small divisions of cavalry (Kilpatrick's and Garrard's). General Elliott was the chief of cavalry to the Army of the Cumberland, and was the senior officer of that arm of service present for duty with me.

We had strong railroad guards at Marietta and Kenesaw, Allatoona, Etowah Bridge, Kingston, Rome, Resaca, Dalton, Ringgold, and Chattanooga. All the important bridges were likewise protected by good block-houses, admirably constructed, and capable of a strong defense against cavalry or infantry; and at nearly all the regular railroad-stations we had smaller detachments intrenched. I had little fear of the enemy's cavalry damaging our roads seriously, for they rarely made a break which could not be repaired in a few days; but it was absolutely necessary to keep General Hood's infantry off our main route of communication and supply. Forrest had with him in Middle Tennessee about eight thousand cavalry, and Hood's army was estimated at from thirty-five to forty thousand men, infantry and artillery, including Wheeler's cavalry, then about three thousand strong.

We crossed the Chattahoochee River during the 3d and 4th of October, rendezvoused at the old battle-field of Smyrna Camp, and the next day reached Marietta and Kenesaw. The telegraph-wires had been cut above Marietta, and learning that heavy masses of infantry, artillery, and cavalry, had been seen from Kenesaw (marching north), I inferred that Allatoona was their objective point; and on the 4th of October I signaled from Vining's Station to Kenesaw, and from Kenesaw to Allatoona, over the heads of the enemy, a message for General Corse, at Rome, to hurry back to the assistance of the garrison at Allatoona. Allatoona was held by a small brigade, commanded by Lieutenant-Colonel Tourtellotte, my present aide-de-camp. He had two small redoubts on either side of the railroad, overlooking the village of Allatoona, and the warehouses, in which were stored over a million rations of bread.

Reaching Kenesaw Mountain about 8 A. M. of October 5th (a beautiful day), I had a superb view of the vast panorama to the north and west. To the southwest, about Dallas, could be seen the smoke of camp-fires, indicating the presence of a large force of the enemy, and the whole line of railroad from Big Shanty up to Allatoona (full fifteen miles) was marked by the fires of the burning railroad. We could plainly see the smoke of battle about Allatoona, and hear the faint reverberation of the cannon.

From Kenesaw I ordered the Twenty-third Corps (General Cox) to march due west on the Burnt Hickory road, and to burn houses or piles of brush as it progressed, to indicate the head of column, hoping to interpose this corps between Hood's main army at Dallas and the detachment then assailing Allatoona. The rest of the army was directed straight for Allatoona, northwest, distant eighteen miles. The signal-officer on Kenesaw reported that since daylight he had failed to obtain any answer to his call for Allatoona; but, while I was with him, he caught a faint glimpse of the tell-tale flag through an embrasure, and after much time he made out these letters—" C.," " R.," " S.," " E.," " H.," " E.," " R.," and translated the message—" Corse is here." It was a source of great relief, for it gave me the first assurance that General Corse had received his orders, and that the place was adequately garrisoned.

I watched with painful suspense the indications of the battle raging there, and was dreadfully impatient at the slow progress of the relieving column, whose advance was marked by the smokes which were made according to orders, but about 2 P. M. I noticed with satisfaction that the smoke of battle about Allatoona grew less and less, and ceased altogether about 4 P. M. For a time I attributed this result to the effect of General Cox's march, but later in the afternoon the signal-flag announced the welcome tidings that the attack had been fairly repulsed, but that General Corse was wounded. The next day my aide, Colonel Dayton, received this characteristic dispatch:

ALLATOONA, GEORGIA, *October* 6, 1864—2 P. M.

Captain L. M. DAYTON, *Aide-de-Camp :*

I am short a cheek-bone and an ear, but am able to whip all h—l yet!

My losses are very heavy. A force moving from Stilesboro' to Kingston gives me some anxiety. Tell me where Sherman is.

JOHN M. CORSE, Brigadier-General.

Inasmuch as the enemy had retreated southwest, and would probably next appear at Rome, I answered General Corse with orders to get back to Rome with his troops as quickly as possible.

General Corse's report of this fight at Allatoona is very full and graphic. It is dated Rome, October 27, 1864; recites the fact that he received his orders by signal to go to the assistance of Allatoona on the 4th, when he telegraphed to Kingston for cars, and a train of thirty empty cars was started for him, but about ten of them got off the track and caused delay. By 7 P. M. he had at Rome a train of twenty cars, which he loaded up with Colonel Rowett's brigade, and part of the Twelfth Illinois Infantry; started at 8 P. M., reached Allatoona (distant thirty-five miles) at 1 A. M. of the 5th, and sent the train back for more men; but the road was in bad order, and no more men came in time. He found Colonel Tourtellotte's garrison composed of eight hundred and ninety men; his reënforcement was one thousand and fifty-four: total for the defense, nineteen hundred and forty-four. The outposts were already engaged, and as soon as daylight came he drew back the men from the village to the ridge on which the redoubts were built.

The enemy was composed of French's division of three brigades, variously reported from four to five thousand strong. This force gradually surrounded the place by 8 A. M., when General French sent in by flag of truce this note:

AROUND ALLATOONA, October 5, 1864.

Commanding Officer, United States Forces, Allatoona:

I have placed the forces under my command in such positions that you are surrounded, and to avoid a needless effusion of blood I call on you to surrender your forces at once, and unconditionally.

Five minutes will be allowed you to decide. Should you accede to this, you will be treated in the most honorable manner as prisoners of war.

I have the honor to be, very respectfully yours,

S. G. FRENCH,
Major-General commanding forces Confederate States.

General Corse answered immediately:

HEADQUARTERS FOURTH DIVISION, FIFTEENTH CORPS, }
ALLATOONA, GEORGIA, 8.30 A. M., *October* 5, 1864. }

Major-General S. G. FRENCH, *Confederate States, etc.:*

Your communication demanding surrender of my command I acknowledge receipt of, and respectfully reply that we are prepared for the "needless effusion of blood" whenever it is agreeable to you.

I am, very respectfully, your obedient servant,

JOHN M. CORSE,
Brigadier-General commanding forces United States.

Of course the attack began at once, coming from front, flank,
and rear. There were two small redoubts, with slight parapets
and ditches, one on each side of the deep railroad-cut. These
redoubts had been located by Colonel Poe, United States Engineers, at the time of our advance on Kenesaw, the previous
June. Each redoubt overlooked the storehouses close by the
railroad, and each could aid the other defensively by catching in
flank the attacking force of the other. Our troops at first endeavored to hold some ground outside the redoubts, but were
soon driven inside, when the enemy made repeated assaults, but
were always driven back. About 11 A. M., Colonel Redfield, of
the Thirty-ninth Iowa, was killed, and Colonel Rowett was
wounded, but never ceased to fight and encourage his men. Colonel Tourtellotte was shot through the hips, but continued to
command. General Corse was, at 1 P. M., shot across the face,
the ball cutting his ear, which stunned him, but he continued to
encourage his men and to give orders. The enemy (about 1.30
P. M.) made a last and desperate effort to carry one of the redoubts, but was badly cut to pieces by the artillery and infantry
fire from the other, when he began to draw off, leaving his dead
and wounded on the ground.

Before finally withdrawing, General French converged a
heavy fire of his cannon on the block-house at Allatoona Creek,
about two miles from the depot, set it on fire, and captured its
garrison, consisting of four officers and eighty-five men. By
4 P. M. he was in full retreat south, on the Dallas road, and got
by before the head of General Cox's column had reached it;

still several ambulances and stragglers were picked up by this command on that road. General Corse reported two hundred and thirty-one rebel dead, four hundred and eleven prisoners, three regimental colors, and eight hundred muskets captured.

Among the prisoners was a Brigadier-General Young, who thought that French's aggregate loss would reach two thousand. Colonel Tourtellotte says that, for days after General Corse had returned to Rome, his men found and buried at least a hundred more dead rebels, who had doubtless been wounded, and died in the woods near Allatoona. I know that when I reached Allatoona, on the 9th, I saw a good many dead men, which had been collected for burial.

Corse's entire loss, officially reported, was:

GARRISON.	Killed.	Wounded.	Missing.	Total.
Officers............	6	23	6	35
Men...............	136	330	206	672
Total............	142	353	212	707

I esteemed this defense of Allatoona so handsome and important, that I made it the subject of a general order, viz., No. 86, of October 7, 1864:

The general commanding avails himself of the opportunity, in the handsome defense made of Allatoona, to illustrate the most important principle in war, that fortified posts should be defended to the last, regardless of the relative numbers of the party attacking and attacked. . . . The thanks of this army are due and are hereby accorded to General Corse, Colonel Tourtellotte, Colonel Rowett, officers, and men, for their determined and gallant defense of Allatoona, and it is made an example to illustrate the importance of preparing in time, and meeting the danger, when present, boldly, manfully, and well.

Commanders and garrisons of the posts along our railroad are hereby instructed that they must hold their posts to the last minute, sure that the time gained is valuable and necessary to their comrades at the front.

By order of Major-General W. T. Sherman,

L. M. DAYTON, *Aide-de-Camp.*

The rebels had struck our railroad a heavy blow, burning

every tie, bending the rails for eight miles, from Big Shanty to above Acworth, so that the estimate for repairs called for thirty-five thousand new ties, and six miles of iron.   Ten thousand men were distributed along the break to replace the ties, and to prepare the road-bed, while the regular repair-party, under Colonel W. W. Wright, came down from Chattanooga with iron, spikes, etc., and in about seven days the road was all right again.   It was by such acts of extraordinary energy that we discouraged our adversaries, for the rebel soldiers felt that it was a waste of labor for them to march hurriedly, on wide circuits, day and night, to burn a bridge and tear up a mile or so of track, when they knew that we could lay it back so quickly.   They supposed that we had men and money without limit, and that we always kept on hand, distributed along the road, duplicates of every bridge and culvert of any importance.

A good story is told of one who was on Kenesaw Mountain during our advance in the previous June or July.   A group of rebels lay in the shade of a tree, one hot day, overlooking our camps about Big Shanty.   One soldier remarked to his fellows:

"Well, the Yanks will have to git up and git now, for I heard General Johnston himself say that General Wheeler had blown up *the tunnel* near Dalton, and that the Yanks would have to retreat, because they could get no more rations."

"Oh, hell!" said a listener, "don't you know that old Sherman carries a *duplicate* tunnel along?"

After the war was over, General Johnston inquired of me who was our chief railroad-engineer.   When I told him that it was Colonel W. W. Wright, a civilian, he was much surprised, said that our feats of bridge-building and repairs of roads had excited his admiration; and he instanced the occasion at Kenesaw in June, when an officer from Wheeler's cavalry had reported to him in person that he had come from General Wheeler, who had made a bad break in our road about Tilton Station, which he said would take at least a fortnight to repair; and, while they were talking, a train was seen coming down the road, which had passed that very break, and had reached me at

Big Shanty as soon as the fleet horseman had reached him (General Johnston) at Marietta!

I doubt whether the history of war can furnish more examples of skill and bravery than attended the defense of the railroad from Nashville to Atlanta during the year 1864.

In person I reached Allatoona on the 9th of October, still in doubt as to Hood's immediate intentions. Our cavalry could do little against his infantry in the rough and wooded country about Dallas, which masked the enemy's movements; but General Corse, at Rome, with Spencer's First Alabama Cavalry and a mounted regiment of Illinois Infantry, could feel the country south of Rome about Cedartown and Villa Rica; and reported the enemy to be in force at both places. On the 9th I telegraphed to General Thomas, at Nashville, as follows:

I came up here to relieve our road. The Twentieth Corps remains at Atlanta. Hood reached the road and broke it up between Big Shanty and Acworth. He attacked Allatoona, but was repulsed. We have plenty of bread and meat, but forage is scarce. I want to destroy all the road below Chattanooga, including Atlanta, and to make for the sea-coast. We cannot defend this long line of road.

And on the same day I telegraphed to General Grant, at City Point:

It will be a physical impossibility to protect the roads, now that Hood, Forrest, Wheeler, and the whole batch of devils, are turned loose without home or habitation. I think Hood's movements indicate a diversion to the end of the Selma & Talladega road, at Blue Mountain, about sixty miles southwest of Rome, from which he will threaten Kingston, Bridgeport, and Decatur, Alabama. I propose that we break up the railroad from Chattanooga forward, and that we strike out with our wagons for Milledgeville, Millen, and Savannah. Until we can repopulate Georgia, it is useless for us to occupy it; but the utter destruction of its roads, houses, and people, will cripple their military resources. By attempting to hold the roads, we will lose a thousand men each month, and will gain no result. I can make this march, and make Georgia howl! We have on hand over eight thousand head of cattle and three million rations of bread, but no corn. We can find plenty of forage in the interior of the State.

Meantime the rebel General Forrest had made a bold circuit in Middle Tennessee, avoiding all fortified points, and breaking up the railroad at several places; but, as usual, he did his work so hastily and carelessly that our engineers soon repaired the damage—then, retreating before General Rousseau, he left the State of Tennessee, crossing the river near Florence, Alabama, and got off unharmed.

On the 10th of October the enemy appeared south of the Etowah River at Rome, when I ordered all the armies to march to Kingston, rode myself to Cartersville with the Twenty-third Corps (General Cox), and telegraphed from there to General Thomas at Nashville:

> It looks to me as though Hood was bound for Tuscumbia. He is now crossing the Coosa River below Rome, looking west. Let me know if you can hold him with your forces now in Tennessee and the expected reënforcements, as, in that event, you know what I propose to do.
>
> I will be at Kingston to-morrow. I think Rome is strong enough to resist any attack, and the rivers are all high. If he turns up by Summerville, I will get in behind him.

And on the same day to General Grant, at City Point:

> Hood is now crossing the Coosa, twelve miles below Rome, bound west. If he passes over to the Mobile & Ohio Railroad, had I not better execute the plan of my letter sent you by Colonel Porter, and leave General Thomas, with the troops now in Tennessee, to defend the State? He will have an ample force when the reënforcements ordered reach Nashville.

I found General John E. Smith at Cartersville, and on the 11th rode on to Kingston, where I had telegraphic communications in all directions.

From General Corse, at Rome, I learned that Hood's army had disappeared, but in what direction he was still in doubt; and I was so strongly convinced of the wisdom of my proposition to change the whole tactics of the campaign, to leave Hood to General Thomas, and to march across Georgia for Savannah or Charleston, that I again telegraphed to General Grant:

> We cannot now remain on the defensive. With twenty-five thousand infantry and the bold cavalry he has, Hood can constantly break my road. I would infinitely prefer to make a wreck of the road and of the country

from Chattanooga to Atlanta, including the latter city; send back all my wounded and unserviceable men, and with my effective army move through Georgia, smashing things to the sea. Hood may turn into Tennessee and Kentucky, but I believe he will be forced to follow me. Instead of being on the defensive, I will be on the offensive. Instead of my guessing at what he means to do, he will have to guess at my plans. The difference in war would be fully twenty-five per cent. I can make Savannah, Charleston, or the mouth of the Chattahoochee (Appalachicola). Answer quick, as I know we will not have the telegraph long.

I received no answer to this at the time, and the next day went on to Rome, where the news came that Hood had made his appearance at Resaca, and had demanded the surrender of the place, which was commanded by Colonel Weaver, reënforced by Brevet Brigadier-General Raum. General Hood had evidently marched with rapidity up the Chattooga Valley, by Summerville, Lafayette, Ship's Gap, and Snake-Creek Gap, and had with him his whole army, except a small force left behind to watch Rome. I ordered Resaca to be further reënforced by rail from Kingston, and ordered General Corse to make a bold reconnoissance down the Coosa Valley, which captured and brought into Rome some cavalrymen and a couple of field-guns, with their horses and men. At first I thought of interposing my whole army in the Chattooga Valley, so as to prevent Hood's escape south; but I saw at a glance that he did not mean to fight, and in that event, after damaging the road all he could, he would be likely to retreat eastward by Spring Place, which I did not want him to do; and, hearing from General Raum that he still held Resaca safe, and that General Edward McCook had also got there with some cavalry reënforcements, I turned all the heads of columns for Resaca, viz., General Cox's, from Rome; General Stanley's, from McGuire's; and General Howard's, from Kingston. We all reached Resaca during that night, and the next morning (13th) learned that Hood's whole army had passed up the valley toward Dalton, burning the railroad and doing all the damage possible.

On the 12th he had demanded the surrender of Resaca in the following letter:

HEADQUARTERS ARMY OF TENNESSEE, }
IN THE FIELD, *October* 12, 1864. }

To the Officer commanding the United States Forces at Resaca, Georgia.

SIR: I demand the immediate and unconditional surrender of the post and garrison under your command, and, should this be acceded to, all white officers and soldiers will be parolled in a few days. If the place is carried by assault, no prisoners will be taken. Most respectfully, your obedient servant,   J. B. HOOD, *General.*

To this Colonel Weaver, then in command, replied:

HEADQUARTERS SECOND BRIGADE, THIRD DIVISION, FIFTEENTH CORPS, }
RESACA, GEORGIA, *October* 12, 1864. }

To General J. B. HOOD:

Your communication of this date just received. In reply, I have to state that I am somewhat surprised at the concluding paragraph, to the effect that, if the place is carried by assault, no prisoners will be taken. In my opinion I can hold this post. If you want it, come and take it.

I am, general, very respectfully, your most obedient servant,
CLARK R. WEAVER, *Commanding Officer.*

This brigade was very small, and as Hood's investment extended only from the Oostenaula, below the town, to the Connesauga above, he left open the approach from the south, which enabled General Raum and the cavalry of General Edward McCook to reënforce from Kingston. In fact, Hood, admonished by his losses at Allatoona, did not attempt an assault at all, but limited his attack to the above threat, and to some skirmishing, giving his attention chiefly to the destruction of the railroad, which he accomplished all the way up to Tunnel Hill, nearly twenty miles, capturing *en route* the regiment of black troops at Dalton (Johnson's Forty-fourth United States colored). On the 14th, I turned General Howard through Snake-Creek Gap, and sent General Stanley around by Tilton, with orders to cross the mountain to the west, so as to capture, if possible, the force left by the enemy in Snake-Creek Gap. We found this gap very badly obstructed by fallen timber, but got through that night, and the next day the main army was at Villanow. On the morning of the 16th, the leading division of General Howard's column, commanded by General Charles R.

Woods, carried Ship's Gap, taking prisoners part of the Twenty-fourth South Carolina Regiment, which had been left there to hold us in check.

The best information there obtained located Hood's army at Lafayette, near which place I hoped to catch him and force him to battle; but, by the time we had got enough troops across the mountain at Ship's Gap, Hood had escaped down the valley of the Chattooga, and all we could do was to follow him as closely as possible. From Ship's Gap I dispatched couriers to Chattanooga, and received word back that General Schofield was there, endeavoring to coöperate with me, but Hood had broken up the telegraph, and thus had prevented quick communication. General Schofield did not reach me till the army had got down to Gaylesville, about the 21st of October.

It was at Ship's Gap that a courier brought me the cipher message from General Halleck which intimated that the authorities in Washington were willing I should undertake the march across Georgia to the sea. The translated dispatch named "Horse-i-bar Sound" as the point where the fleet would await my arrival. After much time I construed it to mean, "Ossabaw Sound," below Savannah, which was correct.

On the 16th I telegraphed to General Thomas, at Nashville:

Send me Morgan's and Newton's old divisions. Reëstablish the road, and I will follow Hood wherever he may go. I think he will move to Blue Mountain. We can maintain our men and animals on the country.

General Thomas's reply was:

NASHVILLE, *October* 17, 1864—10.30 A. M.
Major-General SHERMAN:

Your dispatch from Ship's Gap, 5 P. M. of the 16th, just received. Schofield, whom I placed in command of the two divisions (Wagner's and Morgan's), was to move up Lookout Valley this A. M., to intercept Hood, should he be marching for Bridgeport. I will order him to join you with the two divisions, and will reconstruct the road as soon as possible. Will also reorganize the guards for posts and block-houses. . . . Mower and Wilson have arrived, and are on their way to join you. I hope you will adopt Grant's idea of turning Wilson loose, rather than undertake the plan of a march

with the whole force through Georgia to the sea, inasmuch as General
Grant cannot coöperate with you as at first arranged.

        GEORGE H. THOMAS, *Major-General.*

So it is clear that at that date neither General Grant nor
General Thomas heartily favored my proposed plan of campaign. On the same day, I wrote to General Schofield at Chattanooga:

Hood is not at Dear Head Cove. We occupy Ship's Gap and Lafayette.
Hood is moving south *via* Summerville, Alpine, and Gadsden. If he enters
Tennessee, it will be to the west of Huntsville, but I think he has given up
all such idea. I want the road repaired to Atlanta; the sick and wounded
men sent north of the Tennessee; my army recomposed; and I will then
make the interior of Georgia feel the weight of war. It is folly for us
to be moving our armies on the reports of scouts and citizens. We must
maintain the offensive. Your first move on Trenton and Valley Head was
right—the move to defend Caperton's Ferry is wrong. Notify General
Thomas of these my views. We must follow Hood till he is beyond the
reach of mischief, and then resume the offensive.

The correspondence between me and the authorities at Washington, as well as with the several army commanders, given at
length in the report of the Committee on the Conduct of the
War, is full on all these points.

After striking our road at Dalton, Hood was compelled to
go on to Chattanooga and Bridgeport, or to pass around by Decatur and abandon altogether his attempt to make us let go
our hold of Atlanta by attacking our communications. It was
clear to me that he had no intention to meet us in open battle,
and the lightness and celerity of his army convinced me that I
could not possibly catch him on a stern-chase. We therefore
quietly followed him down the Chattooga Valley to the neighborhood of Gadsden, but halted the main armies near the Coosa
River, at the mouth of the Chattooga, drawing our supplies of
corn and meat from the farms of that comparatively rich valley and of the neighborhood.

General Slocum, in Atlanta, had likewise sent out, under
strong escort, large trains of wagons to the east, and brought

back corn, bacon, and all kinds of provisions, so that Hood's efforts to cut off our supplies only reacted on his own people. So long as the railroads were in good order, our supplies came full and regular from the North; but when the enemy broke our railroads we were perfectly justified in stripping the inhabitants of all they had. I remember well the appeal of a very respectable farmer against our men driving away his fine flock of sheep. I explained to him that General Hood had broken our railroad; that we were a strong, hungry crowd, and needed plenty of food; that Uncle Sam was deeply interested in our continued health and would soon repair these roads, but meantime we must eat; we preferred Illinois beef, but mutton would have to answer. Poor fellow! I don't believe he was convinced of the wisdom or wit of my explanation. Very soon after reaching Lafayette we organized a line of supply from Chattanooga to Ringgold by rail, and thence by wagons to our camps about Gaylesville. Meantime, also, Hood had reached the neighborhood of Gadsden, and drew his supplies from the railroad at Blue Mountain.

On the 19th of October I telegraphed to General Halleck, at Washington:

Hood has retreated rapidly by all the roads leading south. Our advance columns are now at Alpine and Melville Post-Office. I shall pursue him as far as Gaylesville. The enemy will not venture toward Tennessee except around by Decatur. I propose to send the Fourth Corps back to General Thomas, and leave him, with that corps, the garrisons, and new troops, to defend the line of the Tennessee River; and with the rest I will push into the heart of Georgia and come out at Savannah, destroying all the railroads of the State. The break in our railroad at Big Shanty is almost repaired, and that about Dalton should be done in ten days. We find abundance of forage in the country.

On the same day I telegraphed to General L. C. Easton, chief-quartermaster, who had been absent on a visit to Missouri, but had got back to Chattanooga:

Go in person to superintend the repairs of the railroad, and make all orders in my name that will expedite its completion. I want it finished, to bring back from Atlanta to Chattanooga the sick and wounded men and surplus stores. On the 1st of November I want nothing in front of Chattanooga except what we can use as food and clothing and haul in our wagons. There is plenty of corn in the country, and we only want forage for the posts. I allow ten days for all this to be done, by which time I expect to be at or near Atlanta.

I telegraphed also to General Amos Beckwith, chief-commissary in Atlanta, who was acting as chief-quartermaster during the absence of General Easton:

> Hood will escape me. I want to prepare for my big raid. On the 1st of November I want nothing in Atlanta but what is necessary for war. Send all trash to the rear at once, and have on hand thirty days' food and but little forage. I propose to abandon Atlanta, and the railroad back to Chattanooga, to sally forth to ruin Georgia and bring up on the seashore. Make all dispositions accordingly. I will go down the Coosa until I am sure that Hood has gone to Blue Mountain.

On the 21st of October I reached Gaylesville, had my bivouac in an open field back of the village, and remained there till the 28th. During that time General Schofield arrived, with the two divisions of Generals Wagner (formerly Newton's) and Morgan, which were returned to their respective corps (the Fourth and Fourteenth), and General Schofield resumed his own command of the Army of the Ohio, then on the Coosa River, near Cedar Bluff. General Joseph A. Mower also arrived, and was assigned to command a division in the Seventeenth Corps; and General J. H. Wilson came, having been sent from Virginia by General Grant, for the purpose of commanding all my cavalry. I first intended to organize this cavalry into a corps of three small divisions, to be commanded by General Wilson; but the horses were well run down, and, at Wilson's instance, I concluded to retain only one division of four thousand five hundred men, with selected horses, under General Kilpatrick, and to send General Wilson back with all the rest to Nashville, to be reorganized and to act under General Thomas in the defense of Tennessee. Orders to this effect were made on the 24th of October.

General Grant, in designating General Wilson to command

my cavalry, predicted that he would, by his personal activity, increase the effect of that arm "fifty per cént.," and he advised that he should be sent south, to accomplish all that I had proposed to do with the main army; but I had not so much faith in cavalry as he had, and preferred to adhere to my original intention of going myself with a competent force.

About this time I learned that General Beauregard had reached Hood's army at Gadsden; that, without assuming direct command of that army, he had authority from the Confederate Government to direct all its movements, and to call to his assistance the whole strength of the South. His orders, on assuming command, were full of alarm and desperation, dated—

HEADQUARTERS MILITARY DIVISION OF THE WEST, }
October 17, 1864. }

In assuming command, at this critical juncture, of the Military Division of the West, I appeal to my countrymen, of all classes and sections, for their generous support. In assigning me to this responsible position, the President of the Confederate States has extended to me the assurance of his earnest support. The Executives of your States meet me with similar expressions of their devotion to our cause. The noble army in the field, composed of brave men and gallant officers, are strangers to me, but I know they will do all that patriots can achieve. . . .

The army of Sherman still defiantly holds Atlanta. He can and must be driven from it. It is only for the good people of Georgia and surrounding States to speak the word, and the work is done. We have abundant provisions. There are men enough in the country, liable to and able for service, to accomplish the result. . . .

My countrymen, respond to this call as you have done in days that are past, and, with the blessing of a kind and overruling Providence, the enemy shall be driven from your soil. The security of your wives and daughters from the insults and outrages of a brutal foe shall be established soon, and be followed by a permanent and honorable peace. The claims of home and country, wife and children, uniting with the demands of honor and patriotism, summon us to the field. We cannot, dare not, will not fail to respond. Full of hope and confidence, I come to join you in your struggles, sharing your privations, and, with your brave and true men, to strike the blow that shall bring success to our arms, triumph to our cause, and peace to our country!

.   .   .   .

G. T. BEAUREGARD, *General.*

Notwithstanding this somewhat boastful order or appeal, General Beauregard did not actually accompany General Hood on his disastrous march to Nashville, but took post at Corinth, Mississippi, to control the movement of his supplies and to watch me.

At Gaylesville the pursuit of Hood by the army under my immediate command may be said to have ceased. During this pursuit, the Fifteenth Corps was commanded by its senior major-general present, P. J. Osterhaus, in the absence of General John A. Logan; and the Seventeenth Corps was commanded by Briga-dier-General T. E. G. Ransom, the senior officer present, in the absence of General Frank P. Blair.

General Ransom was a young, most gallant, and promis-ing officer, son of the Colonel Ransom who was killed at Cha-pultepec, in the Mexican War. He had served with the Army of the Tennessee in 1862 and 1863, at Vicksburg, where he was severely wounded. He was not well at the time we started from Atlanta, but he insisted on going along with his command. His symptoms became more aggravated on the march, and when we were encamped near Gaylesville, I visited him in company with Surgeon John Moore, United States Army, who said that the case was one of typhoid fever, which would likely prove fatal. A few days after, viz., the 28th, he was being carried on a litter toward Rome; and as I rode from Gaylesville to Rome, I passed him by the way, stopped, and spoke with him, but did not then suppose he was so near his end. The next day, however, his escort reached Rome, bearing his dead body. The officer in charge reported that, shortly after I had passed, his symptoms became so much worse that they stopped at a farm-house by the road-side, where he died that evening. His body was at once sent to Chicago for burial, and a monument has been ordered by the Society of the Army of the Tennessee to be erected in his memory.

On the 26th of October I learned that Hood's whole army had made its appearance about Decatur, Alabama, and at once caused a strong reconnoissance to be made down the Coosa to near Gadsden, which revealed the truth that the enemy was gone, except a small force of cavalry, commanded by General Wheeler, which had been left to watch us. I then finally resolved on my future course, which was to leave Hood to be encountered by General Thomas, while I should carry into full effect the long-contemplated project of marching for the sea-coast, and thence to operate toward Richmond. But it was all-important to me and to our cause that General Thomas should have an ample force, equal to any and every emergency.

He then had at Nashville about eight or ten thousand new troops, and as many more civil employés of the Quartermaster's Department, which were not suited for the field, but would be most useful in manning the excellent forts that already covered Nashville. At Chattanooga, he had General Steedman's division, about five thousand men, besides garrisons for Chattanooga, Bridgeport, and Stevenson; at Murfreesboro' he also had General Rousseau's division, which was full five thousand strong, independent of the necessary garrisons for the railroad. At Decatur and Huntsville, Alabama, was the infantry division of General R. S. Granger, estimated at four thousand; and near Florence, Alabama, watching the crossings of the Tennessee, were General Edward Hatch's division of cavalry, four thousand; General Croxton's brigade, twenty-five hundred; and Colonel Capron's brigade, twelve hundred; besides which, General J. H. Wilson had collected in Nashville about ten thousand dismounted cavalry, for which he was rapidly collecting the necessary horses for a remount. All these aggregated about forty-five thousand men. General A. J. Smith at that time was in Missouri, with the two divisions of the Sixteenth Corps which had been diverted to that quarter to assist General Rosecrans in driving the rebel General Price out of Missouri. This object had been accomplished, and these troops, numbering from eight to ten thousand, had been ordered to Nashville. To these I proposed at first to add only the Fourth Corps (General Stanley), fifteen thousand; and that corps was ordered from Gaylesville to march to Chattanooga, and thence report for orders to General Thomas; but subsequently, on the 30th of October, at Rome, Georgia, learning from General Thomas that the new troops promised by General Grant were coming forward very slowly, I concluded to further reënforce him by General Schofield's corps (Twenty-third), twelve thousand, which corps accordingly marched for Resaca, and there took the cars for Chattanooga. I then knew that General Thomas would have an ample force with which to encounter General Hood anywhere in the open field, besides garrisons to secure the railroad to his rear and as far forward as Chattanooga. And, moreover, I was more than convinced that he would have ample time for preparation; for, on that very day, General R. S. Granger had telegraphed me from Decatur, Alabama:

I omitted to mention another reason why Hood will go to Tuscumbia before crossing the Tennessee River. He was evidently out of supplies. His men were all grumbling; the first thing the prisoners asked for was something to eat. Hood could not get any thing if he should cross this side of Rogersville.

I knew that the country about Decatur and Tuscumbia, Alabama, was bare of provisions, and inferred that General Hood would have to draw his supplies, not only of food, but of stores, clothing, and ammunition, from Mobile, Montgomery, and Selma, Alabama, by the railroad around by Meridian and Corinth, Mississippi, which we had most effectually disabled the previous winter.

General Hood did not make a serious attack on Decatur, but hung around it from October 26th to the 30th, when he drew off and marched for a point on the south side of the Tennessee River, opposite Florence, where he was compelled to remain nearly a month, to collect the necessary supplies for his contemplated invasion of Tennessee and Kentucky.

The Fourth Corps (Stanley) had already reached Chattanooga, and had been transported by rail to Pulaski, Tennessee; and General Thomas ordered General Schofield, with the Twenty-third Corps, to Columbia, Tennessee, a place intermediate between Hood (then on the Tennessee River, opposite Florence) and Forrest, opposite Johnsonville.

On the 31st of October General Croxton, of the cavalry, reported that the enemy had crossed the Tennessee River four miles above Florence, and that he had endeavored to stop him, but without success. Still, I was convinced that Hood's army was in no condition to march for Nashville, and that a good deal of further delay might reasonably be counted on. I also rested with much confidence on the fact that the Tennessee River below Muscle Shoals was strongly patrolled by gunboats, and that the reach of the river above Muscle Shoals, from Decatur as high up as our railroad at Bridgeport, was also guarded by gunboats, so that Hood, to cross over, would be compelled to select a point inaccessible to these gunboats. He actually did choose such a place, at the old railroad-piers, four miles above Florence, Alabama, which is below Muscle Shoals and above Colbert Shoals.

On the 31st of October Forrest made his appearance on the Tennessee River opposite Johnsonville (whence a new railroad led to Nashville), and with his cavalry and field-pieces actually crippled and captured two gunboats with five of our transports, a feat of arms which, I confess, excited my admiration.

There is no doubt that the month of October closed to us looking decidedly squally; but, somehow, I was sustained in the belief that in a very few days the tide would turn.

On the 1st of November I telegraphed very fully to General Grant, at City Point, who must have been disturbed by the wild rumors that filled the country, and on the 2d of November received (at Rome) this dispatch:

CITY POINT, *November* 1, 1864—6 P. M.

Major-General SHERMAN:

Do you not think it advisable, now that Hood has gone so far north, to entirely ruin him before starting on your proposed campaign? With Hood's army destroyed, you can go where you please with impunity. I believed and still believe, if you had started south while Hood was in the neighborhood of you, he would have been forced to go after you. Now that he is far away he might look upon the chase as useless, and he will go in one direction while you are pushing in the other. If you can see a chance of destroying Hood's army, attend to that first, and make your other move secondary.

U. S. GRANT, *Lieutenant-General.*

My answer is dated—

ROME, GEORGIA, *November* 2, 1864.

Lieutenant-General U. S. GRANT, *City Point, Virginia:*

Your dispatch is received. If I could hope to overhaul Hood, I would turn against him with my whole force; then he would retreat to the southwest, drawing me as a decoy away from Georgia, which is his chief object. If he ventures north of the Tennessee River, I may turn in that direction, and endeavor to get below him on his line of retreat; but thus far he has not gone above the Tennessee River. General Thomas will have a force strong enough to prevent his reaching any country in which we have an interest; and he has orders, if Hood turns to follow me, to push for Selma, Alabama. No single army can catch Hood, and I am convinced the best results will follow from our defeating Jeff. Davis's cherished plan of making me leave Georgia by manœuvring. Thus far I have confined my efforts to thwart this plan, and have reduced baggage so that I can pick up and start in any direction; but I regard the pursuit of Hood as useless. Still, if he attempts to invade Middle Tennessee, I will hold Decatur, and be prepared to move in that direction; but, unless I let go of Atlanta, my force will not be equal to his.   W. T. SHERMAN, *Major-General.*

By this date, under the intelligent and energetic action of Colonel W. W. Wright, and with the labor of fifteen hundred men, the railroad break of fifteen miles about Dalton was repaired so far as to admit of the passage of cars, and I transferred my headquarters to Kingston as more central; and from that place, on the same day (November 2d), again telegraphed to General Grant.

KINGSTON, GEORGIA, *November* 2, 1864.

Lieutenant-General U. S. GRANT, *City Point, Virginia:*

If I turn back, the whole effect of my campaign will be lost. By my movements I have thrown Beauregard (Hood) well to the west, and Thomas will have ample time and sufficient troops to hold him until the reënforcements from Missouri reach him. We have now ample supplies at Chattanooga and Atlanta, and can stand a month's interruption to our communications. I do not believe the Confederate army can reach our railroad-lines except by cavalry-raids, and Wilson will have cavalry enough to checkmate them. I am clearly of opinion that the best results will follow my contemplated movement through Georgia.
W. T. SHERMAN, *Major-General.*

That same day I received, in answer to the Rome dispatch, the following:

CITY POINT, VIRGINIA, *November* 2, 1864—11.30 A. M.
Major-General SHERMAN :

Your dispatch of 9 A. M. yesterday is just received. I dispatched you the same date, advising that Hood's army, now that it had worked so far north, ought to be looked upon now as the "object." With the force, however, that you have left with General Thomas, he must be able to take care of Hood and destroy him.

I do not see that you can withdraw from where you are to follow Hood, without giving up all we have gained in territory. I say, then, go on as you propose.   U. S. GRANT, *Lieutenant-General.*

This was the first time that General Grant assented to the " march to the sea," and, although many of his warm friends and admirers insist that he was the author and projector of that march, and that I simply executed his plans, General Grant has never, in my opinion, thought so or said so. The truth is fully given in an original letter of President Lincoln, which I received at Savannah, Georgia, and have at this instant before me, every word of which is in his own familiar handwriting. It is dated—

WASHINGTON, *December* 26, 1864.

When you were about leaving Atlanta for the Atlantic coast, I was anxious, if not fearful ; but, feeling that you were the better judge, and remembering "nothing risked, nothing gained," I did not interfere. Now, the undertaking being a success, the honor is all yours ; for I believe none of us went further than to acquiesce ; and, taking the work of General Thomas into account, as it should be taken, it is indeed a great success. Not only does it afford the obvious and immediate military advantages, but, in showing to the world that your army could be divided, putting the stronger part to an important new service, and yet leaving enough to vanquish the old opposing force of the whole, Hood's army, it brings those who sat in darkness to see a great light. But what next ? I suppose it will be safer if I leave General Grant and yourself to decide.   A. LINCOLN.

Of course, this judgment, made after the event, was extremely flattering and was all I ever expected, a recognition of the truth and of its importance. I have often been asked, by well-meaning friends, when the thought of that march first entered my mind. I knew that an army which had penetrated Georgia as far as Atlanta could not turn back. It must go ahead, but when, how, and where, depended on many considerations. As soon as Hood had shifted across from Lovejoy's to Palmetto, I saw the move in my "mind's eye;" and, after Jeff. Davis's speech at Palmetto, of September 26th, I was more positive in my conviction, but was in doubt as to the time and manner. When General Hood first struck our railroad above Marietta, we were not ready, and I was forced to watch his movements further, till he had "carromed" off to the west of Decatur. Then I was perfectly convinced, and had no longer a shadow of doubt. The only possible question was as to Thomas's strength and ability to meet Hood in the open field. I did not suppose that General Hood, though rash, would venture to attack fortified places like Allatoona, Resaca, Decatur, and Nashville; but he did so, and in so doing he played into our hands perfectly.

On the 2d of November I was at Kingston, Georgia, and my four corps—the Fifteenth, Seventeenth, Fourteenth, and Twentieth—with one division of cavalry, were strung from Rome to Atlanta. Our railroads and telegraph had been repaired, and I deliberately prepared for the march to Savannah, distant three hundred miles from Atlanta. All the sick and wounded men had been sent back by rail to Chattanooga; all our wagon-trains had been carefully overhauled and loaded, so as to be ready to start on an hour's notice, and there was no serious enemy in our front.

General Hood remained still at Florence, Alabama, occupying both banks of the Tennessee River, busy in collecting shoes and clothing for his men, and the necessary ammunition and stores with which to invade Tennessee, most of which had to come from Mobile, Selma, and Montgomery, Alabama, over railroads that were still broken. Beauregard was at Corinth, hastening forward these necessary preparations.

General Thomas was at Nashville, with Wilson's dismounted cavalry and a mass of new troops and quartermaster's employés amply sufficient to defend the place. The Fourth and Twenty-third Corps, under Generals Stanley and Schofield, were posted at Pulaski, Tennessee, and the cavalry of Hatch, Croxton, and Capron, were about Florence, watching Hood.

Smith's (A. J.) two divisions of the Sixteenth Corps were still in Missouri, but were reported as ready to embark at Lexington for the Cumberland River and Nashville. Of course, General Thomas saw that on him would likely fall the real blow, and was naturally anxious. He still kept Granger's division at Decatur, Rousseau's at Murfreesboro', and Steedman's at Chattanooga, with strong railroad guards at all the essential points intermediate, confident that by means of this very railroad he could make his concentration sooner than Hood could possibly march up from Florence.

Meantime, General F. P. Blair had rejoined his corps (Seventeenth), and we were receiving at Kingston recruits and returned furlough-men, distributing them to their proper companies. Paymasters had come down to pay off our men before their departure to a new sphere of action, and commissioners were also on hand from the several States to take the vote of our men in the presidential election then agitating the country.

On the 6th of November, at Kingston, I wrote and telegraphed to General Grant, reviewing the whole situation, gave him my full plan of action, stated that I was ready to march as soon as the election was over, and appointed November 10th as the day for starting. On the 8th I received this dispatch.

CITY POINT, VIRGINIA, *November* 7, 1864—10.30 P. M.

Major-General SHERMAN :

Your dispatch of this evening received. I see no present reason for changing your plan. Should any arise, you will see it, or if I do I will inform you. I think every thing here is favorable now. Great good fortune attend you! I believe you will be eminently successful, and, at worst, can only make a march less fruitful of results than hoped for.

U. S. GRANT, *Lieutenant-General.*

Meantime trains of cars were whirling by, carrying to the rear an immense amount of stores which had accumulated at Atlanta, and at the other stations along the railroad; and General Steedman had come down to Kingston, to take charge of the final evacuation and withdrawal of the several garrisons below Chattanooga.

On the 10th of November the movement may be said to have fairly begun. All the troops designed for the campaign were ordered to march for Atlanta, and General Corse, before evacuating his post at Rome, was ordered to burn all the mills, factories, etc., etc., that could be useful to the enemy, should he undertake to pursue us, or resume military possession of the country. This was done on the night of the 10th, and next day Corse reached Kingston. On the 11th General Thomas and I interchanged full dispatches. He had heard of the arrival of General A. J. Smith's two divisions at Paducah, which would surely reach Nashville much sooner than General Hood could possibly do from Florence, so that he was perfectly satisfied with his share of the army.

On the 12th, with a full staff, I started from Kingston for Atlanta; and about noon of that day we reached Cartersville, and sat on the edge of a porch to rest, when the telegraph operator, Mr. Van Valkenburg, or Eddy, got the wire down from the poles to his lap, in which he held a small pocket instrument. Calling "Chattanooga," he received this message from General Thomas, dated—

NASHVILLE, *November* 12, 1864—8.30. A. M.

Major-General SHERMAN:

Your dispatch of twelve o'clock last night is received. I have no fears that Beauregard can do us any harm now, and, if he attempts to follow you, I will follow him as far as possible. If he does not follow you, I will then thoroughly organize my troops, and believe I shall have men enough to ruin him unless he gets out of the way very rapidly.

The country of Middle Alabama, I learn, is teeming with supplies this year, which will be greatly to our advantage. I have no additional news to report from the direction of Florence.

I am now convinced that the greater part of Beauregard's army is near Florence and Tuscumbia, and that you will have at least a clear road before you for several days, and that your success will fully equal your expectations.   GEORGE H. THOMAS, *Major-General.*

I answered simply: "Dispatch received—all right." About that instant of time, some of our men burnt a bridge, which severed the telegraph-wire, and all communication with the rear ceased thenceforth.

As we rode on toward Atlanta that night, I remember the railroad-trains going to the rear with a furious speed ; the engineers and the few men about the trains waving us an affectionate adieu. It surely was a strange event—two hostile armies marching in opposite directions, each in the full belief that it was achieving a final and conclusive result in a great war; and I was strongly inspired with the feeling that the movement on our part was a direct attack upon the rebel army and the rebel capital at Richmond, though a full thousand miles of hostile country intervened, and that, for better or worse, it would end the war.

CHAPTER XX.

ON the 12th of November the railroad and telegraph communications with the rear were broken, and the army stood detached from all friends, dependent on its own resources and supplies. No time was to be lost; all the detachments were ordered to march rapidly for Atlanta, breaking up the railroad *en route*, and generally to so damage the country as to make it untenable to the enemy. By the 14th all the troops had arrived at or near Atlanta, and were, according to orders, grouped into two wings, the right and left, commanded respectively by Major-Generals O. O. Howard and H. W. Slocum, both comparatively young men, but educated and experienced officers, fully competent to their command.

The right wing was composed of the Fifteenth Corps, Major-General P. J. Osterhaus commanding, and the Seventeenth Corps, Major-General Frank P. Blair commanding.

The left wing was composed of the Fourteenth Corps, Major-General Jefferson C. Davis commanding, and the Twentieth Corps, Brigadier-General A. S. Williams commanding.

The Fifteenth Corps had four divisions, commanded by Brigadier-Generals Charles R. Woods, W. B. Hazen, John E. Smith, and John M. Corse.

The Seventeenth Corps had three divisions, commanded by

Major-General J. A. Mower, and Brigadier-Generals M. D. Leggett and Giles A. Smith.

The Fourteenth Corps had three divisions, commanded by Brigadier-Generals W. P. Carlin, James D. Morgan, and A. Baird.

The Twentieth Corps had also three divisions, commanded by Brigadier-Generals N. J. Jackson, John W. Geary, and W. T. Ward.

The cavalry division was held separate, subject to my own orders. It was commanded by Brigadier-General Judson Kilpatrick, and was composed of two brigades, commanded by Colonels Eli H. Murray, of Kentucky, and Smith D. Atkins, of Illinois.

The strength of the army, as officially reported, is given in the following tables, and shows an aggregate of fifty-five thousand three hundred and twenty-nine infantry, five thousand and sixty-three cavalry, and eighteen hundred and twelve artillery—in all, sixty-two thousand two hundred and four officers and men. (*See* table for December 1st.)

RECAPITULATION—ATLANTA TO SAVANNAH.

ARM.	November 10.	December 1.	December 20.
Infantry	52,796	55,329	54,255
Cavalry	4,961	5,063	4,584
Artillery	1,788	1,812	1,759
Aggregate	59,545	62,204	60,598

The most extraordinary efforts had been made to purge this army of non-combatants and of sick men, for we knew well that there was to be no place of safety save with the army itself; our wagons were loaded with ammunition, provisions, and forage, and we could ill afford to haul even sick men in the ambulances, so that all on this exhibit may be assumed to have been able-bodied, experienced soldiers, well armed, well equipped and provided, as far as human foresight could, with all the essentials of life, strength, and vigorous action.

Effective Strength of the Army commanded by General W. T. SHERMAN during the March from Atlanta to Savannah, Georgia, 1864.

COMMANDS.	NOVEMBER 10.						DECEMBER 1.						DECEMBER 20.					
	Infantry.		Cavalry.		Artillery.		Infantry.		Cavalry.		Artillery.		Infantry.		Cavalry.		Artillery.	
	Commissioned Officers.	Enlisted Men.	Commissioned Officers.	Enlisted Men.	Commissioned Officers.	Enlisted Men.	Commissioned Officers.	Enlisted Men.	Commissioned Officers.	Enlisted Men.	Commissioned Officers.	Enlisted Men.	Commissioned Officers.	Enlisted Men.	Commissioned Officers.	Enlisted Men.	Commissioned Officers.	Enlisted Men.
Fifteenth Army Corps	724	14,568	……	……	11	376	750	15,144	……	……	17	862	758	14,441	……	……	12	367
Seventeenth Army Corps	420	10,607	2	43	5	266	418	11,814	2	30	10	818	436	11,293	2	80	7	278
Total—Right Wing	1,144	25,235	2	43	16	642	1,168	26,458	2	30	27	680	1,189	25,734	2	80	19	645
Fourteenth Army Corps	556	12,897	……	……	11	388	623	13,839	……	……	11	448	621	18,170	……	……	11	494
Twentieth Army Corps	602	12,862	……	……	25	607	638	18,103	……	……	22	529	631	12,910	……	……	24	526
Total—Left Wing	1,158	25,259	……	……	36	995	1,261	26,442	……	……	33	972	1,252	26,080	……	……	35	960
Kilpatrick's Cavalry	……	……	244	4,672	4	95	……	……	251	4,780	4	96	……	……	201	4,851	4	96
Grand Aggregate	2,302	50,494	246	4,715	56	1,732	2,429	52,900	253	4,810	64	1,748	2,441	51,814	208	4,881	58	1,701

The two general orders made for this march appear to me, even at this late day, so clear, emphatic, and well-digested, that no account of that historic event is perfect without them, and I give them entire, even at the seeming appearance of repetition; and, though they called for great sacrifice and labor on the part of the officers and men, I insist that these orders were obeyed as well as any similar orders ever were, by an army operating wholly in an enemy's country, and dispersed, as we necessarily were, during the subsequent period of nearly six months.

[Special Field Orders, No. 119.]

HEADQUARTERS MILITARY DIVISION OF THE MISSISSIPPI, }
IN THE FIELD, KINGSTON, GEORGIA, *November* 8, 1864. }

The general commanding deems it proper at this time to inform the officers and men of the Fourteenth, Fifteenth, Seventeenth, and Twentieth Corps, that he has organized them into an army for a special purpose, well known to the War Department and to General Grant.   It is sufficient for you to know that it involves a departure from our present base, and a long and difficult march to a new one.   All the chances of war have been considered and provided for, as far as human sagacity can.   All he asks of you is to maintain that discipline, patience, and courage, which have characterized you in the past; and he hopes, through you, to strike a blow at our enemy that will have a material effect in producing what we all so much desire, his complete overthrow.   Of all things, the most important is, that the men, during marches and in camp, keep their places and do not scatter about as stragglers or foragers, to be picked up by a hostile people in detail. It is also of the utmost importance that our wagons should not be loaded with any thing but provisions and ammunition.   All surplus servants, noncombatants, and refugees, should now go to the rear, and none should be encouraged to encumber us on the march.   At some future time we will be able to provide for the poor whites and blacks who seek to escape the bondage under which they are now suffering.   With these few simple cautions, he hopes to lead you to achievements equal in importance to those of the past.

By order of Major-General W. T. Sherman,

L. M. DAYTON, *Aide-de-Camp.*

[Special Field Orders, No. 120.]

HEADQUARTERS MILITARY DIVISION OF THE MISSISSIPPI, }
IN THE FIELD, KINGSTON, GEORGIA, *November* 9, 1864. }

1. For the purpose of military operations, this army is divided into two wings viz.:

The right wing, Major-General O. O. Howard commanding, composed of the Fifteenth and Seventeenth Corps; the left wing, Major-General H. W. Slocum commanding, composed of the Fourteenth and Twentieth Corps.

2. The habitual order of march will be, wherever practicable, by four roads, as nearly parallel as possible, and converging at points hereafter to be indicated in orders. The cavalry, Brigadier-General Kilpatrick commanding, will receive special orders from the commander-in-chief.

3. There will be no general train of supplies, but each corps will have its ammunition-train and provision-train, distributed habitually as follows: Behind each regiment should follow one wagon and one ambulance; behind each brigade should follow a due proportion of ammunition-wagons, provision-wagons, and ambulances. In case of danger, each corps commander should change this order of march, by having his advance and rear brigades unencumbered by wheels. The separate columns will start habitually at 7 A. M., and make about fifteen miles per day, unless otherwise fixed in orders.

4. The army will forage liberally on the country during the march. To this end, each brigade commander will organize a good and sufficient foraging party, under the command of one or more discreet officers, who will gather, near the route traveled, corn or forage of any kind, meat of any kind, vegetables, corn-meal, or whatever is needed by the command, aiming at all times to keep in the wagons at least ten days' provisions for his command, and three days' forage. Soldiers must not enter the dwellings of the inhabitants, or commit any trespass; but, during a halt or camp, they may be permitted to gather turnips, potatoes, and other vegetables, and to drive in stock in sight of their camp. To regular foraging-parties must be intrusted the gathering of provisions and forage, at any distance from the road traveled.

5. To corps commanders alone is intrusted the power to destroy mills, houses, cotton-gins, etc.; and for them this general principle is laid down: In districts and neighborhoods where the army is unmolested, no destruction of such property should be permitted; but should guerrillas or bushwhackers molest our march, or should the inhabitants burn bridges, obstruct roads, or otherwise manifest local hostility, then army commanders should order and enforce a devastation more or less relentless, according to the measure of such hostility.

6. As for horses, mules, wagons, etc., belonging to the inhabitants, the cavalry and artillery may appropriate freely and without limit; discriminating, however, between the rich, who are usually hostile, and the poor and industrious, usually neutral or friendly. Foraging-parties may also take mules or horses, to replace the jaded animals of their trains, or to serve as pack-mules for the regiments or brigades. In all foraging, of whatever

kind, the parties engaged will refrain from abusive or threatening language, and may, where the officer in command thinks proper, give written certificates of the facts, but no receipts; and they will endeavor to leave with each family a reasonable portion for their maintenance,

7. Negroes who are able-bodied and can be of service to the several columns may be taken along; but each army commander will bear in mind that the question of supplies is a very important one, and that his first duty is to see to those who bear arms.

8. The organization, at once, of a good pioneer battalion for each army corps, composed if possible of negroes, should be attended to. This battalion should follow the advance-guard, repair roads and double them if possible, so that the columns will not be delayed after reaching bad places. Also, army commanders should practise the habit of giving the artillery and wagons the road, marching their troops on one side, and instruct their troops to assist wagons at steep hills or bad crossings of streams.

9. Captain O. M. Poe, chief-engineer, will assign to each wing of the army a pontoon-train, fully equipped and organized; and the commanders thereof will see to their being properly protected at all times.

By order of Major-General W. T. Sherman,

L. M. DAYTON, *Aide-de-Camp*.

The greatest possible attention had been given to the artillery and wagon trains. The number of guns had been reduced to sixty-five, or about one gun to each thousand men, and these were generally in batteries of four guns each.

Each gun, caisson, and forge, was drawn by four teams of horses. We had in all about twenty-five hundred wagons, with teams of six mules to each, and six hundred ambulances, with two horses to each. The loads were made comparatively light, about twenty-five hundred pounds net; each wagon carrying in addition the forage needed by its own team. Each soldier carried on his person forty rounds of ammunition, and in the wagons were enough cartridges to make up about two hundred rounds per man, and in like manner two hundred rounds of assorted ammunition were carried for each gun.

The wagon-trains were divided equally between the four corps, so that each had about eight hundred wagons, and these usually on the march occupied five miles or more of road. Each corps commander managed his own train; and habitually the artillery and wagons had the road, while the men, with the exception of the advance and rear guards, pursued paths improvised by the side of the wagons, unless they were forced to use a bridge or causeway in common.

I reached Atlanta during the afternoon of the 14th, and found that all preparations had been made—Colonel Beckwith, chief commissary, reporting one million two hundred thousand rations in possession of the troops, which was about twenty days' supply, and he had on hand a good supply of beef-cattle to be driven along on the hoof. Of forage, the supply was limited, being of oats and corn enough for five days, but I knew that within that time we would reach a country well stocked with corn, which had been gathered and stored in cribs, seemingly for our use, by Governor Brown's militia.

Colonel Poe, United States Engineers, of my staff, had been busy in his special task of destruction. He had a large force at work, had leveled the great depot, round-house, and the machine-shops of the Georgia Railroad, and had applied fire to the wreck. One of these machine-shops had been used by the rebels as an arsenal, and in it were stored piles of shot and shell, some of which proved to be loaded, and that night was made hideous by the bursting of shells, whose fragments came uncomfortably near Judge Lyon's house, in which I was quartered. The fire also reached the block of stores near the depot, and the heart of the city was in flames all night, but the fire did not reach the parts of Atlanta where the court-house was, or the great mass of dwelling-houses.

The march from Atlanta began on the morning of November 15th, the right wing and cavalry following the railroad southeast toward Jonesboro', and General Slocum with the Twentieth Corps leading off to the east by Decatur and Stone Mountain, toward Madison. These were divergent lines, designed to threaten both Macon and Augusta at the same time, so as to prevent a concentration at our intended destination, or "objective," Milledgeville, the capital of Georgia, distant southeast about one hundred miles. The time allowed each column for reaching Milledgeville was seven days. I remained in Atlanta during the 15th with the Fourteenth Corps, and the rear-guard of the right wing, to complete the loading of the trains, and the destruction of the buildings of Atlanta which could be converted to hostile uses, and on the morning of the 16th started with my personal staff, a company of Alabama cavalry, commanded by Lieutenant Snelling, and an infantry company, commanded by Lieutenant McCrory, which guarded our small train of wagons.

My staff was then composed of Major L. M. Dayton, aide-de-camp and acting adjutant-general, Major J. C. McCoy, and Major J. C. Audenried, aides.   Major Ward Nichols had joined some weeks before at Gaylesville, Alabama, and was attached as an acting aide-de-camp.   Also Major Henry Hitchcock had joined at the same time as judge-advocate.   Colonel Charles Ewing was inspector-general, and Surgeon John Moore medical director.   These constituted our mess.   We had no tents, only the flies, with which we nightly made bivouacs with the assistance of the abundant pine-boughs, which made excellent shelter, as well as beds.

Colonel L. C. Easton was chief-quartermaster ; Colonel Amos Beckwith, chief-commissary ; Colonel O. M. Poe, chief-engineer; and Colonel T. G. Baylor, chief of ordnance.   These invariably rode with us during the day, but they had a separate camp and mess at night.

General William F. Barry had been chief of artillery in the previous campaign, but at Kingston his face was so swollen with erysipelas that he was reluctantly compelled to leave us for the rear, and he could not, on recovering, rejoin us till we had reached Savannah.

About 7 A. M. of November 16th we rode out of Atlanta by the Decatur road, filled by the marching troops and wagons of the Fourteenth Corps ; and reaching the hill, just outside of the old rebel works, we naturally paused to look back upon the scenes of our past battles.   We stood upon the very ground whereon was fought the bloody battle of July 22d, and could see the copse of wood where McPherson fell.   Behind us lay Atlanta, smouldering and in ruins, the black smoke rising high in air, and hanging like a pall over the ruined city.   Away off in the distance, on the McDonough road, was the rear of Howard's column, the gun-barrels glistening in the sun, the white-topped wagons stretching away to the south ; and right before us the Fourteenth Corps, marching steadily and rapidly, with a cheery look and swinging pace, that made light of the thousand miles that lay between us and Richmond. Some band, by accident, struck up the anthem of "John Brown's soul goes marching on;" the men caught up the strain, and never before or since have I heard the chorus of "Glory, glory, hallelujah!" done with more spirit, or in better harmony of time and place.

Then we turned our horses' heads to the east ; Atlanta was soon lost behind the screen of trees, and became a thing of the past. Around it clings many a thought of desperate battle, of hope and fear, that now seem like the memory of a dream ; and I have never seen the place since. The day was extremely beautiful, clear sunlight, with bracing air, and an unusual feeling of exhilaration seemed to pervade all minds—a feeling of something to come, vague and undefined, still full of venture and intense interest. Even the common soldiers caught the inspiration, and many a group called out to me as I worked my way past them, "Uncle Billy, I guess Grant is waiting for us at Richmond!" Indeed, the general sentiment was that we were marching for Richmond, and that there we should end the war, but how and when they seemed to care not ; nor did they measure the distance, or count the cost in life, or bother their brains about the great rivers to be crossed, and the food required for man and beast, that had to be gathered by the way. There was a "devil-may-care" feeling pervading officers and men, that made me feel the full load of responsibility, for success would be accepted as a matter of course, whereas, should we fail, this "march" would be adjudged the wild adventure of a crazy fool. I had no purpose to march direct for Richmond by way of Augusta and Charlotte, but always designed to reach the sea-coast first at Savannah or Port Royal, South Carolina, and even kept in mind the alternative of Pensacola.

The first night out we camped by the road-side near Lithonia. Stone Mountain, a mass of granite, was in plain view, cut out in clear outline against the blue sky; the whole horizon was lurid with the bonfires of rail-ties, and groups of men all night were carrying the heated rails to the nearest trees, and bending them around the trunks. Colonel Poe had provided tools for ripping up the rails and twisting them when hot; but the best and easiest way is the one I have described, of heating the middle of the iron-rails on bonfires made of the cross-ties, and then winding them around a telegraph-pole or the trunk of some convenient sapling. I attached much importance to this destruction of the railroad, gave it my own personal attention, and made reiterated orders to others on the subject.

The next day we passed through the handsome town of Covington, the soldiers closing up their ranks, the color-bearers unfurling their flags, and the bands striking up patriotic airs. The white people came out of their houses to behold the sight, spite of their deep hatred of the invaders, and the negroes were simply frantic with joy. Whenever they heard my name, they clustered about my horse, shouted and prayed in their peculiar style, which had a natural eloquence that would have moved a stone. I have witnessed hundreds, if not thousands, of such scenes; and can now see a poor girl, in the very ecstasy of the Methodist "shout," hugging the banner of one of the regiments, and jumping up to the "feet of Jesus."

I remember, when riding around by a by-street in Covington, to avoid the crowd that followed the marching column, that some one brought me an invitation to dine with a sister of Sam. Anderson, who was a cadet at West Point with me; but the messenger reached me after we had passed the main part of the town. I asked to be excused, and rode on to a place designated for camp, at the crossing of the Ulcofauhachee River, about four miles to the east of the town. Here we made our bivouac, and I walked up to a plantation-house close by, where were assembled many negroes, among them an old, gray-haired man, of as fine a head as I ever saw. I asked him if he understood about the war and its progress. He said he did; that he had been looking for the "angel of the Lord" ever since he was knee-high, and, though we professed to be fighting for the Union, he supposed that slavery was the cause, and that our success was to be his freedom. I asked him if all the negro slaves comprehended this fact, and he said they surely did. I then explained to him that we wanted the slaves to remain where they were, and not to load us down with useless mouths, which would eat up the food needed for our fighting-men; that our success was their assured freedom; that we could receive a few of their young, hearty men as pioneers; but that, if they followed us in swarms of old and young, feeble and helpless, it would simply load us down and cripple us in our great task. I think Major Henry Hitchcock was with me on that occasion, and made a note of the conversation, and I believe that old man spread this message to the slaves, which was carried from mouth to mouth, to the very end of our journey, and that it in part saved us from the great danger we incurred of swelling our numbers so that famine would have attended our progress. It was at this very plantation that a soldier passed me with a ham on his musket, a jug of sorghum-molasses under his arm, and a big piece of honey in his hand, from which he was eating, and, catching my eye, he remarked *sotto voce* and carelessly to a comrade, "Forage liberally on the country," quoting from my general orders. On this occasion, as on many others that fell under my personal observation, I reproved the man, explained that foraging must be limited to the regular parties properly detailed, and that all provisions thus obtained must be delivered to the regular commissaries, to be fairly distributed to the men who kept their ranks.

From Covington the Fourteenth Corps (Davis's), with which I was traveling, turned to the right for Milledgeville, *via* Shady Dale. General Slocum was ahead at Madison, with the Twentieth Corps, having torn up the railroad as far as that place, and thence had sent Geary's division on to the Oconee, to burn the bridges across that stream, when this corps turned south by Eatonton, for Milledgeville, the common "objective" for the first stage of the "march." We found abundance of corn, molasses, meal, bacon, and sweet-potatoes. We also took a good many cows and oxen, and a large number of mules. In all these the country was quite rich, never before having been visited by a hostile army; the recent crop had been excellent, had been just gathered and laid by for the winter. As a rule, we destroyed none, but kept our wagons full, and fed our teams bountifully.

The skill and success of the men in collecting forage was one of the features of this march. Each brigade commander had authority to detail a company of foragers, usually about fifty men, with one or two commissioned officers selected for their boldness and enterprise. This party would be dispatched before daylight with a knowledge of the intended day's march and camp; would proceed on foot five or six miles from the route traveled by their brigade, and then visit every plantation and farm within range. They would usually procure a wagon or family carriage, load it with bacon, corn-meal, turkeys, chickens, ducks, and every thing that could be used as food or forage, and would then regain the main road, usually in advance of their train. When this came up, they would deliver to the brigade commissary the supplies thus gathered by the way. Often would I pass these foraging-parties at the roadside, waiting for their wagons to come up, and was amused at their strange collections—mules, horses, even cattle, packed with old saddles and loaded with hams, bacon, bags of corn-meal, and poultry of every character and description. Although this foraging was attended with great danger and hard work, there seemed to be a charm about it that attracted the soldiers, and it was a privilege to be detailed on such a party. Daily they returned mounted on all sorts of beasts, which were at once taken from them and appropriated to the general use; but the next day they would start out again on foot, only to repeat the experience of the day before. No doubt, many acts of pillage, robbery, and violence, were committed by these parties of foragers, usually called "bummers;" for I have since heard of jewelry taken from women, and the plunder of articles that never reached the commissary; but these acts were exceptional and incidental. I never heard of any cases of murder or rape; and no army could have carried along sufficient food and forage for a march of three hundred miles; so that foraging in some shape was necessary. The country was sparsely settled, with no magistrates or civil authorities who could respond to requisitions, as is done in all the wars of Europe; so that this system of foraging was simply indispensable to our success. By it our men were well supplied with all the essentials of life and health, while the wagons retained enough in case of unexpected delay, and our animals were well fed. Indeed, when we reached Savannah, the trains were pronounced by experts to be the finest in flesh and appearance ever seen with any army.

Habitually each corps followed some main road, and the foragers, being kept out on the exposed flank, served all the military uses of flankers. The main columns gathered, by the roads traveled, much forage and food, chiefly meat, corn, and sweet-potatoes, and it was the duty of each division and brigade quartermaster to fill his wagons as fast as the contents were issued to the troops. The wagon-trains had the right to the road *always*, but each wagon was required to keep closed up, so as to leave no gaps in the column. If for any purpose any wagon or group of wagons dropped out of place, they had to wait for the rear. And this was always dreaded, for each brigade commander wanted his train up at camp as soon after reaching it with his men as possible.

I have seen much skill and industry displayed by these quartermasters on the march, in trying to load their wagons with corn and fodder by the way without losing their place in column. They would, while marching, shift the loads of wagons, so as to have six or ten of them empty. Then, riding well ahead, they would secure possession of certain stacks of fodder near the road, or cribs of corn, leave some men in charge, then open fences and a road back for a couple of miles, return to their trains, divert the empty wagons out of column, and conduct them rapidly to their forage, load up and regain their place in column without losing distance. On one occasion I remem-

ber to have seen ten or a dozen wagons thus loaded with corn
from two or three full cribs, almost without halting. These
cribs were built of logs, and roofed. The train-guard, by a
lever, had raised the whole side of the crib a foot or two; the
wagons drove close alongside, and the men in the cribs, lying on
their backs, kicked out a wagon-load of corn in the time I have
taken to describe it.

In a well-ordered and well-disciplined army, these things
might be deemed irregular, but I am convinced that the in-
genuity of these younger officers accomplished many things far
better than I could have ordered, and the marches were thus
made, and the distances were accomplished, in the most admirable way. Habitually we started from camp at the earliest break
of dawn, and usually reached camp soon after noon. The
marches varied from ten to fifteen miles a day, though some-
times on extreme flanks it was necessary to make as much as
twenty, but the rate of travel was regulated by the wagons; and,
considering the nature of the roads, fifteen miles per day was
deemed the limit.

The pontoon-trains were in like manner distributed in about
equal proportions to the four corps, giving each a section of
about nine hundred feet. The pontoons were of the skeleton
pattern, with cotton-canvas covers, each boat, with its proportion of balks and chesses, constituting a load for one wagon. By
uniting two such sections together, we could make a bridge of
eighteen hundred feet, enough for any river we had to traverse;
but habitually the leading brigade would, out of the abundant
timber, improvise a bridge before the pontoon-train could come
up, unless in the cases of rivers of considerable magnitude, such
as the Ocmulgee, Oconee, Ogeechee, Savannah, etc.

On the 20th of November I was still with the Fourteenth
Corps, near Eatonton Factory, waiting to hear of the Twentieth
Corps; and on the 21st we camped near the house of a man
named Vann; the next day, about 4 P. M., General Davis had
halted his head of column on a wooded ridge, overlooking an
extensive slope of cultivated country, about ten miles short of
Milledgeville, and was deploying his troops for camp when I got

up. There was a high, raw wind blowing, and I asked him why he had chosen so cold and bleak a position. He explained that he had accomplished his full distance for the day, and had there an abundance of wood and water. He explained further that his advance-guard was a mile or so ahead; so I rode on, asking him to let his rear division, as it came up, move some distance ahead into the depression or valley beyond. Riding on some distance to the border of a plantation, I turned out of the main road into a cluster of wild-plum bushes, that broke the force of the cold November wind, dismounted, and instructed the staff to pick out the place for our camp.

The afternoon was unusually raw and cold. My orderly was at hand with his invariable saddle-bags, which contained a change of under-clothing, my maps, a flask of whiskey, and bunch of cigars. Taking a drink and lighting a cigar, I walked to a row of negro-huts close by, entered one and found a soldier or two warming themselves by a wood-fire. I took their place by the fire, intending to wait there till our wagons had got up, and a camp made for the night. I was talking to the old negro woman, when some one came and explained to me that, if I would come farther down the road, I could find a better place. So I started on foot, and found on the main road a good double-hewed-log house, in one room of which Colonel Poe, Dr. Moore, and others, had started a fire. I sent back orders to the "plum-bushes" to bring our horses and saddles up to this house, and an orderly to conduct our headquarter wagons to the same place. In looking around the room, I saw a small box, like a candle-box, marked "Howell Cobb," and, on inquiring of a negro, found that we were at the plantation of General Howell Cobb, of Georgia, one of the leading rebels of the South, then a general in the Southern army, and who had been Secretary of the United States Treasury in Mr. Buchanan's time. Of course, we confiscated his property, and found it rich in corn, beans, pea-nuts, and sorghum-molasses. Extensive fields were all round the house; I sent word back to General Davis to explain whose plantation it was, and instructed him to spare nothing. That night huge bonfires consumed the fence-rails, kept our soldiers warm, and the teamsters and men, as well as the slaves, carried off an immense quantity of corn and provisions of all sorts.

In due season the headquarter wagons came up, and we got supper. After supper I sat on a chair astride, with my back to a good fire, musing, and became conscious that an old negro, with a tallow-candle in his hand, was scanning my face closely. I inquired, "What do you want, old man?" He answered, "Dey say you is Massa Sherman." I answered that such was the case, and inquired what he wanted. He only wanted to look at me, and kept muttering, "Dis nigger can't sleep dis night." I asked him why he trembled so, and he said that he wanted to be sure that we were in fact "Yankees," for on a former occasion some rebel cavalry had put on light-blue overcoats, personating Yankee troops, and many of the negroes were deceived thereby, himself among the number—had shown them sympathy, and had in consequence been unmercifully beaten therefor. This time he wanted to be certain before committing himself; so I told him to go out on the porch, from which he could see the whole horizon lit up with camp-fires, and he could then judge whether he had ever seen any thing like it before. The old man became convinced that the "Yankees" had come at last, about whom he had been dreaming all his life; and some of the staff-officers gave him a strong drink of whiskey, which set his tongue going. Lieutenant Snelling, who commanded my escort, was a Georgian, and recognized in this old negro a favorite slave of his uncle, who resided about six miles off; but the old slave did not at first recognize his young master in our uniform. One of my staff-officers asked him what had become of his young master, George. He did not know, only that he had gone off to the war, and he supposed him killed, as a matter of course. His attention was then drawn to Snelling's face, when he fell on his knees and thanked God that he had found his young master alive and along with the Yankees. Snelling inquired all about his uncle and the family, asked my permission to go and pay his uncle a visit, which I granted, of course, and the next morning he described to me his visit. The uncle was not cordial, by any means, to find his nephew in the ranks of the host that was desolating the land, and Snelling came back, having exchanged his tired horse for a fresher one out of his uncle's stables, explaining that surely some of the "bummers" would have got the horse had he not.

The next morning, November 23d, we rode into Milledgeville, the capital of the State, whither the Twentieth Corps had preceded us; and during that day the left wing was all united, in and around Milledgeville. From the inhabitants we learned that some of Kilpatrick's cavalry had preceded us by a couple of days, and that all of the right wing was at and near Gordon, twelve miles off, viz., the place where the branch railroad came to Milledgeville from the Macon & Savannah road. The first stage of the journey was, therefore, complete, and absolutely successful.

General Howard soon reported by letter the operations of his right wing, which, on leaving Atlanta, had substantially followed the two roads toward Macon, by Jonesboro' and McDonough, and reached the Ocmulgee at Planters' Factory, which they crossed, by the aid of the pontoon-train, during the 18th and 19th of November. Thence, with the Seventeenth Corps (General Blair's) he (General Howard) had marched *via* Monticello toward Gordon, having dispatched Kilpatrick's cavalry, supported by the Fifteenth Corps (Osterhaus's), to feign on Macon. Kilpatrick met the enemy's cavalry about four miles out of Macon, and drove them rapidly back into the bridge-defenses held by infantry. Kilpatrick charged these, got inside the parapet, but could not hold it, and retired to his infantry supports, near Griswold Station. The Fifteenth Corps tore up the railroad-track eastward from Griswold, leaving Charles R. Wood's division behind as a rear-guard—one brigade of which was intrenched across the road, with some of Kilpatrick's cavalry on the flanks. On the 22d of November General G. W. Smith, with a division of troops, came out of Macon, attacked this brigade (Walcutt's) in position, and was handsomely repulsed and driven back into Macon. This brigade was in part armed with Spencer repeating-rifles, and its fire was so rapid that General Smith insists to this day that he encountered a whole division ; but he is mistaken ; he was beaten by one brigade (Walcutt's), and made no further effort to molest our operations from that direction. General Walcutt was wounded in the leg, and had to ride the rest of the distance to Savannah in a carriage.

Therefore, by the 23d, I was in Milledgeville with the left wing, and was in full communication with the right wing at Gordon. The people of Milledgeville remained at home, except the Governor (Brown), the State officers, and Legislature, who had ignominiously fled, in the utmost disorder and confusion ; standing not on the order of their going, but going at once— some by rail, some by carriages, and many on foot. Some of the citizens who remained behind described this flight of the " brave and patriotic" Governor Brown. He had occupied a public building known as the " Governor's Mansion," and had hastily stripped it of carpets, curtains, and furniture of all sorts, which were removed to a train of freight-cars, which carried away these things—even the cabbages and vegetables from his kitchen and cellar—leaving behind muskets, ammunition, and the public archives. On arrival at Milledgeville I occupied the same public mansion, and was soon overwhelmed with appeals for protection. General Slocum had previously arrived with the Twentieth Corps, had taken up his quarters at the Milledgeville Hotel, established a good provost-guard, and excellent order was maintained. The most frantic appeals had been made by the Governor and Legislature for help from every quarter, and the people of the State had been called out *en masse* to resist and destroy the invaders of their homes and firesides. Even the prisoners and convicts of the penitentiary were released on condition of serving as soldiers, and the cadets were taken from their military college for the same purpose. These constituted a small battalion, under General Harry Wayne, a former officer of the United States Army, and son of the then Justice Wayne of the Supreme Court. But these hastily retreated east across the Oconee River, leaving us a good bridge, which we promptly secured.

At Milledgeville we found newspapers from all the South, and learned the consternation which had filled the Southern mind at our temerity; many charging that we were actually fleeing for our lives and seeking safety at the hands of our fleet on the sea-coast. All demanded that we should be assailed, "front, flank, and rear;" that provisions should be destroyed in advance, so that we would starve; that bridges should be burned, roads obstructed, and no mercy shown us. Judging from the tone of the Southern press of that day, the outside world must have supposed us ruined and lost. I give a few of these appeals as samples, which to-day must sound strange to the parties who made them:

CORINTH, MISSISSIPPI, *November* 18, 1864.

To the People of Georgia:

Arise for the defense of your native soil! Rally around your patriotic Governor and gallant soldiers! Obstruct and destroy all the roads in Sherman's front, flank, and rear, and his army will soon starve in your midst. Be confident. Be resolute. Trust in an overruling Providence, and success will soon crown your efforts. I hasten to join you in the defense of your homes and firesides.   G. T. BEAUREGARD.

RICHMOND, *November* 18, 1864.

To the People of Georgia:

You have now the best opportunity ever yet presented to destroy the enemy. Put every thing at the disposal of our generals; remove all provisions from the path of the invader, and put all obstructions in his path.

Every citizen with his gun, and every negro with his spade and axe, can do the work of a soldier. You can destroy the enemy by retarding his march.

Georgians, be firm! Act promptly, and fear not!

B. H. HILL, *Senator.*

I most cordially approve the above.

JAMES A. SEDDON, *Secretary of War.*

RICHMOND, *November* 19, 1864.

To the People of Georgia:

We have had a special conference with President Davis and the Secretary of War, and are able to assure you that they have done and are still doing all that can be done to meet the emergency that presses upon you. Let every man fly to arms! Remove your negroes, horses, cattle, and provisions from Sherman's army, and burn what you cannot carry. Burn all bridges, and block up the roads in his route. Assail the invader in front, flank, and rear, by night and by day. Let him have no rest.

JULIAN HARTRIDGE,   MARK BLAUFORD,

J. H. REYNOLDS,   General N. LESTER,

JOHN T. SHOEMAKER,   JOSEPH M. SMITH,

Members of Congress.

Of course, we were rather amused than alarmed at these threats, and made light of the feeble opposition offered to our progress. Some of the officers (in the spirit of mischief) gathered together in the vacant hall of Representatives, elected a Speaker, and constituted themselves the Legislature of the State of Georgia! A proposition was made to repeal the ordinance of secession, which was well debated, and resulted in its repeal by a fair vote! I was not present at these frolics, but heard of them at the time, and enjoyed the joke.

Meantime orders were made for the total destruction of the arsenal and its contents, and of such public buildings as could be easily converted to hostile uses. But little or no damage was done to private property, and General Slocum, with my approval, spared several mills, and many thousands of bales of cotton, taking what he knew to be worthless bonds, that the cotton should not be used for the Confederacy. Meantime the right wing continued its movement along the railroad toward Savannah, tearing up the track and destroying its iron. At the Oconee was met a feeble resistance from Harry Wayne's troops, but soon the pontoon-bridge was laid, and that wing crossed over. Kilpatrick's cavalry was brought into Milledgeville, and crossed the Oconee by the bridge near the town; and on the 23d I made the general orders for the next stage of the march as far as Millen. These were, substantially, for the right wing to follow the Savannah Railroad, by roads on its south; the left wing was to move to Sandersville, by Davisboro' and Louisville, while the cavalry was ordered by a circuit to the north, and to march rapidly for Millen, to rescue our prisoners of war confined there. The distance was about a hundred miles.

General Wheeler, with his division of rebel cavalry, had succeeded in getting ahead of us between Milledgeville and Augusta;

and General W. J. Hardee had been dispatched by General Beauregard from Hood's army to oppose our progress directly in front. He had, however, brought with him no troops, but relied on his influence with the Georgians (of whose State he was a native) to arouse the people, and with them to annihilate Sherman's army !

On the 24th we renewed the march, and I accompanied the Twentieth Corps, which took the direct road to Sandersville, which we reached simultaneously with the Fourteenth Corps, on the 26th. A brigade of rebel cavalry was deployed before the town, and was driven in and through it by our skirmish-line. I myself saw the rebel cavalry apply fire to stacks of fodder standing in the fields at Sandersville, and gave orders to burn some unoccupied dwellings close by. On entering the town, I told certain citizens (who would be sure to spread the report) that, if the enemy attempted to carry out their threat to burn their food, corn, and fodder, in our route, I would most un-doubtedly execute to the letter the general orders of devastation made at the outset of the campaign. With this exception, and one or two minor cases near Savannah, the people did not destroy food, for they saw clearly that it would be ruin to themselves.

At Sandersville I halted the left wing until I heard that the right wing was abreast of us on the railroad. During the evening a negro was brought to me, who had that day been to the station (Tenille), about six miles south of the town. I inquired of him if there were any Yankees there, and he answered, "Yes." He described in his own way what he had seen. "First, there come along some cavalry-men, and they burned the depot; then come along some infantry-men, and they tore up the track, and burned it;" and just before he left they had "sot fire to the well !"

The next morning, viz., the 27th, I rode down to the station, and found General Corse's division (of the Fifteenth Corps) engaged in destroying the railroad, and saw the well which my negro informant had seen " burnt." It was a square pit about twenty-five feet deep, boarded up, with wooden steps lead-

ing to the bottom, wherein was a fine copper pump, to lift
the water to a tank above. The soldiers had broken up the
pump, heaved in the steps and lining, and set fire to the mass
of lumber in the bottom of the well, which corroborated the
negro's description.

From this point Blair's corps, the Seventeenth, took up the
work of destroying the railroad, the Fifteenth Corps following another road leading eastward, farther to the south of the railroad.
While the left wing was marching toward Louisville, north of
the railroad, General Kilpatrick had, with his cavalry division,
moved rapidly toward Waynesboro', on the branch railroad leading from Millen to Augusta. He found Wheeler's division of
rebel cavalry there, and had considerable skirmishing with it;
but, learning that our prisoners had been removed two days before from Millen, he returned to Louisville on the 29th, where
he found the left wing. Here he remained a couple of days to
rest his horses, and, receiving orders from me to engage Wheeler
and give him all the fighting he wanted, he procured from
General Slocum the assistance of the infantry division of General
Baird, and moved back for Waynesboro' on the 2d of December,
the remainder of the left wing continuing its march on toward
Millen. Near Waynesboro' Wheeler was again encountered,
and driven through the town and beyond Brier Creek, toward
Augusta, thus keeping up the delusion that the main army was
moving toward Augusta. General Kilpatrick's fighting and
movements about Waynesboro' and Brier Creek were spirited,
and produced a good effect by relieving the infantry column and
the wagon-trains of all molestation during their march on Millen.
Having thus covered that flank, he turned south and followed
the movement of the Fourteenth Corps to Buckhead Church,
north of Millen and near it.

On the 3d of December I entered Millen with the Seventeenth Corps (General Frank P. Blair), and there paused one day,
to communicate with all parts of the army. General Howard
was south of the Ogeechee River, with the Fifteenth Corps,
opposite Scarboro'. General Slocum was at Buckhead Church,
four miles north of Millen, with the Twentieth Corps. The

Fourteenth (General Davis) was at Lumpkin's Station, on the Augusta road, about ten miles north of Millen, and the cavalry division was within easy support of this wing. Thus the whole army was in good position and in good condition. We had largely subsisted on the country; our wagons were full of forage and provisions; but, as we approached the sea-coast, the country became more sandy and barren, and food became more scarce; still, with little or no loss, we had traveled two-thirds of our distance, and I concluded to push on for Savannah. At Millen I learned that General Bragg was in Augusta, and that General Wade Hampton had been ordered there from Richmond, to organize a large cavalry force with which to resist our progress.

General Hardee was ahead, between us and Savannah, with McLaw's division, and other irregular troops, that could not, I felt assured, exceed ten thousand men. I caused the fine depot at Millen to be destroyed, and other damage done, and then resumed the march directly on Savannah, by the four main roads. The Seventeenth Corps (General Blair) followed substantially the railroad, and, along with it, on the 5th of December, I reached Ogeechee Church, about fifty miles from Savannah, and found there fresh earthworks, which had been thrown up by McLaw's division; but he must have seen that both his flanks were being turned, and prudently retreated to Savannah without a fight. All the columns then pursued leisurely their march toward Savannah, corn and forage becoming more and more scarce, but rice-fields beginning to occur along the Savannah and Ogeechee Rivers, which proved a good substitute, both as food and forage. The weather was fine, the roads good, and every thing seemed to favor us. Never do I recall a more agreeable sensation than the sight of our camps by night, lit up by the fires of fragrant pine-knots. The trains were all in good order, and the men seemed to march their fifteen miles a day as though it were nothing. No enemy opposed us, and we could only occasionally hear the faint reverberation of a gun to our left rear, where we knew that General Kilpatrick was skirmishing with Wheeler's cavalry, which persistently followed him. But the infantry columns had met with no opposition whatsoever. McLaw's division was falling back before us, and we occasionally picked up a few of his men as prisoners, who insisted that we would meet with strong opposition at Savannah.

On the 8th, as I rode along, I found the column turned out of the main road, marching through the fields. Close by, in the corner of a fence, was a group of men standing around a handsome young officer, whose foot had been blown to pieces by a torpedo planted in the road. He was waiting for a surgeon to amputate his leg, and told me that he was riding along with the rest of his brigade-staff of the Seventeenth Corps, when a torpedo trodden on by his horse had exploded, killing the horse and literally blowing off all the flesh from one of his legs. I saw the terrible wound, and made full inquiry into the facts. There had been no resistance at that point, nothing to give warning of danger, and the rebels had planted eight-inch shells in the road, with friction-matches to explode them by being trodden on. This was not war, but murder, and it made me very angry. I immediately ordered a lot of rebel prisoners to be brought from the provost-guard, armed with picks and spades, and made them march in close order along the road, so as to explode their own torpedoes, or to discover and dig them up. They begged hard, but I reiterated the order, and could hardly help laughing at their stepping so gingerly along the road, where it was supposed sunken torpedoes might explode at each step, but they found no other torpedoes till near Fort McAllister. That night we reached Pooler's Station, eight miles from Savannah, and during the next two days, December 9th and 10th, the several corps reached the defenses of Savannah—the Fourteenth Corps on the left, touching the river; the Twentieth Corps next; then the Seventeenth; and the Fifteenth on the extreme right; thus completely investing the city. Wishing to reconnoitre the place in person, I rode forward by the Louisville road, into a dense wood of oak, pine, and cypress, left the horses, and walked down to the railroad-track, at a place where there was a side-track, and a cut about four feet deep. From that point the railroad was straight, leading into Savannah, and about eight hundred yards off were a rebel parapet and battery. I could see the cannoneers preparing to fire, and cautioned the officers near me to scatter, as we would likely attract a shot. Very soon I saw the white puff of smoke, and, watching close, caught sight of the ball as it rose in its flight, and, finding it coming pretty straight, I stepped a short distance to one side, but noticed a negro very near me in the act of crossing the track at right angles. Some one called to him to look out; but, before the poor fellow understood his danger, the ball (a thirty-two-pound round shot) struck the ground, and rose in its first ricochet, caught the negro under the right jaw, and literally carried away his head, scattering blood and brains about. A soldier close by spread an overcoat over the body, and we all concluded to get out of that railroad-cut. Meantime, General Mower's division of the Seventeenth Corps had crossed the canal to the right of the Louisville road, and had found the line of parapet continuous; so at Savannah we had again run up against the old familiar parapet, with its deep ditches, canals, and bayous, full of water; and it looked as though another siege was inevitable. I accordingly made a camp or bivouac near the Louisville road, about five miles from Savannah, and proceeded to invest the place closely, pushing forward reconnoissances at every available point.

As soon as it was demonstrated that Savannah was well fortified, with a good garrison, commanded by General William J. Hardee, a competent soldier, I saw that the first step was to open communication with our fleet, supposed to be waiting for us with supplies and clothing in Ossabaw Sound.

General Howard had, some nights previously, sent one of his best scouts, Captain Duncan, with two men, in a canoe, to drift past Fort McAllister, and to convey to the fleet a knowledge of our approach. General Kilpatrick's cavalry had also been transferred to the south bank of the Ogeechee, with orders to open communication with the fleet. Leaving orders with General Slocum to press the siege, I instructed General Howard to send a division with all his engineers to King's Bridge, fourteen and a half miles southwest from Savannah, to rebuild it. On the evening of the 12th I rode over myself, and spent the night at Mr. King's house, where I found General Howard, with General Hazen's division of the Fifteenth Corps. His engineers were hard at work on the bridge, which they finished that night, and at sunrise Hazen's division passed over. I gave General Hazen, in person, his orders to march rapidly down the right bank of the Ogeechee, and without hesitation to assault and carry Fort McAllister by storm. I knew it to be strong in heavy artillery, as against an approach from the sea, but believed it open and weak to the rear. I explained to General Hazen, fully, that on his action depended the safety of the whole army, and the success of the campaign. Kilpatrick had already felt the fort, and had gone farther down the coast to Kilkenny Bluff, or St. Catharine's Sound, where, on the same day, he had communication with a vessel belonging to the blockading fleet; but, at the time, I was not aware of this fact, and trusted entirely to General Hazen and his division of infantry, the Second of the Fifteenth Corps, the same old division which I had commanded at Shiloh and Vicksburg, in which I felt a special pride and confidence.

Having seen General Hazen fairly off, accompanied by General Howard, I rode with my staff down the left bank of the Ogeechee, ten miles to the rice-plantation of a Mr. Cheeves, where General Howard had established a signal-station to overlook the lower river, and to watch for any vessel of the blockading squadron, which the negroes reported to be expecting us, because they nightly sent up rockets, and daily dispatched a steamboat up the Ogeechee as near to Fort McAllister as it was safe.

On reaching the rice-mill at Cheeves's, I found a guard and a couple of twenty-pound Parrott guns, of De Gres's battery, which fired an occasional shot toward Fort McAllister, plainly seen over the salt-marsh, about three miles distant. Fort McAllister had the rebel flag flying, and occasionally sent a heavy shot back across the marsh to where we were, but otherwise every thing about the place looked as peaceable and quiet as on the Sabbath.

The signal-officer had built a platform on the ridge-pole of the rice-mill. Leaving our horses behind the stacks of rice-straw, we all got on the roof of a shed attached to the mill, wherefrom I could communicate with the signal-officer above, and at the same time look out toward Ossabaw Sound, and across the Ogeechee River at Fort McAllister. About 2 p. m. we observed signs of commotion in the fort, and noticed one or two guns fired inland, and some musket-skirmishing in the woods close by.

This betokened the approach of Hazen's division, which had been anxiously expected, and soon thereafter the signal-officer discovered about three miles above the fort a signal-flag, with which he conversed, and found it to belong to General Hazen, who was preparing to assault the fort, and wanted to know if I were there. On being assured of this fact, and that I expected the fort to be carried before night, I received by signal the assurance of General Hazen that he was making his preparations, and would soon attempt the assault. The sun was rapidly declining, and I was dreadfully impatient. At that very moment some one discovered a faint cloud of smoke, and an object gliding, as it were, along the horizon above the tops of the sedge toward the sea, which little by little grew till it was pronounced to be the smoke-stack of a steamer coming up the river. "It must be one of our squadron!" Soon the flag of the United States was plainly visible, and our attention was divided between this approaching steamer and the expected assault. When the sun was about an hour high, another signal-message came from General Hazen that he was all ready, and I replied to go ahead, as a friendly steamer was approaching from below. Soon we made out a group of officers on the deck of this vessel, signaling with a flag, "Who are you?" The answer went back promptly, "General Sherman." Then followed the question, "Is Fort McAllister taken?" "Not yet, but it will be in a minute!" Almost at that instant of time, we saw Hazen's troops come out of the dark fringe of woods that encompassed the fort, the lines dressed as on parade, with colors flying, and moving forward with a quick, steady pace. Fort McAllister was then all alive, its big guns belching forth dense clouds of smoke, which soon enveloped our assaulting lines. One color went down, but was up in a moment. On the lines advanced, faintly seen in the white, sulphurous smoke; there was a pause, a cessation of fire; the smoke cleared away, and the parapets were blue with our men, who fired their muskets in the air, and shouted so that we actually heard them, or felt that we did. Fort McAllister was taken, and the good news was instantly sent by the signal-officer to our navy friends on the approaching gun-boat, for a point of timber had shut out Fort McAllister from their view, and they had not seen the action at all, but must have heard the cannonading.

During the progress of the assault, our little group on Cheeves's mill hardly breathed; but no sooner did we see our flags on the parapet than I exclaimed, in the language of the poor negro at Cobb's plantation, " This nigger will have no sleep this night!"

I was resolved to communicate with our fleet that night, which happened to be a beautiful moonlight one. At the wharf belonging to Cheeves's mill was a small skiff, that had been used by our men in fishing or in gathering oysters. I was there in a minute, called for a volunteer crew, when several young officers, Nichols and Merritt among the number, said they were good oarsmen, and volunteered to pull the boat down to Fort McAllister. General Howard asked to accompany me; so we took seats in the stern of the boat, and our crew of officers pulled out with a will. The tide was setting in strong, and they had a hard pull, for, though the distance was but three miles in an air-line, the river was so crooked that the actual distance was fully six miles. On the way down we passed the wreck of a steamer which had been sunk some years before, during a naval attack on Fort McAllister.

Night had fairly set in when we discovered a soldier on the beach. I hailed him, and inquired if he knew where General Hazen was. He answered that the general was at the house of the overseer of the plantation (McAllister's), and that he could guide me to it. We accordingly landed, tied our boat to a drift-log, and followed our guide through bushes to a frame-house, standing in a grove of live-oaks, near a row of negro quarters.

General Hazen was there with his staff, in the act of getting supper; he invited us to join them, which we accepted promptly, for we were really very hungry. Of course, I congratulated Hazen most heartily on his brilliant success, and praised its execution very highly, as it deserved, and he explained to me more in detail the exact results. The fort was an inclosed work, and its land-front was in the nature of a bastion and curtains, with good parapet, ditch, *fraise*, and *chevaux-de-frise*, made out of the large branches of live-oaks. Luckily, the rebels had left the larger and unwieldy trunks on the ground, which served as a good cover for the skirmish-line, which crept behind these logs, and from them kept the artillerists from loading and firing their guns accurately.

The assault had been made by three parties in line, one from below, one from above the fort, and the third directly in rear, along the capital. All were simultaneous, and had to pass a good abatis and line of torpedoes, which actually killed more of the assailants than the heavy guns of the fort, which generally overshot the mark. Hazen's entire loss was reported, killed and wounded, ninety-two. Each party reached the parapet about the same time, and the garrison inside, of about two hundred and fifty men (about fifty of them killed or wounded), were in his power. The commanding officer, Major Anderson, was at that moment a prisoner, and General Hazen invited him in to take supper with us, which he did.

Up to this time General Hazen did not know that a gunboat was in the river below the fort; for it was shut off from sight by a point of timber, and I was determined to board her that night, at whatever risk or cost, as I wanted some news of what was going on in the outer world. Accordingly, after supper, we all walked down to the fort, nearly a mile from the house where we had been, entered Fort McAllister, held by a regiment of Hazen's troops, and the sentinel cautioned us to be very careful, as the ground outside the fort was full of torpedoes. Indeed, while we were there, a torpedo exploded, tearing to pieces a poor fellow who was hunting for a dead comrade. Inside the fort lay the dead as they had fallen, and they could hardly be distinguished from their living comrades, sleeping soundly side by side in the pale moonlight. In the river, close by the fort, was a good yawl tied to a stake, but the tide was high, and it required some time to get it in to the bank; the commanding officer, whose name I cannot recall, manned the boat with a good crew of his men, and, with General Howard, I entered, and pulled down-stream, regardless of the warnings of all about the torpedoes.

The night was unusually bright, and we expected to find the gunboat within a mile or so; but, after pulling down the river fully three miles, and not seeing the gunboat, I began to think she had turned and gone back to the sound; but we kept on, following the bends of the river, and about six miles below McAllister we saw her light, and soon were hailed by the vessel at anchor. Pulling alongside, we announced ourselves, and were received with great warmth and enthusiasm on deck by half a dozen naval officers, among them Captain Williamson, United States Navy. She proved to be the Dandelion, a tender of the regular gunboat Flag, posted at the mouth of the Ogeechee. All sorts of questions were made and answered, and we learned that Captain Duncan had safely reached the squadron, had communicated the good news of our approach, and they had been expecting us for some days. They explained that Admiral Dahlgren commanded the South-Atlantic Squadron, which was then engaged in blockading the coast from Charleston south, and was on his flag-ship, the Harvest Moon, lying in Wassaw Sound; that General J. G. Foster was in command of the Department of the South, with his headquarters at Hilton Head; and that several ships loaded with stores for the army were lying in Tybee Roads and in Port Royal Sound. From these officers I also learned that General Grant was still besieging Petersburg and Richmond, and that matters and things generally remained pretty much the same as when we had left Atlanta. All thoughts seemed to have been turned to us in Georgia, cut off from all communication with our friends; and the rebel papers had reported us to be harassed, defeated, starving, and fleeing for safety to the coast. I then asked for pen and paper, and wrote several hasty notes to General Foster, Admiral Dahlgren, General Grant, and the Secretary of War, giving in general terms the actual state of affairs, the fact of the capture of Fort Mc-Allister, and of my desire that means should be taken to establish a line of supply from the vessels in port up the Ogeechee to the rear of the army. As a sample, I give one of these notes, addressed to the Secretary of War, intended for publication to relieve the anxiety of our friends at the North generally:

ON BOARD DANDELION, OSSABAW SOUND, *December* 13, 1864—11.50 P. M.

To Hon. E. M. STANTON, *Secretary of War, Washington, D. C.:*

To-day, at 5 P. M., General Hazen's division of the Fifteenth Corps carried Fort McAllister by assault, capturing its entire garrison and stores. This opened to us Ossabaw Sound, and I pushed down to this gunboat to communicate with the fleet. Before opening communication we had completely destroyed all the railroads leading into Savannah, and invested the city. The left of the army is on the Savannah River three miles above the city, and the right on the Ogeechee, at King's Bridge. The army is in splendid order, and equal to any thing. The weather has been fine, and supplies were abundant. Our march was most agreeable, and we were not at all molested by guerrillas.

We reached Savannah three days ago, but, owing to Fort McAllister, could not communicate; but, now that we have McAllister, we can go ahead.

We have already captured two boats on the Savannah River, and prevented their gunboats from coming down.

I estimate the population of Savannah at twenty-five thousand, and the garrison at fifteen thousand. General Hardee commands.

We have not lost a wagon on the trip; but have gathered a large supply of negroes, mules, horses, etc., and our teams are in far better condition than when we started.

My first duty will be to clear the army of surplus negroes, mules, and horses. We have utterly destroyed over two hundred miles of rails, and consumed stores and provisions that were essential to Lee's and Hood's armies.

The quick work made with McAllister, the opening of communication with our fleet, and our consequent independence as to supplies, dissipate all their boasted threats to head us off and starve the army.

I regard Savannah as already *gained.* Yours truly,

W. T. SHERMAN, *Major-General.*

By this time the night was well advanced, and the tide was

running ebb-strong; so I asked Captain Williamson to tow us up
as near Fort McAllister as he would venture for the torpedoes,
of which the navy-officers had a wholesome dread. The Dandelion steamed up some three or four miles, till the lights of Fort
McAllister could be seen, when she anchored, and we pulled to
the fort in our own boat. General Howard and I then walked
up to the McAllister House, where we found General Hazen and
his officers asleep on the floor of one of the rooms. Lying
down on the floor, I was soon fast asleep, but shortly became conscious that some one in the room was inquiring for me among
the sleepers. Calling out, I was told that an officer of General
Foster's staff had just arrived from a steamboat anchored below
McAllister; that the general was extremely anxious to see me
on important business, but that he was lame from an old Mexi-
can-War wound, and could not possibly come to me. I was
extremely weary from the incessant labor of the day and
night before, but got up, and again walked down the sandy
road to McAllister, where I found a boat awaiting us, which carried us some three miles down the river, to the steamer W. W.
Coit (I think), on board of which we found General Foster.
He had just come from Port Royal, expecting to find Admiral
Dahlgren in Ossabaw Sound, and, hearing of the capture of
Fort McAllister, he had come up to see me. He described fully
the condition of affairs with his own command in South Carolina. He had made several serious efforts to effect a lodgment
on the railroad which connects Savannah with Charleston near
Pocotaligo, but had not succeeded in reaching the railroad itself,
though he had a full division of troops, strongly intrenched, near
Broad River, within cannon-range of the railroad. He explained, moreover, that there were at Port Royal abundant supplies of bread and provisions, as well as of clothing, designed
for our use. We still had in our wagons and in camp abundance of meat, but we needed bread, sugar, and coffee, and it
was all-important that a route of supply should at once be
opened, for which purpose the aid and assistance of the navy
were indispensable. We accordingly steamed down the Ogeechee
River to Ossabaw Sound, in hopes to meet Admiral Dahlgren,

but he was not there, and we continued on by the inland channel to Wassaw Sound, where we found the Harvest Moon, and
Admiral Dahlgren.   I was not personally acquainted with him
at the time, but he was so extremely kind and courteous that
I was at once attracted to him.   There was nothing in his
power, he said, which he would not do to assist us, to make our
campaign absolutely successful.   He undertook at once to find
vessels of light draught to carry our supplies from Port Royal
to Cheeves's Mill, or to King's Bridge above, whence they could
be hauled by wagons to our several camps; he offered to return
with me to Fort McAllister, to superintend the removal of the
torpedoes, and to relieve me of all the details of this most difficult
work.   General Foster then concluded to go on to Port Royal,
to send back to us six hundred thousand rations, and all the
rifled guns of heavy calibre, and ammunition on hand, with which
I thought we could reach the city of Savannah, from the positions already secured.   Admiral Dahlgren then returned with
me in the Harvest Moon to Fort McAllister.   This consumed all
of the 14th of December; and by the 15th I had again reached
Cheeves's Mill, where my horse awaited me, and rode on to General Howard's headquarters at Anderson's plantation, on the
plank-road, about eight miles back of Savannah.   I reached
this place about noon, and immediately sent orders to my
own headquarters, on the Louisville road, to have them brought
over to the plank-road, as a place more central and convenient;
gave written notice to Generals Slocum and Howard of all
the steps taken, and ordered them to get ready to receive
the siege-guns, to put them in position to bombard Savannah,
and to prepare for the general assault.   The country back of
Savannah is very low, and intersected with innumerable salt-
water creeks, swamps, and rice-fields.   Fortunately the weather
was good and the roads were passable, but, should the winter
rains set in, I knew that we would be much embarrassed.   Therefore, heavy details of men were at once put to work to prepare
a wharf and depot at King's Bridge, and the roads leading thereto
were corduroyed in advance.   The Ogeechee Canal was also
cleared out for use; and boats, such as were common on the river

plantations, were collected, in which to float stores from our proposed base on the Ogeechee to the points most convenient to the several camps.

Slocum's wing extended from the Savannah River to the canal, and Howard's wing from the canal to the extreme right, along down the Little Ogeechee. The enemy occupied not only the city itself, with its long line of outer works, but the many forts which had been built to guard the approaches from the sea—such as at Beaulieu, Rosedew, White Bluff, Bonaventura, Thunderbolt, Cansten's Bluff, Forts Tatnall, Boggs, etc., etc. I knew that General Hardee could not have a garrison strong enough for all these purposes, and I was therefore anxious to break his lines before he could receive reënforcements from Virginia or Augusta. General Slocum had already captured a couple of steamboats trying to pass down the Savannah River from Augusta, and had established some of his men on Argyle and Hutchinson Islands above the city, and wanted to transfer a whole corps to the South Carolina bank; but, as the enemy had iron-clad gunboats in the river, I did not deem it prudent, because the same result could be better accomplished f om General Foster's position at Broad River.

Fort McAllister was captured as described, late in the evening of December 13th, and by the 16th many steamboats had passed up as high as King's Bridge; among them one which General Grant had dispatched with the mails for the army, which had accumulated since our departure from Atlanta, under charge of Colonel A. H. Markland. These mails were most welcome to all the officers and soldiers of the army, which had been cut off from friends and the world for two months, and this prompt receipt of letters from home had an excellent effect, making us feel that home was near. By this vessel also came Lieutenant Dunn, aide-de-camp, with the following letter of December 3d, from General Grant, and on the next day Colonel Babcock, United States Engineers, arrived with the letter of December 6th, both of which are in General Grant's own handwriting, and are given entire:

HEADQUARTERS ARMIES OF THE UNITED STATES,
CITY POINT, VIRGINIA, *December* 3, 1864.

Major - General W. T. SHERMAN, *commanding Armies near Savannah, Georgia.*

GENERAL: The little information gleaned from the Southern press indicating no great obstacle to your progress, I have directed your mails (which had been previously collected in Baltimore by Colonel Markland, special agent of the Post-Office Department) to be sent as far as the blockading squadron off Savannah, to be forwarded to you as soon as heard from on the coast.

Not liking to rejoice before the victory is assured, I abstain from congratulating you and those under your command, until bottom has been struck. I have never had a fear, however, for the result.

Since you left Atlanta no very great progress has been made here. The enemy has been closely watched, though, and prevented from detaching against you. I think not one man has gone from here, except some twelve or fifteen hundred dismounted cavalry. Bragg has gone from Wilmington. I am trying to take advantage of his absence to get possession of that place. Owing to some preparations Admiral Porter and General Butler are making to blow up Fort Fisher (which, while hoping for the best, I do not believe a particle in), there is a delay in getting this expedition off. I hope they will be ready to start by the 7th, and that Bragg will not have started back by that time.

In this letter I do not intend to give you any thing like directions for future action, but will state a general idea I have, and will get your views after you have established yourself on the sea-coast. With your veteran army I hope to get control of the only two through routes from east to west possessed by the enemy before the fall of Atlanta. The condition will be filled by holding Savannah and Augusta, or by holding any other port to the east of Savannah and Branchville. If Wilmington falls, a force from there can coöperate with you.

Thomas has got back into the defenses of Nashville, with Hood close upon him. Decatur has been abandoned, and so have all the roads, except the main one leading to Chattanooga. Part of this falling back was undoubtedly necessary, and all of it may have been. It did not look so, however, to me. In my opinion, Thomas far outnumbers Hood in infantry. In cavalry Hood has the advantage in *morale* and numbers. I hope yet that Hood will be badly crippled, if not destroyed. The general news you will learn from the papers better than I can give it.

After all becomes quiet, and roads become so bad up here that there is likely to be a week or two when nothing can be done, I will run down the coast to see you. If you desire it, I will ask Mrs. Sherman to go with me.

Yours truly,   U. S. GRANT, *Lieutenant-General.*

HEADQUARTERS ARMIES OF THE UNITED STATES, }
CITY POINT, VIRGINIA, *December* 6, 1864. }

Major-General W. T. SHERMAN, *commanding Military Division of the Mississippi.*

GENERAL : On reflection since sending my letter by the hands of Lieutenant Dunn, I have concluded that the most important operation toward closing out the rebellion will be to close out Lee and his army.

You have now destroyed the roads of the South so that it will probably take them three months without interruption to reëstablish a through line from east to west. In that time I think the job here will be effectually completed.

My idea now is that you establish a base on the sea-coast, fortify and leave in it all your artillery and cavalry, and enough infantry to protect them, and at the same time so threaten the interior that the militia of the South will have to be kept at home. With the balance of your command come here by water with all dispatch. Select yourself the officer to leave in command, but you I want in person. Unless you see objections to this plan which I cannot see, use every vessel going to you for purposes of transportation.

Hood has Thomas close in Nashville. I have said all I can to force him to attack, without giving the positive order until to-day. To-day, however, I could stand it no longer, and gave the order without any reserve. I think the battle will take place to-morrow. The result will probably be known in New York before Colonel Babcock (the bearer of this) will leave it. Colonel Babcock will give you full information of all operations now in progress. Very respectfully your obedient servant,

        U. S. GRANT, *Lieutenant-General.*

The contents of these letters gave me great uneasiness, for I had set my heart on the capture of Savannah, which I believed to be practicable, and to be near ; for me to embark for Virginia by sea was so complete a change from what I had supposed would be the course of events that I was very much concerned. I supposed, as a matter of course, that a fleet of vessels would soon pour in, ready to convey the army to Virginia, and as General Grant's orders contemplated my leaving the cavalry, trains, and artillery, behind, I judged Fort McAllister to be the best place for the purpose, and sent my chief-engineer, Colonel Poe, to that fort, to reconnoitre the ground, and to prepare it so as to make a fortified camp large enough to accommodate the vast herd of mules and horses that would thus be left behind. And as some time might be required to collect the necessary shipping, which I estimated at little less than a hundred steamers and sailing-vessels, I determined to push operations, in hopes to secure the city of Savannah before the necessary fleet could be available. All these ideas are given in my answer to General Grant's letters (dated December 16, 1864) herewith, which is a little more full than the one printed in the report of the Committee on the Conduct of the War, because in that copy I omitted the matter concerning General Thomas, which now need no longer be withheld:

HEADQUARTERS MILITARY DIVISION OF THE MISSISSIPPI,
IN THE FIELD, NEAR SAVANNAH, *December* 16, 1864.

Lieutenant-General U. S. GRANT, *Commander-in-Chief, City Point, Virginia.*

GENERAL : I received, day before yesterday, at the hands of Lieutenant Dunn, your letter of December 3d, and last night, at the hands of Colonel Babcock, that of December 6th. I had previously made you a hasty scrawl from the tugboat Dandelion, in Ogeechee River, advising you that the army had reached the sea-coast, destroying all the railroads across the State of Georgia, investing closely the city of Savannah, and had made connection with the fleet.

Since writing that note, I have in person met and conferred with General Foster and Admiral Dahlgren, and made all the arrangements which were deemed essential for reducing the city of Savannah to our possession. But, since the receipt of yours of the 6th, I have initiated measures looking principally to coming to you with fifty or sixty thousand infantry, and incidentally to capture Savannah, if time will allow.

At the time we carried Fort McAllister by assault so handsomely, with its twenty-two guns and entire garrison, I was hardly aware of its importance ; but, since passing down the river with General Foster and up with Admiral Dahlgren, I realize how admirably adapted are Ossabaw Sound and Ogeechee River to supply an army operating against Savannah. Sea-going vessels can easily come to King's Bridge, a point on Ogeechee River, fourteen and a half miles due west of Savannah, from which point we have roads leading to all our camps. The country is low and sandy, and cut up with marshes, which in wet weather will be very bad, but we have been so favored with weather that they are all now comparatively good, and heavy details are constantly employed in double-corduroying the marshes, so that I have no fears even of bad weather. Fortunately, also, by liberal and judicious foraging, we reached the sea-coast abundantly supplied with forage and provisions, needing nothing on arrival except bread. Of this we started from Atlanta, with from eight to twenty days' supply per corps, and some of the troops only had one day's issue of bread during the trip of thirty days; yet they did not want, for sweet-potatoes were very abun-dant, as well as corn-meal, and our soldiers took to them naturally. We started with about five thousand head of cattle, and arrived with over ten thousand, of course consuming mostly turkeys, chickens, sheep, hogs, and the cattle of the country. As to our mules and horses, we left Atlanta with about twenty-five hundred wagons, many of which were drawn by mules which had not recovered from the Chattanooga starvation, all of which were replaced, the poor mules shot, and our transportation is now in superb condition. I have no doubt the State of Georgia has lost, by our operations, fifteen thousand first-rate mules. As to horses, Kilpatrick collected all his remounts, and it looks to me, in riding along our columns, as though every officer had three or four led horses, and each regiment seems to be followed by at least fifty negroes and foot-sore soldiers, riding on horses and mules. The custom was for each brigade to send out daily a foraging-party of about fifty men, on foot, who invariably returned mounted, with several wagons loaded with poultry, potatoes, etc., and as the army is composed of about forty brigades, you can estimate approximately the number of horses collected. Great numbers of these were shot by my order, because of the disorganizing effect on our infantry of having too many idlers mounted. General Easton is now engaged in collecting statistics on this subject, but I know the Government will never receive full accounts of our captures, although the result aimed at was fully attained, viz., to deprive our enemy of them. All these animals I will have sent to Port Royal, or collected behind Fort McAllister, to be used by General Saxton in his farming operations, or by the Quartermaster's Department, after they are systematically accounted for. While General Easton is collecting transportation for my troops to James River, I will throw to Port Royal Island all our means of transportation I can, and collect the rest near Fort McAllister, covered by the Ogeechee River and intrenchments to be erected, and for which Captain Poe, my chief-engineer, is now reconnoitring the ground, but in the mean time will act as I have begun, as though the city of Savannah were my objective: namely, the troops will continue to invest Savannah closely, making attacks and feints wherever we have fair ground to stand upon, and I will place some thirty-pound Parrotts, which I have got from General Foster, in position, near enough to reach the centre of the city, and then will demand its surrender. If General Hardee is alarmed, or fears starvation, he may surrender; otherwise I will bombard the city, but not risk the lives of our men by assaults across the narrow causeways, by which alone I can now reach it.

If I had time, Savannah, with all its dependent fortifications, would surely fall into our possession, for we hold all its avenues of supply.

The enemy has made two desperate efforts to get boats from above to the city, in both of which he has been foiled—General Slocum (whose left flank rests on the river) capturing and burning the first boat, and in the second instance driving back two gunboats and capturing the steamer Resolute, with seven naval officers and a crew of twenty-five seamen. General Slocum occupies Argyle Island and the upper end of Hutchinson Island, and has a brigade on the South Carolina shore opposite, and is very urgent to pass one of his corps over to that shore. But, in view of the change of plan made necessary by your order of the 6th, I will maintain things *in statu quo* till I have got all my transportation to the rear and out of the way, and until I have sea-transportation for the troops you require at James River, which I will accompany and command in person. Of course, I will leave Kilpatrick, with his cavalry (say five thousand three hundred), and, it may be, a division of the Fifteenth Corps; but, before determining on this, I must see General Foster, and may arrange to shift his force (now over above the Charleston Railroad, at the head of Broad River) to the Ogeechee, where, in coöperation with Kilpatrick's cavalry, he can better threaten the State of Georgia than from the direction of Port Royal. Besides, I would much prefer not to detach from my regular corps any of its veteran divisions, and would even prefer that other less valuable troops should be sent to reenforce Foster from some other quarter. My four corps, full of experience and full of ardor, coming to you *en masse*, equal to sixty thousand fighting-men, will be a reënforcement that Lee cannot disregard. Indeed, with my present command, I had expected, after reducing Savannah, instantly to march to Columbia, South Carolina; thence to Raleigh, and thence to report to you. But this would consume, it may be, six weeks' time after the fall of Savannah; whereas, by sea, I can probably reach you with my men and arms before the middle of January.

I myself am somewhat astonished at the attitude of things in Tennessee. I purposely delayed at Kingston until General Thomas assured me that he was all ready, and my last dispatch from him of the 12th of November was full of confidence, in which he promised me that he would ruin Hood if he dared to advance from Florence, urging me to go ahead, and give myself no concern about Hood's army in Tennessee.

Why he did not turn on him at Franklin, after checking and discomfiting him, surpasses my understanding. Indeed, I do not approve of his evacuating Decatur, but think he should have assumed the offensive against Hood from Pulaski, in the direction of Waynesburg. I know full well that General Thomas is slow in mind and in action; but he is judicious and brave, and the troops feel great confidence in him. I still hope he will outmanœuvre and destroy Hood.

As to matters in the Southeast, I think Hardee, in Savannah, has good artillerists, some five or six thousand good infantry, and, it may be, a mongrel mass of eight to ten thousand militia. In all our marching through Georgia, he has not forced us to use any thing but a skirmish-line, though at several points he had erected fortifications and tried to alarm us by bombastic threats. In Savannah he has taken refuge in a line constructed behind swamps and overflowed rice-fields, extending from a point on the Savannah River about three miles above the city, around by a branch of the Little Ogeechee, which stream is impassable from its salt-marshes and boggy swamps, crossed only by narrow causeways or common corduroy-roads.

There must be twenty-five thousand citizens, men, women, and children, in Savannah, that must also be fed, and how he is to feed them beyond a few days I cannot imagine. I know that his requisitions for corn on the interior counties were not filled, and we are in possession of the rice-fields and mills, which could alone be of service to him in this neighborhood. He can draw nothing from South Carolina, save from a small corner down in the southeast, and that by a disused wagon-road. I could easily get possession of this, but hardly deem it worth the risk of making a detachment, which would be in danger by its isolation from the main army. Our whole army is in fine condition as to health, and the weather is splendid. For that reason alone I feel a personal dislike to turning northward. I will keep Lieutenant Dunn here until I know the result of my demand for the surrender of Savannah, but, whether successful or not, shall not delay my execution of your order of the 6th, which will depend alone upon the time it will require to obtain transportation by sea.

I am, with respect, etc., your obedient servant,

W. T. SHERMAN, *Major-General United States Army.*

Having concluded all needful preparations, I rode from my headquarters, on the plank-road, over to General Slocum's headquarters, on the Macon road, and thence dispatched (by flag of truce) into Savannah, by the hands of Colonel Ewing, inspector-general, a demand for the surrender of the place. The following letters give the result. General Hardee refused to surrender, and I then resolved to make the attempt to break his line of defense at several places, trusting that some one would succeed.

HEADQUARTERS MILITARY DIVISION OF THE MISSISSIPPI,
IN THE FIELD, SAVANNAH, GEORGIA, *December* 17, 1864.

General WILLIAM J. HARDEE, *commanding Confederate Forces in Savannah.*

GENERAL: You have doubtless observed, from your station at Rosedew, that sea-going vessels now come through Ossabaw Sound and up the Ogeechee to the rear of my army, giving me abundant supplies of all kinds, and more especially heavy ordnance necessary for the reduction of Savannah. I

have already received guns that can cast heavy and destructive shot as far
as the heart of your city; also, I have for some days held and controlled
every avenue by which the people and garrison of Savannah can be supplied, and I am therefore justified in demanding the surrender of the city
of Savannah, and its dependent forts, and shall wait a reasonable time for
your answer, before opening with heavy ordnance. Should you entertain
the proposition, I am prepared to grant liberal terms to the inhabitants and
garrison; but should I be forced to resort to assault, or the slower and surer
process of starvation, I shall then feel justified in resorting to the harshest
measures, and shall make little effort to restrain my army—burning to avenge
the national wrong which they attach to Savannah and other large cities
which have been so prominent in dragging our country into civil war. I
inclose you a copy of General Hood's demand for the surrender of the town
of Resaca, to be used by you for what it is worth.

I have the honor to be your obedient servant,

W. T. Sherman, *Major-General.*

Headquarters Department South Carolina, Georgia, and Florida, }
Savannah, Georgia, *December* 17, 1864.   }

Major-General W. T. Sherman, *commanding Federal Forces near Savannah,*
Georgia.

General: I have to acknowledge the receipt of a communication from
you of this date, in which you demand "the surrender of Savannah and its
dependent forts," on the ground that you "have received guns that can
cast heavy and destructive shot into the heart of the city," and for the
further reason that you "have, for some days, held and controlled every
avenue by which the people and garrison can be supplied." You add that,
should you be "forced to resort to assault, or to the slower and surer process of starvation, you will then feel justified in resorting to the harshest
measures, and will make little effort to restrain your army," etc., etc. The
position of your forces (a half-mile beyond the outer line for the land-de-
fense of Savannah) is, at the nearest point, at least four miles from the heart
of the city. That and the interior line are both intact.

Your statement that you have, for some days, held and controlled every
avenue by which the people and garrison can be supplied, is incorrect. I
am in free and constant communication with my department.

Your demand for the surrender of Savannah and its dependent forts is
refused.

With respect to the threats conveyed in the closing paragraphs of your
letter (of what may be expected in case your demand is not complied with),
I have to say that I have hitherto conducted the military operations intrusted
to my direction in strict accordance with the rules of civilized warfare, and I
should deeply regret the adoption of any course by you that may force me

to deviate from them in future. I have the honor to be, very respectfully, your obedient servant,

W. J. HARDEE, Lieutenant-General.

HEADQUARTERS MILITARY DIVISION OF THE MISSISSIPPI,
IN THE FIELD, NEAR SAVANNAH, GEORGIA, <i>December</i> 18, 1864—8 P. M.</div>

Lieutenant-General U. S. GRANT, City Point, Virginia.

GENERAL: I wrote you at length (by Colonel Babcock) on the 16th instant. As I therein explained my purpose, yesterday I made a demand on General Hardee for the surrender of the city of Savannah, and to-day received his answer—refusing; copies of both letters are herewith inclosed. You will notice that I claim that my lines are within easy cannon-range of the heart of Savannah; but General Hardee asserts that we are four and a half miles distant. But I myself have been to the intersection of the Charleston and Georgia Central Railroads, and the three-mile post is but a few yards beyond, within the line of our pickets. The enemy has no pickets outside of his fortified line (which is a full quarter of a mile within the three-mile post), and I have the evidence of Mr. R. R. Cuyler, President of the Georgia Central Railroad (who was a prisoner in our hands), that the mile-posts are measured from the Exchange, which is but two squares back from the river. By to-morrow morning I will have six thirty-pound Parrotts in position, and General Hardee will learn whether I am right or not. From the left of our line, which is on the Savannah River, the spires can be plainly seen; but the country is so densely wooded with pine and live-oak, and lies so flat, that we can see nothing from any other portion of our lines. General Slocum feels confident that he can make a successful assault at one or two points in front of General Davis's (Fourteenth) corps. All of General Howard's troops (the right wing) lie behind the Little Ogeechee, and I doubt if it can be passed by troops in the face of an enemy. Still, we can make strong feints, and if I can get a sufficient number of boats, I shall make a coöperative demonstration up Vernon River or Wassaw Sound. I should like very much indeed to take Savannah before coming to you; but, as I wrote to you before, I will do nothing rash or hasty, and will embark for the James River as soon as General Easton (who is gone to Port Royal for that purpose) reports to me that he has an approximate number of vessels for the transportation of the contemplated force. I fear even this will cost more delay than you anticipate, for already the movement of our transports and the gunboats has required more time than I had expected. We have had dense fogs; there are more mud-banks in the Ogeechee than were reported, and there are no pilots whatever. Admiral Dahlgren promised to have the channel buoyed and staked, but it is not done yet. We find only six feet of water up to King's Bridge at low tide, about ten feet up to the rice-mill, and sixteen to Fort McAllister. All these points may be used by us, and we have a good, strong bridge across Ogeechee at King's, by which our wagons can go to Fort McAllister, to which point I am sending all wagons not absolutely necessary for daily use, the negroes, prisoners of war, sick, etc., *en route* for Port Royal. In relation to Savannah, you will remark that General Hardee refers to his still being in communication with his department. This language he thought would deceive me ; but I am confirmed in the belief that the route to which he refers (the Union Plank-road on the South Carolina shore) is inadequate to feed his army and the people of Savannah, and General Foster assures me that he has his force on that very road, near the head of Broad River, so that cars no longer run between Charleston and Savannah. We hold this end of the Charleston Railroad, and have destroyed it from the three-mile post back to the bridge (about twelve miles). In anticipation of leaving this country, I am continuing the destruction of their railroads, and at this moment have two divisions and the cavalry at work breaking up the Gulf Railroad from the Ogeechee to the Altamaha ; so that, even if I do not take Savannah, I will leave it in a bad way. But I still hope that events will give me time to take Savannah, even if I have to assault with some loss. I am satisfied that, unless we take it, the gunboats never will, for they can make no impression upon the batteries which guard every approach from the sea. I have a faint belief that, when Colonel Babcock reaches you, you will delay operations long enough to enable me to succeed here. With Savannah in our possession, at some future time if not now, we can punish South Carolina as she deserves, and as thousands of the people in Georgia hoped we would do. I do sincerely believe that the whole United States, North and South, would rejoice to have this army turned loose on South Carolina, to devastate that State in the manner we have done in Georgia, and it would have a direct and immediate bearing on your campaign in Virginia.

I have the honor to be your obedient servant,

W. T. SHERMAN, *Major-General United States Army.*

As soon as the army had reached Savannah, and had opened communication with the fleet, I endeavored to ascertain what had transpired in Tennessee since our departure. We received our letters and files of newspapers, which contained full accounts of all the events there up to about the 1st of December. As before described, General Hood had three full corps of infantry—S. D. Lee's, A. P. Stewart's, and Cheatham's, at Florence, Alabama—with Forrest's corps of cavalry, numbering in the aggregate about forty-five thousand men. General Thomas was in Nashville, Tennessee, quietly engaged in reorganizing his army out of the somewhat broken forces at his disposal. He had posted his only two regular corps, the Fourth and Twenty-third, under the general command of Major-General J. M. Schofield, at Pulaski, directly in front of Florence, with the three brigades of cavalry (Hatch, Croxton, and Capron), commanded by Major-General Wilson, watching closely for Hood's initiative.

This force aggregated about thirty thousand men, was therefore inferior to the enemy; and General Schofield was instructed, in case the enemy made a general advance, to fall back slowly toward Nashville, fighting, till he should be reenforced by General Thomas in person. Hood's movement was probably hurried by reason of my advance into Georgia; for on the 17th his infantry columns marched from Florence in the direction of Waynesboro', turning Schofield's position at Pulaski. The latter at once sent his trains to the rear, and on the 21st fell back to Columbia, Tennessee. General Hood followed up this movement, skirmished lightly with Schofield at Columbia, began the passage of Duck River, below the town, and Cheatham's corps reached the vicinity of Spring Hill, whither General Schofield had sent General Stanley, with two of his divisions, to cover the movement of his trains. During the night of November 29th General Schofield passed Spring Hill with his trains and army, and took post at Franklin, on the south side of Harpeth River. General Hood now attaches serious blame to General Cheatham for not attacking General Schofield in flank while in motion at Spring Hill, for he was bivouacked within eight hundred yards of the road at the time of the passage of our army. General Schofield reached Franklin on the morning of November 30th, and posted his army in front of the town, where some rifle-intrenchments had been constructed in advance. He had the two corps of Stanley and Cox (Fourth and Twenty-third), with Wilson's cavalry on his flanks, and sent his trains behind the Harpeth.

General Hood closed upon him the same day, and assaulted his position with vehemence, at one time breaking the line and wounding General Stanley seriously; but our men were veterans, cool and determined, and fought magnificently. The rebel officers led their men in person to the several persistent assaults, continuing the battle far into the night, when they drew off, beaten and discomfited.

Their loss was very severe, especially in general officers; among them Generals Cleburn and Adams, division commanders. Hood's loss on that day was afterward ascertained to be (Thomas's report): Buried on the field, seventeen hundred and fifty; left in hospital at Franklin, thirty-eight hundred; and seven hundred and two prisoners captured and held: aggregate, six thousand two hundred and fifty-two. General Schofield's loss, reported officially, was one hundred and eighty-nine killed, one thousand and thirty-three wounded, and eleven hundred and four prisoners or missing: aggregate, twenty-three hundred and twenty-six. The next day General Schofield crossed the Harpeth without trouble, and fell back to the defenses of Nashville.

Meantime General Thomas had organized the employés of the Quartermaster's Department into a corps, commanded by the chief-quartermaster, General J. L. Donaldson, and placed them in the fortifications of Nashville, under the general direction of Major-General Z. B. Tower, now of the United States Engineers. He had also received the two veteran divisions of the Sixteenth Corps, under General A. J. Smith, long absent and long expected; and he had drawn from Chattanooga and Decatur (Alabama) the divisions of Steedman and of R. S. Granger. These, with General Schofield's army and about ten thousand good cavalry, under General J. H. Wilson, constituted a strong army, capable not only of defending Nashville, but of beating Hood in the open field. Yet Thomas remained inside of Nashville, seemingly passive, until General Hood had closed upon him and had intrenched his position.

General Thomas had furthermore held fast to the railroad leading from Nashville to Chattanooga, leaving strong guards at its principal points, as at Murfreesboro', Deckerd, Stevenson, Bridgeport, Whitesides, and Chattanooga. At Murfreesboro' the division of Rousseau was reënforced and strengthened up to about eight thousand men.

At that time the weather was cold and sleety, the ground

was covered with ice and snow, and both parties for a time rested on the defensive. Thus matters stood at Nashville, while we were closing down on Savannah, in the early part of December, 1864; and the country, as well as General Grant, was alarmed at the seeming passive conduct of General Thomas; and General Grant at one time considered the situation so dangerous that he thought of going to Nashville in person, but General John A. Logan, happening to be at City Point, was sent out to supersede General Thomas; luckily for the latter, he acted in time, gained a magnificent victory, and thus escaped so terrible a fate.

On the 18th of December, at my camp by the side of the plank-road, eight miles back of Savannah, I received General Hardee's letter declining to surrender, when nothing remained but to assault. The ground was difficult, and, as all former assaults had proved so bloody, I concluded to make one more effort to completely surround Savannah on all sides, so as further to excite Hardee's fears, and, in case of success, to capture the whole of his army. We had already completely invested the place on the north, west, and south, but there remained to the enemy, on the east, the use of the old dike or plank-road leading into South Carolina, and I knew that Hardee would have a pontoon-bridge across the river. On examining my maps, I thought that the division of John P. Hatch, belonging to General Foster's command, might be moved from its then position at Broad River, by water, down to Bluffton, from which it could reach this plank-road, fortify and hold it—at some risk, of course, because Hardee could avail himself of his central position to fall on this detachment with his whole army. I did not want to make a mistake like "Ball's Bluff" at that period of the war; so, taking one or two of my personal staff, I rode back to King's Bridge, leaving with Generals Howard and Slocum orders to make all possible preparations, but not to attack, during my two or three days' absence; and there I took a boat for Wassaw Sound, whence Admiral Dahlgren conveyed me in his own boat (the Harvest Moon) to Hilton Head, where I represented the matter to General Foster, and he promptly agreed to give his personal attention to it. During the night of the 20th we started back, the wind blowing strong, Admiral Dahlgren ordered the pilot of the Harvest Moon to run into Tybee, and to work his way through to Wassaw Sound and the Ogeechee River by the Romney Marshes. We were caught by a low tide and stuck in the mud. After laboring some time, the admiral ordered out his barge; in it we pulled through this intricate and shallow channel, and toward evening of December 21st we discovered, coming toward us, a tug, called the Red Legs, belonging to the Quartermaster's Department, with a staff-officer on board, bearing letters from Colonel Dayton to myself and the admiral, reporting that the city of Savannah had been found evacuated on the morning of December 21st, and was then in our possession. General Hardee had crossed the Savannah River by a pontoon-bridge, carrying off his men and light artillery, blowing up his iron-clads and navy-yard, but leaving for us all the heavy guns, stores, cotton, railway-cars, steamboats, and an immense amount of public and private property. Admiral Dahlgren concluded to go toward a vessel (the Sonoma) of his blockading fleet, which lay at anchor near Beaulieu, and I transferred to the Red Legs, and hastened up the Ogeechee River to King's Bridge, whence I rode to my camp that same night. I there learned that, early on the morning of December 21st, the skirmishers had detected the absence of the enemy, and had occupied his lines simultaneously along their whole extent; but the left flank (Slocum), especially Geary's division of the Twentieth Corps, claimed to have been the first to reach the heart of the city.

Generals Slocum and Howard moved their headquarters at once into the city, leaving the bulk of their troops in camps outside. On the morning of December 22d I followed with my own headquarters, and rode down Bull Street to the custom-house, from the roof of which we had an extensive view over the city, the river, and the vast extent of marsh and rice-fields on the South Carolina side. The navy-yard, and the wreck of the iron-clad ram Savannah, were still smouldering, but all else looked quiet enough. Turning back, we rode to the Pulaski

Hotel, which I had known in years long gone, and found it kept by a Vermont man with a lame leg, who used to be a clerk in the St. Louis Hotel, New Orleans, and I inquired about the capacity of his hotel for headquarters. He was very anxious to have us for boarders, but I soon explained to him that we had a full mess equipment along, and that we were not in the habit of paying board; that one wing of the building would suffice for our use, while I would allow him to keep an hotel for the accommodation of officers and gentlemen in the remainder. I then dispatched an officer to look around for a livery-stable that could accommodate our horses, and, while waiting there, an English gentleman, Mr. Charles Green, came and said that he had a fine house completely furnished, for which he had no use, and offered it as headquarters. He explained, moreover, that General Howard had informed him, the day before, that I would want his house for headquarters. At first I felt strongly disinclined to make use of any private dwelling, lest complaints should arise of damage and loss of furniture, and so expressed myself to Mr. Green; but, after riding about the city, and finding his house so spacious, so convenient, with large yard and stabling, I accepted his offer, and occupied that house during our stay in Savannah. He only reserved for himself the use of a couple of rooms above the dining-room, and we had all else, and a most excellent house it was in all respects.

I was disappointed that Hardee had escaped with his army, but on the whole we had reason to be content with the substantial fruits of victory. The Savannah River was found to be badly obstructed by torpedoes, and by log piers stretched across the channel below the city, which piers were filled with the cobble stones that formerly paved the streets. Admiral Dahlgren was extremely active, visited me repeatedly in the city, while his fleet still watched Charleston, and all the avenues, for the blockade-runners that infested the coast, which were notoriously owned and managed by Englishmen, who used the island of New Providence (Nassau) as a sort of entrepot. One of these small blockade-runners came into Savannah after we were in full possession, and the master did not discover his mistake till he came ashore to visit the custom-house. Of course his vessel fell a prize to the navy. A heavy force was at once set to work to remove the torpedoes and obstructions in the main channel of the river, and, from that time forth, Savannah became the great depot of supply for the troops operating in that quarter.

Meantime, on the 15th and 16th of December, were fought, in front of Nashville, the great battles in which General Thomas so nobly fulfilled his promise to ruin Hood, the details of which are fully given in his own official reports, long since published. Rumors of these great victories reached us at Savannah by piecemeal, but his official report came on the 24th of December, with a letter from General Grant, giving in general terms the events up to the 18th, and I wrote at once through my chief of staff, General Webster, to General Thomas, complimenting him in the highest terms. His brilliant victory at Nashville was necessary to mine at Savannah to make a complete whole, and this fact was perfectly comprehended by Mr. Lincoln, who recognized it fully in his personal letter of December 26th, hereinbefore quoted at length, and which I also claimed at the time, in my Special Field Order No. 6, of January 8, 1865, here given:

[Special Field Order No. 6.]

HEADQUARTERS MILITARY DIVISION OF THE MISSISSIPPI, }
IN THE FIELD, SAVANNAH, GEORGIA, *January* 8, 1865. }

The general commanding announces to the troops composing the Military Division of the Mississippi that he has received from the President of the United States, and from Lieutenant-General Grant, letters conveying their high sense and appreciation of the campaign just closed, resulting in the capture of Savannah and the defeat of Hood's army in Tennessee.

In order that all may understand the importance of events, it is proper to revert to the situation of affairs in September last. We held Atlanta, a city of little value to us, but so important to the enemy that Mr. Davis, the head of the rebellious faction in the South, visited his army near Palmetto, and commanded it to regain the place and also to ruin and destroy us, by a series of measures which he thought would be effectual. That army, by a rapid march, gained our railroad near Big Shanty, and afterward about Dalton. We pursued it, but it moved so rapidly that we could not overtake it, and General Hood led his army successfully far over toward Mississippi, in hope to decoy us out of Georgia. But we were not thus to be led away by him, and preferred to lead and control events ourselves. Generals Thomas and Schofield, commanding the departments to our rear, returned to their posts and prepared to decoy General Hood into their meshes, while we came on to complete the original journey. We quietly and deliberately destroyed Atlanta, and all the railroads which the enemy had used to carry on war against us, occupied his State capital, and then captured his commercial capital, which had been so strongly fortified from the sea as to defy approach from that quarter. Almost at the moment of our victorious entry into Savannah came the welcome and expected news that our comrades in Tennessee had also fulfilled nobly and well their part, had decoyed General Hood to Nashville and then turned on him, defeating his army thoroughly, capturing all his artillery, great numbers of prisoners, and were still pursuing the fragments down in Alabama. So complete a success in military operations, extending over half a continent, is an achievement that entitles it to a place in the military history of the world. The armies serving in Georgia and Tennessee, as well as the local garrisons of Decatur, Bridgeport, Chattanooga, and Murfreesboro', are alike entitled to the common honors, and each regiment may inscribe on its colors, at pleasure, the word "Savannah" or "Nashville." The general commanding embraces, in the same general success, the operations of the cavalry under Generals Stoneman, Burbridge, and Gillem, that penetrated into Southwest Virginia, and paralyzed the efforts of the enemy to disturb the peace and safety of East Tennessee. Instead of being put on the defensive, we have at all points assumed the bold offensive, and have completely thwarted the designs of the enemies of our country.

By order of Major-General W. T. Sherman,

L. M. DAYTON, *Aide-de-Camp.*

Here terminated the "March to the Sea," and I only add a few letters, selected out of many, to illustrate the general feeling of rejoicing throughout the country at the time. I only regarded the march from Atlanta to Savannah as a "shift of base," as the transfer of a strong army, which had no opponent, and had finished its then work, from the interior to a point on the sea-coast, from which it could achieve other important results. I considered this march as a means to an end, and not as an essential act of war. Still, then, as now, the march to the sea was generally regarded as something extraordinary, something anomalous, something out of the usual order of events; whereas, in fact, I simply moved from Atlanta to Savannah, as one step in the direction of Richmond, a movement that had to be met and defeated, or the war was necessarily at an end.

Were I to express my measure of the relative importance of the march to the sea, and of that from Savannah northward, I would place the former at one, and the latter at ten, or the maximum.

I now close this long chapter by giving a tabular statement of the losses during the march, and the number of prisoners captured. The property captured consisted of horses and mules by the thousand, and of quantities of subsistence stores that aggregate very large, but may be measured with sufficient accuracy by assuming that sixty-five thousand men obtained abundant food for about forty days, and thirty-five thousand animals were fed for a like period, so as to reach Savannah in splendid flesh and condition. I also add a few of the more important letters that passed between Generals Grant, Halleck, and myself, which illustrate our opinions at that stage of the war:

STATEMENT OF CASUALTIES AND PRISONERS CAPTURED BY THE ARMY IN THE FIELD, CAMPAIGN OF GEORGIA.

COMMANDS.	KILLED.		W'UND'D.		MISSING.			CAPTURED.		
	Commissioned Officers.	Enlisted Men.	Commissioned Officers.	Enlisted Men.	Commissioned Officers.	Enlisted Men.	Aggregate.	Commissioned Officers.	Enlisted Men.	Aggregate.
Right Wing, Army of the Tennessee, Major-General O. O. Howard commanding	5	35	11	172	....	19	242	34	632	666
Left Wing, Fourteenth and Twentieth Corps, Major-General H. W. Slocum commanding.	2	23	6	112	1	258	402	30	409	439
Cavalry Division, Brigadier-General J. Kilpatrick commanding	3	35	7	120	....	....	120	13	220	233
Total	10	93	24	404	1	277	764	77	1,261	1,338

L. M. DAYTON, *Assistant Adjutant-General.*

HEADQUARTERS OF THE ARMY, ⎫
WASHINGTON, *December* 16, 1864. ⎰

Major-General SHERMAN (*via Hilton Head*).

GENERAL: Lieutenant-General Grant informs me that, in his last dispatch sent to you, he suggested the transfer of your infantry to Richmond. He now wishes me to say that you will retain your entire force, at least for the present, and, with such assistance as may be given you by General Foster and Admiral Dahlgren, operate from such base as you may establish on the coast.   General Foster will obey such instructions as may be given by you.

Should you have captured Savannah, it is thought that by transferring the water-batteries to the land side that place may be made a good depot and base of operations on Augusta, Branchville, or Charleston.   If Savannah should not be captured, or if captured and not deemed suitable for this purpose, perhaps Beaufort would serve as a depot.   As the rebels have probably removed their most valuable property from Augusta, perhaps Branchville would be the most important point at which to strike in order to sever all connection between Virginia and the Southwestern Railroad.

General Grant's wishes, however, are, that this whole matter of your future actions should be entirely left to your discretion.

We can send you from here a number of complete batteries of field-artillery, with or without horses, as you may desire; also, as soon as General Thomas can spare them, all the fragments, convalescents, and furloughed men of your army.   It is reported that Thomas defeated Hood yesterday, near Nashville, but we have no particulars nor official reports, telegraphic communication being interrupted by a heavy storm.

Our last advices from you was General Howard's note, announcing his approach to Savannah.   Yours truly,

H. W. HALLECK, *Major-General, Chief-of-Staff.*

HEADQUARTERS OF THE ARMY,
WASHINGTON, *December* 18, 1864.

Major-General W. T. SHERMAN, *Savannah (via Hilton Head).*

MY DEAR GENERAL: Yours of the 13th, by Major Anderson, is just received.   I congratulate you on your splendid success, and shall very soon expect to hear of the crowning work of your campaign—the capture of Savannah.   Your march will stand out prominently as the great one of this great war.   When Savannah falls, then for another wide swath through the centre of the Confederacy.   But I will not anticipate.   General Grant is expected here this morning, and will probably write you his own views.

I do not learn from your letter, or from Major Anderson, that you are in want of any thing which we have not provided at Hilton Head.   Thinking it probable that you might want more field-artillery, I had prepared several batteries, but the great difficulty of foraging horses on the sea-coast will prevent our sending any unless you actually need them.   The hay-crop this year is short, and the Quartermaster's Department has great difficulty in procuring a supply for our animals.

General Thomas has defeated Hood, near Nashville, and it is hoped that he will completely crush his army. Breckenridge, at last accounts, was trying to form a junction near Murfreesboro', but, as Thomas is between them, Breckenridge must either retreat or be defeated.

General Rosecrans made very bad work of it in Missouri, allowing Price with a small force to overrun the State and destroy millions of property.

Orders have been issued for all officers and detachments having three months or more to serve, to rejoin your army *via* Savannah. Those having less than three months to serve, will be retained by General Thomas.

Should you capture Charleston, I hope that by *some accident* the place may be destroyed, and, if a little salt should be sown upon its site, it may prevent the growth of future crops of nullification and secession.

Yours truly,

H. W. HALLECK, *Major-General, Chief-of-Staff.*

[CONFIDENTIAL.]

HEADQUARTERS ARMIES OF THE UNITED STATES, }
WASHINGTON, D. C., *December* 18, 1864. }

To Major-General W. T. SHERMAN, *commanding Military Division of the Mississippi.*

MY DEAR GENERAL: I have just received and read, I need not tell you with how much gratification, your letter to General Halleck. I congratulate you and the brave officers and men under your command on the successful termination of your most brilliant campaign. I never had a doubt of the result. When apprehensions for your safety were expressed by the President, I assured him with the army you had, and you in command of it, there was no danger but you would *strike* bottom on salt-water some place; that I would not feel the same security—in fact, would not have intrusted the expedition to any other living commander.

It has been very hard work to get Thomas to attack Hood. I gave him the most peremptory order, and had started to go there myself, before he got off. He has done magnificently, however, since he started. Up to last night, five thousand prisoners and forty-nine pieces of captured artillery, besides many wagons and innumerable small-arms, had been received in Nashville. This is exclusive of the enemy's loss at Franklin, which amounted to thirteen general officers killed, wounded, and captured. The enemy probably lost five thousand men at Franklin, and ten thousand in the last three days' operations. Breckenridge is said to be making for Murfreesboro'.

I think he is in a most excellent place. Stoneman has nearly wiped out John Morgan's old command, and five days ago entered Bristol. I did think the best thing to do was to bring the greater part of your army here, and wipe out Lee. The turn affairs now seem to be taking has shaken me in that opinion. I doubt whether you may not accomplish more toward that result where you are than if brought here, especially as I am informed, since my arrival in the city, that it would take about two months to get you here with all the other calls there are for ocean transportation.

I want to get your views about what ought to be done, and what can be done. If you capture the garrison of Savannah, it certainly will compel Lee to detach from Richmond, or give us nearly the whole South. My own opinion is that Lee is averse to going out of Virginia, and if the cause of the South is lost he wants Richmond to be the last place surrendered. If he has such views, it may be well to indulge him until we get every thing else in our hands.

Congratulating you and the army again upon the splendid results of your campaign, the like of which is not read of in past history, I subscribe myself, more than ever, if possible, your friend,

U. S. GRANT, *Lieutenant-General.*

HEADQUARTERS ARMIES OF THE UNITED STATES, }
CITY POINT, VIRGINIA, *December* 26, 1864. }

Major-General W. T. SHERMAN, *Savannah, Georgia.*

GENERAL: Your very interesting letter of the 22d inst., brought by Major Gray, of General Foster's staff, is just at hand. As the major starts back at once, I can do no more at present than simply acknowledge its receipt. The capture of Savannah, with all its immense stores, must tell upon the people of the South. All well here.

Yours truly,   U. S. GRANT, *Lieutenant-General.*

HEADQUARTERS MILITARY DIVISION OF THE MISSISSIPPI, }
SAVANNAH, GEORGIA, *December* 24, 1864. }

Lieutenant-General U. S. GRANT, *City Point, Virginia.*

GENERAL: Your letter of December 18th is just received. I feel very much gratified at receiving the handsome commendation you pay my army. I will, in general orders, convey to the officers and men the substance of your note.

I am also pleased that you have modified your former orders, for I feared that the transportation by sea would very much disturb the unity and *morale* of my army, now so perfect.

The occupation of Savannah, which I have heretofore reported, completes the first part of our game, and fulfills a great part of your instructions; and we are now engaged in dismantling the rebel forts which bear upon the sea-channels, and transferring the heavy ordnance and ammunition to Fort Pulaski and Hilton Head, where they can be more easily guarded than if left in the city.

The rebel inner lines are well adapted to our purpose, and with slight modifications can be held by a comparatively small force; and in about ten days I expect to be ready to sally forth again. I feel no doubt whatever as to our future plans. I have thought them over so long and well that they appear as clear as daylight. I left Augusta untouched on purpose, because the enemy will be in doubt as to my objective point, after we cross the Savannah River, whether it be Augusta or Charleston, and will naturally divide his forces. I will then move either on Branchville or Columbia, by any curved line that gives us the best supplies, breaking up in our course as much railroad as possible; then, ignoring Charleston and Augusta both, I would occupy Columbia and Camden, pausing there long enough to observe the effect. I would then strike for the Charleston & Wilmington Railroad, somewhere between the Santee and Cape Fear Rivers, and, if possible, communicate with the fleet under Admiral Dahlgren (whom I find a most agreeable gentleman, accommodating himself to our wishes and plans). Then I would favor an attack on Wilmington, in the belief that Porter and Butler will fail in their present undertaking. Charleston is now a mere desolated wreck, and is hardly worth the time it would take to starve it out. Still, I am aware that, historically and politically, much importance is attached to the place, and it may be that, apart from its military importance, both you and the Administration may prefer I should give it more attention; and it would be well for you to give me some general idea on that subject, for otherwise I would treat it as I have expressed, as a point of little importance, after all its railroads leading into the interior have been destroyed or occupied by us. But, on the hypothesis of ignoring Charleston and taking Wilmington, I would then favor a movement direct on Raleigh. The game is then up with Lee, unless he comes out of Richmond, avoids you and fights me; in which case I should reckon on your being on his heels. Now that Hood is used up by Thomas, I feel disposed to bring the matter to an issue as quick as possible. I feel confident that I can break up the whole railroad system of South Carolina and North Carolina, and be on the Roanoke, either at Raleigh or Weldon, by the time spring fairly opens; and, if you feel confident that you can whip Lee outside of his intrenchments, I feel equally confident that I can handle him in the open country.

One reason why I would ignore Charleston is this: that I believe Hardee will reduce the garrison to a small force, with plenty of provisions; I know that the neck back of Charleston can be made impregnable to assault, and we will hardly have time for siege operations.

I will have to leave in Savannah a garrison, and, if Thomas can spare them, I would like to have all detachments, convalescents, etc., belonging to these four corps, sent forward at once. I do not want to cripple Thomas, because I regard his operations as all-important, and I have ordered him to pursue Hood down into Alabama, trusting to the country for supplies.

I reviewed one of my corps to-day, and shall continue to review the whole army. I do not like to boast, but believe this army has a confidence in itself that makes it almost invincible. I wish you could run down and see us; it would have a good effect, and show to both armies that they are acting on a common plan. The weather is now cool and pleasant, and the general health very good. Your true friend,

W. T. SHERMAN, *Major-General.*

HEADQUARTERS MILITARY DIVISION OF THE MISSISSIPPI,
IN THE FIELD, SAVANNAH, *December* 24, 1864.

Major-General H. W. HALLECK, *Chief-of-Staff, Washington, D. C.*

GENERAL: I had the pleasure of receiving your two letters of the 16th and 18th instant to-day, and feel more than usually flattered by the high encomiums you have passed on our recent campaign, which is now complete by the occupation of Savannah.

I am also very glad that General Grant has changed his mind about embarking my troops for James River, leaving me free to make the broad swath you describe through South and North Carolina, and still more gratified at the news from Thomas, in Tennessee, because it fulfills my plans, which contemplated his being able to dispose of Hood, in case he ventured north of the Tennessee River. So, I think, on the whole, I can chuckle over Jeff. Davis's disappointment in not turning my Atlanta campaign into a "Moscow disaster."

I have just finished a long letter to General Grant, and have explained to him that we are engaged in shifting our base from the Ogeechee to the Savannah River, dismantling all the forts made by the enemy to bear upon the salt-water channels, transferring the heavy ordnance, etc., to Fort Pulaski and Hilton Head, and in remodeling the enemy's interior lines to suit our future plans and purposes. I have also laid down the programme for a campaign which I can make this winter, and which will put me in the spring on the Roanoke, in direct communication with General Grant on James River. In general terms, my plan is to turn over to General Foster the city of Savannah, to sally forth with my army resupplied, cross the Savannah, feign on Charleston and Augusta, but strike between, breaking *en route* the Charleston & Augusta Railroad, also a large part of that from Branchville and Camden toward North Carolina, and then rapidly to move for some point of the railroad from Charleston to Wilmington, between the Santee and Cape Fear Rivers; then, communicating with the fleet in the neighborhood of Georgetown, I would turn upon Wilmington or Charleston, according to the importance of either. I rather prefer Wilmington, as a live place, over Charleston, which is dead and unimportant when its railroad communications are broken. I take it for granted that the present movement on Wilmington will fail. If I should determine to take Charleston, I would turn across the country (which I have hunted over many a time) from Santee to Mount Pleasant, throwing one wing on the peninsula between the Ashley and Cooper. After accomplishing one or other of these ends, I would make a bee-line for Raleigh or Weldon, when Lee would be forced to come out of Richmond, or acknowledge himself beaten. He would, I think, by the use of the Danville Railroad, throw himself rapidly between me and Grant, leaving Richmond in the hands of the latter. This would not alarm me, for I have an army which I think can manœuvre, and I would force him to attack me at a disadvantage, always under the supposition that Grant would be on his heels; and, if the worst come to the worst, I can fight my way down to Albermarle Sound, or Newbern.

I think the time has come now when we should attempt the boldest moves, and my experience is, that they are easier of execution than more timid ones, because the enemy is disconcerted by them—as, for instance, my recent campaign.

I also doubt the wisdom of concentration beyond a certain extent, for the roads of this country limit the amount of men that can be brought to bear in any one battle, and I do not believe that any one general can handle more than sixty thousand men in battle.

I think our campaign of the last month, as well as every step I take from this point northward, is as much a direct attack upon Lee's army as though we were operating within the sound of his artillery.

I am very anxious that Thomas should follow up his success to the very utmost point. My orders to him before I left Kingston were, after beating Hood, to follow him as far as Columbus, Mississippi, or Selma, Alabama, both of which lie in districts of country which are rich in corn and meat.

I attach more importance to these deep incisions into the enemy's country, because this war differs from European wars in this particular: we are not only fighting hostile armies, but a hostile people, and must make old and young, rich and poor, feel the hard hand of war, as well as their organized armies. I know that this recent movement of mine through Georgia has had a wonderful effect in this respect. Thousands who had been deceived by their lying newspapers to believe that we were being whipped all the time now realize the truth, and have no appetite for a repetition of the same experience. To be sure, Jeff. Davis has his people under pretty good discipline, but I think faith in him is much shaken in Georgia, and before we have done with her South Carolina will not be quite so tempestuous.

I will bear in mind your hint as to Charleston, and do not think "salt" will be necessary. When I move, the Fifteenth Corps will be on the right of the right wing, and their position will naturally bring them into Charleston first; and, if you have watched the history of that corps, you will have remarked that they generally do their work pretty well. The truth is, the whole army is burning with an insatiable desire to wreak vengeance upon South Carolina. I almost tremble at her fate, but feel that she deserves all that seems in store for her.

Many and many a person in Georgia asked me why we did not go to South Carolina; and, when I answered that we were *en route* for that State, the invariable reply was, "Well, if you will make those people feel the utmost severities of war, we will pardon you for your desolation of Georgia."

I look upon Columbia as quite as bad as Charleston, and I doubt if we shall spare the public buildings there as we did at Milledgeville.

I have been so busy lately that I have not yet made my official report, and I think I had better wait until I get my subordinate reports before attempting it, as I am anxious to explain clearly not only the reasons for every step, but the amount of execution done, and this I cannot do until I get the subordinate reports; for we marched the whole distance in four or more columns, and, of course, I could only be present with one, and generally that one engaged in destroying railroads. This work of destruction was performed better than usual, because I had an engineer-regiment, provided with claws to twist the bars after being heated. Such bars can never be used again, and the only way in which a railroad line can be reconstructed across Georgia is, to make a new road from Fairburn Station (twenty-four miles southwest of Atlanta) to Madison, a distance of one hundred miles; and, before that can be done, I propose to be on the road from Augusta to Charleston, which is a continuation of the same. I felt somewhat disappointed at Hardee's escape, but really am not to blame. I moved as quickly as possible to close up the "Union Causeway," but intervening obstacles were such that, before I could get troops on the road, Hardee had slipped out. Still, I know that the men that were in Savannah will be lost in a measure to Jeff. Davis, for the Georgia troops, under G. W. Smith, declared they would not fight in South Carolina, and they have gone north, *en route* for Augusta, and I have reason to believe the North Carolina troops have gone to Wilmington; in other words, they are scattered. I have reason to believe that Beauregard was present in Savannah at the time of its evacuation, and think that he and Hardee are now in Charleston, making preparations for what they suppose will be my next step.

Please say to the President that I have received his kind message (through Colonel Markland), and feel thankful for his high favor. If I disappoint him in the future, it shall not be from want of zeal or love to the cause.

From you I expect a full and frank criticism of my plans for the future, which may enable me to correct errors before it is too late. I do not wish to be rash, but want to give my rebel friends no chance to accuse us of want of enterprise or courage.

Assuring you of my high personal respect, I remain, as ever, your friend,

W. T. SHERMAN, *Major-General.*

[General Order No. 3.]

WAR DEPARTMENT, ADJUTANT-GENERAL'S OFFICE, }
WASHINGTON, *January* 14, 1865. }

The following resolution of the Senate and House of Representatives is published to the army:

[PUBLIC RESOLUTION—No. 4.]

Joint resolution tendering the thanks of the people and of Congress to Major-General William T. Sherman, and the officers and soldiers of his command, for their gallant conduct in their late brilliant movement through Georgia.

Be it resolved by the Senate and House of Representatives of the United States of America in Congress assembled, That the thanks of the people and of the Congress of the United States are due and are hereby tendered to Major-General William T. Sherman, and through him to the officers and men under his command, for their gallantry and good conduct in their late campaign from Chattanooga to Atlanta, and the triumphal march thence through Georgia to Savannah, terminating in the capture and occupation of that city; and that the President cause a copy of this joint resolution to be engrossed and forwarded to Major-General Sherman.   Approved, January 10, 1865.

By order of the Secretary of War,

W. A. NICHOLS, *Assistant Adjutant-General.*

A CATALOG OF SELECTED DOVER
BOOKS IN ALL FIELDS OF INTEREST

CONCERNING THE SPIRITUAL IN ART, Wassily Kandinsky. Pioneering work by father of abstract art. Thoughts on color theory, nature of art. Analysis of earlier masters. 12 illustrations. 80pp. of text. 5⅜ x 8½. 0-486-23411-8

CELTIC ART: The Methods of Construction, George Bain. Simple geometric techniques for making Celtic interlacements, spirals, Kells-type initials, animals, humans, etc. Over 500 illustrations. 160pp. 9 x 12. (Available in U.S. only.) 0-486-22923-8

AN ATLAS OF ANATOMY FOR ARTISTS, Fritz Schider. Most thorough reference work on art anatomy in the world. Hundreds of illustrations, including selections from works by Vesalius, Leonardo, Goya, Ingres, Michelangelo, others. 593 illustrations. 192pp. 7⅞ x 10¼. 0-486-20241-0

CELTIC HAND STROKE-BY-STROKE (Irish Half-Uncial from "The Book of Kells"): An Arthur Baker Calligraphy Manual, Arthur Baker. Complete guide to creating each letter of the alphabet in distinctive Celtic manner. Covers hand position, strokes, pens, inks, paper, more. Illustrated. 48pp. 8¼ x 11. 0-486-24336-2

EASY ORIGAMI, John Montroll. Charming collection of 32 projects (hat, cup, pelican, piano, swan, many more) specially designed for the novice origami hobbyist. Clearly illustrated easy-to-follow instructions insure that even beginning papercrafters will achieve successful results. 48pp. 8¼ x 11. 0-486-27298-2

BLOOMINGDALE'S ILLUSTRATED 1886 CATALOG: Fashions, Dry Goods and Housewares, Bloomingdale Brothers. Famed merchants' extremely rare catalog depicting about 1,700 products: clothing, housewares, firearms, dry goods, jewelry, more. Invaluable for dating, identifying vintage items. Also, copyright-free graphics for artists, designers. Co-published with Henry Ford Museum & Greenfield Village. 160pp. 8¼ x 11. 0-486-25780-0

THE ART OF WORLDLY WISDOM, Baltasar Gracian. "Think with the few and speak with the many," "Friends are a second existence," and "Be able to forget" are among this 1637 volume's 300 pithy maxims. A perfect source of mental and spiritual refreshment, it can be opened at random and appreciated either in brief or at length. 128pp. 5⅜ x 8½. 0-486-44034-6

JOHNSON'S DICTIONARY: A Modern Selection, Samuel Johnson (E. L. McAdam and George Milne, eds.). This modern version reduces the original 1755 edition's 2,300 pages of definitions and literary examples to a more manageable length, retaining the verbal pleasure and historical curiosity of the original. 480pp. 5¾₆ x 8¼. 0-486-44089-3

ADVENTURES OF HUCKLEBERRY FINN, Mark Twain, Illustrated by E. W. Kemble. A work of eternal richness and complexity, a source of ongoing critical debate, and a literary landmark, Twain's 1885 masterpiece about a barefoot boy's journey of self-discovery has enthralled readers around the world. This handsome clothbound reproduction of the first edition features all 174 of the original black-and-white illustrations. 368pp. 5⅜ x 8½. 0-486-44322-1

THE MALLEUS MALEFICARUM OF KRAMER AND SPRENGER, translated by Montague Summers. Full text of most important witchhunter's "bible," used by both Catholics and Protestants. 278pp. 6⅛ x 10. 0-486-22802-9

SPANISH STORIES/CUENTOS ESPAÑOLES: A Dual-Language Book, Angel Flores (ed.). Unique format offers 13 great stories in Spanish by Cervantes, Borges, others. Faithful English translations on facing pages. 352pp. 5⅜ x 8½. 0-486-25399-6

GARDEN CITY, LONG ISLAND, IN EARLY PHOTOGRAPHS, 1869–1919, Mildred H. Smith. Handsome treasury of 118 vintage pictures, accompanied by carefully researched captions, document the Garden City Hotel fire (1899), the Vanderbilt Cup Race (1908), the first airmail flight departing from the Nassau Boulevard Aerodrome (1911), and much more. 96pp. 8⅞ x 11¾. 0-486-40669-5

OLD QUEENS, N.Y., IN EARLY PHOTOGRAPHS, Vincent F. Seyfried and William Asadorian. Over 160 rare photographs of Maspeth, Jamaica, Jackson Heights, and other areas. Vintage views of DeWitt Clinton mansion, 1939 World's Fair and more. Captions. 192pp. 8⅞ x 11. 0-486-26358-4

CAPTURED BY THE INDIANS: 15 Firsthand Accounts, 1750-1870, Frederick Drimmer. Astounding true historical accounts of grisly torture, bloody conflicts, relentless pursuits, miraculous escapes and more, by people who lived to tell the tale. 384pp. 5⅜ x 8½. 0-486-24901-8

THE WORLD'S GREAT SPEECHES (Fourth Enlarged Edition), Lewis Copeland, Lawrence W. Lamm, and Stephen J. McKenna. Nearly 300 speeches provide public speakers with a wealth of updated quotes and inspiration–from Pericles' funeral oration and William Jennings Bryan's "Cross of Gold Speech" to Malcolm X's powerful words on the Black Revolution and Earl of Spenser's tribute to his sister, Diana, Princess of Wales. 944pp. 5⅜ x 8⅜. 0-486-40903-1

THE BOOK OF THE SWORD, Sir Richard F. Burton. Great Victorian scholar/adventurer's eloquent, erudite history of the "queen of weapons"–from prehistory to early Roman Empire. Evolution and development of early swords, variations (sabre, broadsword, cutlass, scimitar, etc.), much more. 336pp. 6⅛ x 9¼. 0-486-25434-8

AUTOBIOGRAPHY: The Story of My Experiments with Truth, Mohandas K. Gandhi. Boyhood, legal studies, purification, the growth of the Satyagraha (nonviolent protest) movement. Critical, inspiring work of the man responsible for the freedom of India. 480pp. 5⅜ x 8½. (Available in U.S. only.) 0-486-24593-4

CELTIC MYTHS AND LEGENDS, T. W. Rolleston. Masterful retelling of Irish and Welsh stories and tales. Cuchulain, King Arthur, Deirdre, the Grail, many more. First paperback edition. 58 full-page illustrations. 512pp. 5⅜ x 8½. 0-486-26507-2

THE PRINCIPLES OF PSYCHOLOGY, William James. Famous long course complete, unabridged. Stream of thought, time perception, memory, experimental methods; great work decades ahead of its time. 94 figures. 1,391pp. 5⅜ x 8½. 2-vol. set.
Vol. I: 0-486-20381-6 Vol. II: 0-486-20382-4

THE WORLD AS WILL AND REPRESENTATION, Arthur Schopenhauer. Definitive English translation of Schopenhauer's life work, correcting more than 1,000 errors, omissions in earlier translations. Translated by E. F. J. Payne. Total of 1,269pp. 5⅜ x 8½. 2-vol. set. Vol. 1: 0-486-21761-2 Vol. 2: 0-486-21762-0